# Mary Wollaston

*By*

Henry Kitchell Webster

Double9
BOOKS

# Mary Wollaston
## by Henry Kitchell Webster

ISBN: 978-93-59954-51-6
**Published by**

# DOUBLE 9 BOOKS

2/13-B, Ansari Road
Daryaganj, New Delhi – 110002
info@double9books.com
www.double9books.com
Tel. 011-40042856

# ABOUT THE AUTHOR

Henry Kitchell Webster was an American author who lived from September 7, 1875, to December 8, 1932. He was one of the most famous serial writers in the country in the early 1900s. He wrote mystery, family drama, science fiction, and other types of novels and short stories. He also came up with new ways to make books sell a lot of copies. Towner K. Webster and Emma Josephine Kitchell had one son, Henry Kitchell Webster. He was the oldest child. In 1897, he graduated from Hamilton College and started teaching rhetoric at Union College. In any case, he lived in Evanston, Illinois, for most of his life. Their wedding day was September 7, 1901. After his first books did well, he and Mary took a trip around the world in 1910. There were three boys born to them: Henry Kitchell Jr. (1905), Stokely (1912), who became a famous impressionist painter, and Roderick (1915), who was Chairman of the Adler Planetarium and a donor to its Webster Institute. The family lived and traveled in Europe for a year in 1922. Their Paris apartment was on the Rive Gauche, and Stokely learned painting with Lawton S. Parker, an American artist who was a family friend. Webster was friends with a lot of artists and opera singers, like Ethel Barrymore, who played the lead role in his Broadway play June Madness in 1912.

# CONTENTS

# CHAPTER I
# THE CIRCASSIAN GRAND

Miss Lucile Wollaston was set to exude sympathy, like an aphid waiting for an overworked ant to come down to breakfast. But there was no sympathizing with the man who came in from a doctor's all-night vigil like a boy from a ball-game, gave her a hard brisk kiss on the cheek-bone, and then, before taking his place at the table, unfolded the morning paper for a glance at the head-lines.

If there was something rigorous about the way she lighted the alcohol lamp under the silver urn and rang for Nathaniel, the old colored butler, it was from a determination not to let this younger brother of hers put her into a flurry again as he so often did. A very much younger brother indeed, he seemed when this mood was on him.

Miss Wollaston was born on the election day that made James Buchanan president of the United States and Doctor John within a few days of Appomattox. But one would have said, looking at them here at the breakfast table on a morning in March in the year 1919, that there was a good deal more than those ten years between them. He folded his paper and sat down when the butler suggestively pulled out his chair for him and his manner became, for the moment, absent, as his eye fell upon a letter beside his plate addressed in his daughter, Mary's, handwriting.

"I want a big platter of ham and eggs, Nat, sliced thick. And a few of Lucartha's wheat cakes." He made some sort of good-humored, half articulate acknowledgment of the old servitor's pleasure in getting such an order, but one might have seen that his mind was a little out of focus, for it was not exactly dealing with the letter either. He sliced it open with a table knife with the precise movement one would have expected from a surgeon and disengaged it in the same neat way from its envelope. But he read it as if he weren't very sharply aware of what, particularly, it had to say and he laid it beside his plate again without any comment.

"Did you have any sleep last night, at all?" Miss Wollaston asked.

It brought him back like a flash. "Not a wink," he said jovially.

This was a challenge and the look that went with it, one of clear boyish mischief, was one that none of John Wollaston's other intimates—and among these I include his beautiful young wife and his two grown-up children by an earlier marriage—ever saw. It was a special thing for this sister who had been a stately young lady of twenty when he was a bad little boy of ten. She had watched him, admiring yet rather aghast, ever since then.

To the world at large his social charm lay in—or was at least inseparable from—his really exquisite manners, his considerateness, the touch of old-fashioned punctilio there was about him. His first wife would have agreed with her successor about his possession of this quality though they would have appraised it rather differently. Only this elderly unmarried sister of his felt the fascination of the horrible about him.

This was to some extent inherent in his profession. He had a reputation that was growing to amount to fame as a specialist in the very wide field of gynecology, obstetrics and abdominal surgery. The words themselves made Miss Wollaston shudder.

When he replied to her question, whether or not he had had any sleep at all, with an open grin and that triumphant "Not a wink," she had a prophetic sense of what was going to happen. She was going to ask him more questions and he was going to tell her something perfectly ghastly.

She felt herself slipping, but she pulled up. "What's in Mary's letter?" she asked.

She knew that this was not quite fair, and the look that it brought to his face—a twinge of pain like neuralgia—awakened a sharp compunction in her. She did not know why—at least not exactly why—his relation with his daughter should be a sore spot in his emotional life, but she knew quite well that this was true. There was on the surface, nothing, or nowhere near enough, to account for it.

He had always been, Miss Wollaston felt, an adorer to the verge of folly of this lovely pale-blonde daughter of his. He had indulged her outrageously but without any evident bad results. Upon her mother's death, in 1912 that was, when Mary was seventeen years old, she had, to the utmost limit that a daughter could compass, taken her mother's place in the bereaved man's life. She had foregone the college course she was prepared for and had taken over very skillfully the management of her father's household; even, in a surprisingly successful way, too, the motherly guidance of her two-years-younger brother, Rush. Miss Wollaston's testimony on these two points was unbiased as it was ungrudging. She had offered herself for that job and had not then been wanted.

called in on at four o'clock this morning was another thing altogether." A gleam had come into his eyes again as over the memory of some brilliantly successful audacity. The gray old look had gone out of his face.

"I don't altogether wonder that Pollard blew up," he added, "except that a man in that profession has got no business to—ever."

The coffee urn offered Miss Wollaston her only means of escape but she didn't avail herself of it. She let herself go on looking for a breathless minute into her brother's face. Then she asked weakly, "What was it?"

"Why, Pollard...." John Wollaston began but then he stopped short and listened. "I thought I heard Paula coming," he explained.

"Paula won't be down for hours," Miss Wollaston said, "but I do not see why she shouldn't hear, since she is a married woman and your own wife...."

Her brother's "Precisely" cut across that sentence with a snick like a pair of shears and left a little silence behind it.

"I think she'll be along in a minute," he went on. "She always does come to breakfast. Why did you think she wouldn't to-day?"

This was one of Miss Wollaston's minor crosses. The fact was that on the comparatively rare occasions when Doctor John himself was present for the family breakfast at the custom-consecrated hour, Paula managed about two times in five to put in a last-minute appearance. This was not what annoyed Miss Wollaston. She was broad-minded enough to be aware that to an opera singer, the marshaling of one's whole family in the dining-room at eight o'clock in the morning might seem a barbarous and revolting practise and even occasional submissions to it, acts of real devotion. She was not really bitterly annoyed either by Paula's oft repeated assertion that she always came to breakfast. Paula was one of those temperamental persons who have to be forgiven for treating their facts—atmospherically. But that John, a man of science, enlisted under the banner of truth, should back this assertion of his wife's, in the face of overwhelming evidence to the contrary, really required resignation to put up with; argued a blindness, an infatuation, which seemed to his sister hardly decent. Because after all, facts were facts, and you didn't alter them by pretending that they did not exist.

So instead of answering her brother's question, she sat a little straighter in her chair, and compressed her lips.

He smiled faintly at that and added, "Anyhow she said she'd be along in a minute or two."

"Oh," said Miss Wollaston, "you have wakened her then. I would have suggested that the poor child be left asleep this morning."

Now he saw that she had something to tell him. "Nothing went wrong last night after I left, I hope."

"Oh, not wrong," Miss Wollaston conceded, "only the Whitneys went of course, when you did and the Byrnes, and Wallace Hood, but Portia Stanton and that new husband of hers stayed. It was his doing, I suppose. You might have thought he was waiting all the evening for just that thing to happen. They went up to Paula's studio—Paula invited me, of course, but I excused myself—and they played and sang until nearly two o'clock this morning. It was all perfectly natural, I suppose. And still I did think that Paula might have sung earlier, down in the drawing-room when you asked her to."

"She was perfectly right to refuse." He caught his sister up rather short on that, "I shouldn't have asked her. It was very soon after dinner. They weren't a musical crowd anyway, except Novelli. It's utterly unfair to expect a person like Paula to perform unless she happens to be in the mood for it. At that she's extremely amiable about it; never refuses unless she has some real reason. What her reason was last night, I don't know, but you may be perfectly sure it was sufficient."

He would have realized that he was protesting too much even if he had not read that comment in his sister's face. But somehow he couldn't have pulled himself up but for old Nat's appearance with the platter of ham and eggs and the first installment of the wheat cakes. He was really hungry and he settled down to them in silence.

And, watching him between the little bites of dry toast and sips of coffee, Miss Wollaston talked about Portia Stanton. Everybody, indeed, was talking about Portia these days but Miss Wollaston had a special privilege. She had known Portia's mother rather well,—Naomi Rutledge Stanton, the suffrage leader, she was—and she had always liked and admired Portia; liked her better than the younger and more sensational daughter, Rose.

Miss Wollaston hoped, hoped with all her heart that Portia had not made a tragic mistake in this matter of her marriage. She couldn't herself quite see how a sensible girl like Portia could have done anything so reckless as to marry a romantic young Italian pianist, ten years at least her junior. It couldn't be denied that the experiment seemed to have worked well so far. Portia certainly seemed happy enough last night; contented. There was a sort of glow about her there never was before. But the question was how long would it last. How long would it be before those big brown Italian eyes began looking soulfully at somebody else; somebody more....

It was here that Miss Wollaston chopped herself off short, hearing—this time it was no false alarm—Paula's step in the hall. She'd have been amazed, scandalized, profoundly indignant, dear good-hearted lady that she was, had some expert in the psychology of the unconscious pointed out to her that the reason she had begun talking about Portia was that it gave her an outlet for expressing her misgivings about her own brother's marriage. Paula, of course, was a different thing altogether.

What a beautiful creature she was, even at eight o'clock in the morning at the end of an abruptly terminated night's sleep. She looked lovelier than ever as she came in through the shadowy doorway. She wasn't a true blonde like Mary. Her thick strong hair was a sort of golden glorification of brown, her skin a warm tone of ivory. Her eyes, set wide apart, were brown, and the lashes, darker than her hair, enhanced the size of them. The look of power about Paula, inseparable from her beauty, was not one of Miss Wollaston's feminine ideals. It spoke in every line of her figure as well as in the lineaments of her face; in the short, rather broad, yet cleanly defined nose; in the generous width of her mouth; in the sculpturesque poise of her neck upon her shoulders.

Paula's clothes, too, worried her elderly sister-in-law a little, especially the house-dresses that she affected. They were beautiful, heaven knew; more simply beautiful perhaps than it was right that clothes should be. There was nothing indecent about them. Dear Paula was almost surprisingly nice in those ways. But that thing she had on now, for instance;—a tunic of ecru colored silk that she had pulled on over her head, with a little over-dress of corn colored tulle, weighted artfully here and there that it mightn't fly away. And a string of big lumpish amber beads. She could have got into that costume in about two minutes and there was probably next to nothing under it. From the on-looker's point of view, it mightn't violate decorum at all; indeed, clearly did not. But Miss Wollaston herself, if she hadn't been more or less rigidly laced, stayed, gartered, pinched, pried and pulled about; if she could have moved freely in any direction without an admonitory—"take care"—from some bit of whalebone somewhere, wouldn't have felt dressed at all. There ought to be something perpetually penitential about clothes. The biblical story of the fall of man made that clear, didn't it?

John sprang up as his wife came into the room; went around the table and held her chair for her. "My dear, I didn't know I was robbing you of half a night's sleep," he said. "You should have turned me out."

She reached up her strong white arms (the tulle sleeves did fall away from them rather alarmingly, and Miss Wollaston concentrated her attention on the spiggot of the coffee urn) for his head as he bent over her and pulled it down for a kiss.

"I didn't need any more sleep. I had such a joyous time last night. I sang the whole of *Maliela*, and a lot of *Thais*. I don't know what all. Novelli's a marvel; the best accompanist I've found yet. But, oh, my darling, I did feel such a pig about it."

He was back in his own chair by now and his sister breathed a little more freely.

"Pig?" he asked.

"Oh, because you weren't there," said Paula. "Because I didn't sing before, when you asked me to."

"Dearest!" John remonstrated,—pleased though with the apology, you could see with half an eye,—"it was inexcusable of me to have asked you. It was a dull crowd from a musical point of view. The only thing I minded was having, myself, put you into a position where you had to refuse. I am glad you were able to make it up to yourself after."

"That was not why I didn't," Paula said. She always spoke rather deliberately and never interrupted any one. "I mean it wasn't because the others weren't especially musical. But I couldn't have sung without asking Novelli to play. And he couldn't have refused—being new and a little on trial you know. And that drawing-room piano, so badly out of tune, would have been terrible for him. There's no knowing what he mightn't have done."

John's face beamed triumph. "I might have known you had an unselfish reason for it," he said. He didn't look at his sister but, of course, the words slanted her way.

It was perfectly characteristic of Miss Wollaston that she did not, however, make any immediate attempt to set herself right. She attended first very competently to all of Paula's wants in the way of breakfast and saw her fairly launched on her chilled grapefruit. Then she said, "A man is coming to tune the piano this morning."

It was more than a statement of fact. Indeed I despair of conveying to you all the implications and moral reflections which Miss Wollaston contrived to pack into that simple sentence.

The drawing-room piano was what an artillerist would speak of as one of the sensitive points along the family front. It had been a present to the Wollaston household from the eldest of John's brothers, the unmarried one Miss Wollaston had kept house for so many years before he died;

the last present, it turned out, he ever made to anybody. Partly perhaps, because it was a sacred object, the Wollaston children took to treating it rather irreverently. The "Circassian grand" was one of its nicknames and the "Siamese Elephant" another. It did glare in the otherwise old-fashioned Dearborn Avenue drawing-room and its case did express a complete recklessness of expense rather than any more austere esthetic impulse.

Paula ignored it in rather a pointed way; being a musician she might have been expected to see that it was kept in tune. She had a piano of her own up in the big room at the top of the house that had once been the nursery and over this instrument, she made, Miss Wollaston felt, a silly amount of fuss. Supposedly expert tuners were constantly being called in to do things to it and nothing they did ever seemed to afford Paula any satisfaction.

The aura that surrounded Miss Wollaston's remark included, then, the conviction that the drawing-room piano, being a sacred memory, couldn't be out of tune in the first place; that Paula, in the second, ought to have attended to it; and third (this is rather complex but I guarantee the accuracy of it) the fact that it was to be tuned this morning, really made it a perfectly possible instrument for Mr. Novelli to have played upon last night.

John missed none of that. He hadn't been observing his sister during half a century for nothing. He glanced over to see how much of it his wife took in; but the fact, in this instance, was all that interested Paula.

"It was awfully clever of you," she said, "to get hold of a tuner. Who is he? Where did you find him?"

"I found him in the park," said Miss Wollaston brightly, responding to the little thrill you always felt when Paula focused her attention upon you. "He was sitting on a bench when I drove by just after lunch. I don't know why I noticed him but I did and when I came back hours later, he was still sitting there on the same bench. He was in uniform; a private, I think, certainly not an officer. It struck me as rather sad, his sitting there like that, so I stopped the car and spoke to him. He got his discharge just the other day, it seemed. I asked him if he had a job and he said, no, he didn't believe he had. Then I asked him what his trade was and he said he was a piano tuner. So I told him he might come this morning and tune ours."

It was Paula's bewildered stare that touched off John's peal of laughter. Alone with his sister he might have smiled to himself over the lengths she went in the satisfaction of her passion for good works. But Paula, he knew, would just as soon have invited a strange bench-warming dentist to come and work on her teeth by way of being kind to him.

Miss Wollaston, a flush of annoyance on her faded cheeks, began making dignified preparations to leave the table and John hastily apologized. "I laughed," he said,—disingenuously because it wouldn't do to implicate Paula—"over the idea that perhaps he didn't want a job at all and made up on the spur of the moment the unlikeliest trade he could think of. And how surprised he must have been when you took him up."

"He did not seem surprised," Miss Wollaston said. "He thanked me very nicely and said he would come this morning. At ten, if that would be convenient. Of course if you wish to put it off...."

"Not at all," said John. He rose when she did and—this was an extra bit, an act of contrition for having wounded her—went with her to the door. "It was a good idea," he said; "an excellent way of—of killing two birds with one stone."

Paula was smiling over this when he came back to her. "It doesn't matter, does it?" he asked.

She shook her head. "It isn't that it's out of tune, really; it's just—hopeless."

It was strange how like a knife thrust that word of hers—hopeless—went through him. Perfectly illogical, of course; she was not speaking of his life and hers but of that ridiculous drawing-room piano. Somehow the mere glow she had brought into the room with her, the afterglow of an experience he had no share in producing, had become painful to him; made him feel old. He averted his eyes from her with an effort and stared down at his empty plate.

A moment later she came around the table and seated herself, facing him, upon the arm of his chair; clasped his neck with her two hands. "You're tired," she said. "How much sleep did you have last night?" And on his admitting that he hadn't had any, she exclaimed against his working himself to death like that.

No memory, though he made a conscious effort to recover it, of his audacious success during the small hours of that morning in bringing triumphantly into the world the small new life that Pollard would have destroyed, came back to fortify him; no trace of his own afterglow that had so fascinated and alarmed his sister. "I shall sleep fast for an hour or two this morning and make it up," he told Paula.

"I do wish you might have been there last night," she said after a little silence. "I don't believe I've ever sung so well;—could have, at least, if there had been room enough to turn around in. It was all there; it's getting bigger all the time. Not just the voice, if you know what I mean, darling, but what I could do with it."

"It was partly Novelli, I suspect," he said. "Having him for an accompanist, I mean. He's very good indeed, isn't he?"

"Oh, yes, he's good," she assented absently. "Awfully good. And he is a nice furry little enthusiastic thing; like a faun, rather; exciting to play with of course. But it wasn't that. It's you, really—being in love with you the way I am. I suppose that's the very best thing that could possibly have happened to me. I'm another person altogether from that girl you found in Vienna. Just where she left off, I begin."

She uttered a little laugh then of sheer exuberance and with a strong embrace, pressed his head hard against her breast. He yielded passively, made no response of his own beyond a deep-drawn breath or two. A moment later when she had released him and risen to her feet, he rose too.

"Would Novelli be procurable?" he asked. "Could he be engaged regularly, as an accompanist for you and so on?"

She looked at him rather oddly. "Why, I don't need him," she said, "as long as I am just playing. Of course, if I were to go regularly to work, somebody like him would be almost necessary."

There was a tight little silence for a few seconds after that, he once more evading her eyes. "It seems to me you work most of the time as it is," he said. Then he announced his intention of going up-stairs to take a nap. He wasn't going to the hospital until eleven.

He did go up to his room and lay down upon his bed and, eventually, he slept. But for an hour, his mind raced like an idle motor. That nonsense of Lucile's about Portia Stanton's folly in marrying a young musician whose big Italian eyes would presently begin looking soulfully at some one else. Had they already looked like that at Paula? Jealousy itself wasn't a base emotion. Betraying it was all that mattered. You couldn't help feeling it for any one you loved. Paula, bending over that furry faun-like head, reading off the same score with him, responding to the same emotions from the music…. Fantastic, of course. There could be no sane doubt as to who it was that Paula was in love with. That embrace of hers, just now. Curious how it terrified him. He had felt like a mouse under the soft paw of a cat. An odd symptom of fatigue.

What a curious thing life was. How widely it departed from the traditional patterns. Here in his own case, that Fate should save the one real passion of his life for the Indian summer of it. And that it should be a reciprocated passion. The wiseacres were smiling at him, he supposed;

smiling as the world always smiled at the spectacle of infatuate age mating with tolerant, indifferently acquiescent youth. Smiled and wondered how long it would be before youth awoke and turned to its own. Well, he could afford to smile at the wiseacres. And at the green inexperienced young, as well, who thought that love was exclusively their affair—children the age of Mary taking their sentimental thrills so seriously!

Four years now he had been married to Paula and the thing had never chilled,—never gone stale. How different from the love of his youth that had led to his former marriage, was this burning constant flame. Paula was utterly content with him. She had given up her career for him.—No. She hadn't done that. He had not asked her to do that. Had not, on the contrary, her marriage really furthered it? Was she not more of a person to-day than the discouraged young woman he had found singing for pittances the leading dramatic soprano rôles in the minor municipal operas of Germany and Austria? Wasn't that what she had said this morning—that falling in love with him was the best thing that could possibly have happened to her? He had taken it wrong when she said it, as if she were regarding him just as an instrument that served her purpose, a purpose that lay beyond him; outside him.

That was what had given him that momentary pang of terror. Fatigue, of course. He ought to go to sleep. Paula was refraining from her morning practise just so that he could. Or was that why? Was she dreaming, up in the music room where she was never to be disturbed,—of last night—of Novelli? Damnation....

# CHAPTER II
# SEA DRIFT

Paula went up to the music room after breakfast, stood at one of its open windows for a few minutes breathing in the air of an unusually mild March and then abruptly left it; dressed for the street and went out for a walk.

She was quite as much disturbed over the scene in the dining-room as her husband had been. His flash of jealousy over the little Italian pianist, instantly recognizable through its careful disguise, had only endeared John Wollaston to her further, if that were possible. She had laughed and hugged his worried old head tight against her breast.

But his refusal to face facts about her musical career was another thing altogether. Once more he had, patently and rather pitiably, evaded the subject of her going seriously to work. Did he think that she could go on indefinitely parading a parlor accomplishment for his society friends, — singing nice little English songs for Wallace Hood? It was too ridiculous! That hadn't been their understanding when she married him.

What she had been sure of last night as never before, she had tried down there in the dining-room to convey to him; that her powers were ripe, were crying out for use. She had failed simply because he had refused to see what she was driving at. It was just another form of jealousy really, she supposed.

She was not an introspective person, but this, clearly, was something that wanted thinking over. It was to "think" that she went out for the walk. Only, being Paula, the rhythm of her stride, the sparkle of the spring air, the stream of sharp new-minted sensations incessantly assailing eye and ear, soon swamped her problem; sunk it beneath the level of consciousness altogether. Long before ten o'clock when she came swinging along Dearborn Avenue toward her husband's house, she had "walked off" her perplexities.

A block from the house she found herself overtaking a man in uniform and slackened her pace a little in order not to pass him. There was something unmilitary about the look of him that mildly amused her. It was not that he slouched nor shuffled nor that he was ill-made, though he was probably one of those unfortunates whom issue uniforms never fit. He carried a little black leather satchel, and it broke over Paula that here perhaps was Lucile's piano tuner. She half formed the intention to stay away another hour or two until he should have had time to finish. But he interfered with that plan by stopping in front of the house and looking at it as if making up his mind whether to go in.

It was an odd look he had, but distinctly an engaging one. He was not criticizing the architecture, if so it could be called, of the house-front. Yet there was a sort of comfortable detachment about him which precluded the belief that it was a mere paralyzing shyness that held him there.

Paula abandoned her intention of walking by. She stopped instead as she came up to him and said, "Are you coming in here? If you are, I'll let you in." She fished an explanatory latch-key out of her wrist-bag as she went up the steps.

"Why," he said, "I believe this is the house where I'm expected to tune a piano."

In the act of thrusting home her key, Paula stopped short, turned irrepressibly and stared at him. She was one of that very small number of American-born singers who take the English language seriously and she knew good speech when she heard it. It was one of the qualities which had first attracted her to Doctor John. This man's speaking voice would have arrested her attention pleasantly anywhere. Coming from the private soldier Lucile had told to come round to tune the piano, it really startled her. She turned back to the door and opened it.

"Yes," she said, "they're expecting you. Come in and I'll show you the piano."

She might, of course, merely have indicated the drawing-room door to him with a nod and gone up-stairs, but she was determined now to wait and hear him say something more. So she led the way into the drawing-room and quite superfluously indicated the Circassian grand with a gesture. Then she looked back at him quickly enough to surprise the expression that flickered across his face at the sight of it. A mere cocking of one eyebrow it was, but amusingly expressive. So, too, was the way he walked over toward it, with an air of cautious determination, of readiness for anything, that made Paula want to laugh. He dropped down sidewise on the bench, turned up the lid and dug his fingers into the keyboard.

At the noise he evoked from that pampered instrument she did laugh aloud. It was not a piano tuner's arpeggio but a curiously teasing mixed dissonance she couldn't begin to identify. She thought she heard him say, "My God!" but couldn't be sure. He repeated his chord pianissimo and held it down, reached up and echoed it in the upper half of the keyboard; then struck, hard, two octaves in the bass.

"What a piano!" he said. "What a damned piano!" He made a sort of effort to pull himself up; apologized (she thought that was what he meant to do) for the damn. But as he turned back to the piano and struck another chord or two, she could see that his sense of outrage was mounting steadily all the time.

"You can't tune a piano like this." —He pushed up the cover and stared gloomily at the strings. "A mincing sickly thing like this. It's all wrong. The scale is all wrong. The man who designed it ought to be hung. But he called it a piano and sold it for a piano and I'm expected to come in and tune it. Slick and smear it over and leave it sounding sicklier and tubbier and more generally disgusting than ever. You might as well take a painted harlot off the streets" —he glared at the ornate extravagance of the case—"and expect to make a gentlewoman of her with one lesson in deportment. I won't tune it. It's better left as it is. In its shame."

"Well," said Paula, letting go a long breath, "you've said it."

Then she dropped into a chair and began to laugh. Never again, she felt sure, would the drawing-room piano be able to cause her a moment's irritation. This astonishing piano tuner of Lucile's had converted it, with his new christening, into a source of innocent merriment. "The painted harlot" covered the ground. Clear inspiration was what that was. The way he went on glowering at it, digging every now and then a new and more abominable chord out of its entrails made her mirth the more uncontrollable.

"It isn't funny, you know, a thing like this," he remonstrated at last. "It's serious."

"It would be serious," she retorted with sudden severity, "if you had said all that or anything in the least like that to Miss Wollaston. Because she really loves it. She has adopted it."

"Was she the lady who spoke to me in the park?" His evident consternation over this aspect of the case made Paula smile as she nodded yes.

"That was an act of real kindness," he said earnestly. "Not mere good nature. It doesn't grow on every bush."

To this she eagerly agreed. "She is kind; she's a dear." But when she saw him looking unhappily at the piano again, she said (for she hadn't the slightest intention of abandoning him now), "There's another one, quite a different sort of one, in the music room up-stairs. Would you like to come along and look at that?"

He followed her tractably enough, but up in her studio before looking at the piano, he asked her a question or two. Had he the name right? And was the lady related to Doctor Wollaston?

"She's his sister," said Paula, adding, "and I am his wife. Why, do you know him?"

"I talked with him once. He came out to the factory to see my father and I happened to be there. Two or three years ago, that was. He did an operation on my sister that saved her life. He is a great man." He added, "My name's Anthony March, but he wouldn't remember me."

He sat down at the instrument, went over the keyboard from bottom, to top and back again with a series of curious modulations. Then opening his bag and beginning to get out his tools, he said, "Before I went into the army, there was a man named Bernstein in these parts, who used to perpetrate outrages like this on pianos."

"Yes," said Paula, "he tuned this one two weeks ago."

Without so much as a by your leave, Anthony March went to work.

It was Paula's childlike way to take any pleasurable event simply as a gift from heaven without any further scrutiny of its source; with no labored attempt to explain its arrival and certainly with no misgivings as to whether or not she was entitled to it. Anthony March was such a gift. By the time he had got to work on her own piano, she knew he was pure gold and settled down joyously to make the most of him.

It was not until she attempted to give an account to the Wollastons at dinner that night, of the day they had spent together—for they had made a day of it—that she realized there was anything odd, not to say astonishing, about the episode. How in the first place did it happen that it was Paula's piano he tuned instead of the one in the drawing-room? This was, of course, inexplicable until she could get John by himself and tell him about it. One couldn't report to Lucile his phrase about the painted harlot. She had to content herself with stressing the fact that he intended to tune the drawing-room piano after he had finished with hers and then somehow he hadn't got around to it.

But why had an unaccredited wanderer whom Lucile had found in the park even been given a chance at the piano up-stairs? Well, he had looked to Paula like an artist when she had let him in the door. You could tell, with people like that, if you had an eye for such matters. And then his recognition of Bernstein's nefarious handiwork had clenched her conviction. Certainly she had been right about it; he had absolutely bewitched that piano of hers. She didn't believe there was another such tuner in the United States. If they would come up-stairs after dinner, she'd show them. They had always thought she was unnecessarily fussy about it, but now they should see they were mistaken. It was like unveiling a statue. The poor thing had been there all the time, covered up so that you couldn't hear it. She was so excited about it she could hardly leave it alone.

And he had been as delighted with the results as she herself. After he had played it a while for her (oh, he didn't play well, atrociously badly really, but that didn't matter; it only made it all the more exciting) he made her play for him. Paula smiled reminiscently when she added that he had sat all the while she was playing, on the bare floor under the piano where he could feel the vibrations as well as hear them. He had paid her an odd sort of compliment too, when he came crawling out, saying that he had assumed from the scores on the piano that she was a singer but that she played like a musician,—only not a pianist!

He was a genius, absolutely a genius of the first water, when it came to tuning pianos. Whether his talent as a composer ran to any such lengths as that she, of course, didn't know. If what he had played for her had been his own, any of it, it was awfully modern and interesting, at least. You could tell that even though it kept him swearing at himself all the time for not being able to play it. And from something he said at lunch…

"Lunch!" Miss Wollaston gasped (she had been away from home all day). "Do you mean you had lunch with him?"

"Why not?" Paula wanted to know. "Me to have gone down-stairs and eaten all alone and had a tray sent up for him? That would have been so silly, I never even thought of it. He's a real person. I like him a lot. And I don't know when I've had such a nice day."

Here was where Paula's difficulties began. Because when they asked her who he was, where he lived, where he came from, what his experiences in the army had been, and whether he had been to France or not, she had to profess herself upon all these topics totally uninformed. His name she happened to know; it was Anthony March. He told her that, somehow, right at the beginning, though she couldn't remember how the fact had cropped out.

As to the other matters her husband and his sister were seeking information about she simply hadn't had time to get around to things like that. She thought he might have been a farmer once or some such sort of person. He liked the country anyway. He had spent a lot of time, he told her, tramping about in Illinois and Iowa, earning his way by tuning farmers' pianos.

He hated Puccini and spoke rather disrespectfully of Wagner as a spellbinder. He liked Wolf-Ferrari pretty well; the modern he was really crazy about was Montemezzi. But he had made her sing oceans of Gluck,—both the *Iphigenia* and *Euridice*. It was awfully funny too because he would sing the other parts wherever they happened to lie, tenor, bass, contralto, anything, in the most awful voice you ever heard, though his speaking voice was lovely. Let John just wait until he heard it. It was almost as nice as his own. Oh, he was coming back again some time. He had promised to bring over some songs of his own composing for her to try.

It was at this point or thereabouts that John precipitated a crisis by asking how much this paragon of a piano tuner had charged her for his professional services. Paula stared at him, stricken.

"Why," she said, "I don't believe I paid him anything. I know I didn't. I never thought of it at all. Neither did he, for that matter though, I'm sure of it."

This provoked Lucile into an outburst, rare with her, of outspoken indignation. The man, delinquent as he had been in the matter of the drawing-room piano, became once more her protégé, her soldier whom she had found in the park and attempted to do a kindness to. Paula had kept him fussing over her piano all day and then let him go without, for all she knew, money enough to buy his supper or procure a lodging for the night.

John, though he made less commotion about it, took his wife's negligence even more seriously for he set about attempting to repair it. "You're quite sure," he asked in his crisp, consulting-room manner—a manner Paula was happily unfamiliar with—"You're quite sure he told you nothing about himself beyond his bare name? You've got that right, haven't you? Anthony March?"

"Yes," said Paula uncertainly, "I'm absolutely sure of that."

Had he any insignia on his uniform?—little bronze numerals on his collar—anything like that that she could remember? That would tell them what organization he belonged to and might give them a clue.

Here Lucile got drawn into the inquisition. She had seen him and talked to him. Had she noticed anything of the sort? But Lucile had not. She had, naturally, deferred all inquiries until he came to tune the piano; and had she been called as she felt she should have been....

But John, it appeared, was not interested in pursuing that line. He turned back to Paula. "I wish you'd begin at the beginning, my dear, at the time you let him into the house, and try to remember as nearly as you can everything that you said to him and that he said to you. He may have said something casually that you didn't remark at the time which would be of the greatest help to us now."

Paula wasn't very hopeful of obtaining any result in this way, but she dutifully went to work trying to think. She was perfectly amiable about it all. Presently her husband prompted her. "How did he happen to tell you what his name was? Can you remember that?"

After a minute, she did. "Why," she cried, lighting up, "he said he knew you but you wouldn't remember him. He said you did an operation on his sister once—that saved her life."

"An unmarried sister?" he asked.

"What difference ... Oh, I see, because if she was married her name wouldn't be March. No, he didn't say anything about that. He did say something, though, about a factory. You went out to the factory to see his father and he was there."

John Wollaston's face went blank for a minute and his eyelids drooped shut. Then a quick jerk of the head and a sharp expulsion of breath announced success. "That's all right," he said. "Thank the Lord, I've got it now."

It would have seemed absurd to Paula, had she been capable of regarding anything he did in that light, that he should take a trivial matter like this so seriously. He couldn't have looked more relieved over the successful finish of a difficult operation.

"That happens to be a case I'll never forget," he went on to explain. "Professionally speaking, it was unique, but it had points of human interest as well. The girl was a patient in one of the wards at the Presbyterian. I didn't get a look at her until the last minute when it was desperate. Her father was opposed to the operation—a religious scruple, it turned out. Didn't want God's will interfered with. He was a workman, a skilled workman in a piano factory. There was no time to lose so I drove out there and got him; converted him on the way back to the hospital. I remember the son, now I think of it; by his speech, too. I remember thinking that the mother must have been a really cultivated woman. Well, it's all right. I've got the address in the files at the office. I'll send a letter there in the morning and enclose a check. How much ought it to be?"

Once more Paula did not know. Hadn't, she protested, an idea; and when John asked her how much she paid Bernstein, she didn't know that either. It all went on the bill.

"Well, that's easy," said John. "I've got last month's bills in my desk. All right, I'll look into it. You needn't bother about it any more."

An approximation to a sniff from Miss Wollaston conveyed the comment that Paula hadn't bothered appreciably about it from the beginning, but neither of the others paid any attention to that.

As it fell out, John might have spared his labors because at eight o'clock or thereabouts the next morning just as he was sitting down to breakfast, Anthony March came back to repair his omission of the day before and tune the drawing-room piano.

A minor domestic detail of that sort would normally have fallen within Lucile's province, but John decisively took it away from her.

"When I finish breakfast," he said, "I'll write him a check and take it in to him." He added, "I'm curious to see what this new discovery of Paula's looks like."

That was exactly what he felt, an amused comfortable curiosity. Nothing in the least like that flash of jealousy he had felt over Novelli. If it had occurred to him to try to explain the difference to himself and had he taken the trouble to skim off the superficial explanation,—that Portia Stanton's husband belonged in Paula's world and that a tramp genius who came around to tune pianos did not,—he might have got down to the recognition of the fact that the character Paula had sketched for him last night was a grotesque and not therefore to be taken seriously. You could not, at least, do anything but smile over a man who sat on the floor under Paula's piano while she played and came crawling out to express surprise that a singer should be a musician as well.

So the look of the man he found in the drawing-room stopped him rather short. Anthony March had taken off the ill-fitting khaki blouse and the sleeves of his olive-drab uniform shirt were rolled up above the elbows. He was sitting sidewise on the piano bench, his left hand on the keyboard, his right making imperceptible changes in the tension of one of the strings. His implement, John's quick eye noticed, was not the long-handled L shaped affair he had always seen tuners use but a T shaped thing that put the tuner's hand exactly above the pin.

"It must take an immense amount of strength," he observed, "to tune a piano with a wrench like that."

March turned and with a pleasant sort of smile wished him a good morning. But he finished ironing the wave out of a faulty unison before he replied to John's remark. He arose from the bench as he spoke. "It does; but it is more a matter of knack really. A great tuner named Clark taught me, and he learned it from Jonas Chickering himself. Old Jonas wouldn't allow any of his grand pianos to be tuned with an L head wrench."

"My wife," said John, "recalled you to me last night, in the effort to remedy her omission to pay you for your services yesterday. I remember your sister's case very distinctly. I hope she is ..."

"She is quite well, thank you," March said. Oddly enough his manner stiffened a little.

John hastily produced his check. It had struck him as possible that March might suspect him of hinting that one gratuitous service ought to offset the other.

"I hope the amount is satisfactory," he said.

March glanced at the check and smiled. "It's rather more than satisfactory; I should call it handsome. Thank you very much." He tucked the check into the pocket of his shirt.

"My wife's immensely pleased over what you did to her piano. I'm sure she will be glad to do all she can in the way of recommending you among her musical friends."

March looked at him in consternation. "Oh, she mustn't do that!" he cried. "I hope she won't—recommend me to any one."

John's sudden unwelcome surmise must have been legible in his face because March then said earnestly and quite as if the doctor had spoken his thought aloud, "Oh, it isn't that. I mean, I haven't done anything disgraceful. It's only that I know too many musicians as it is—professional pianists and such. If they find out I'm back, they'll simply make a slave of me. I don't need to earn much money and I like to live my own way, but it's hard to deny people what they are determined to get." He added thoughtfully, "I dare say you understand that, sir."

John Wollaston nodded. He understood very well indeed. He checked on his tongue the words, "Only I *have* to earn a lot of money." "You are a composer, too, my wife tells me."

"Yes," March said, "but that isn't the point exactly. Put it that I enjoy traveling light and that I don't like harness. Though this one,"—he glanced down at his uniform,—"hasn't been so bad." He turned toward the piano with the evident idea of going back to work.

"Well," John said, "I must be off. You've a good philosophy of life if you can make it work. Not many men can. Good-by. We'll meet again some time, I hope."

"I hope so too," said Anthony March.

John went out and closed the drawing-room door behind him. Then he left the house without going up-stairs and saying hello to Paula and sitting down on the edge of her bed, as he had meant to do, and telling her all about his talk with the piano tuner.

It really was late and he must be getting started. Only why had he closed the drawing-room door so carefully behind him? So that his wife shouldn't be disturbed by the infernal racket those fellows always made tuning pianos? Or so that she mightn't even know, until he had finished his work and gone, that Anthony March had come back at all? And not knowing, should not come down *en negligée* and ask whether he had brought his songs for her. Had he brought them? Certainly John had given him a good enough chance to say so. And if he had brought them and Paula did not come, would he leave them for her with Nat? Or would he carry them away in his little black satchel?

All the way out to the hospital John kept turning Anthony March over in his mind and the last thing to leave it was what had been the first impression of all. The fine strength of that hand and wrist which tuned grand pianos with a T wrench.

He hated himself for having shut the door.

And as it happened this act did not prevent Paula from finding March. The tyrant who looked after her hair had given her an appointment that morning at ten. So, a little before that hour and just as March was finishing off his job, she came down, dressed for the street. She came into the drawing-room and with good-humored derision, smiled at him.

"I knew you'd come and do it," she told him.

"It isn't going to be so bad," he answered. "Moszkowski, Chaminade,— quite a little of Chopin for that matter,—will go pretty well on it."

"Did you bring my songs?" she asked.

From the chair that he had thrown his blouse upon, he produced a flat package neatly wrapped in brown paper. And as she went over to the window with it, tearing the wrappers away as she walked, he went back to his work at the piano.

"Don't do that," she said, as he struck a chord or two. "I can't read if you do." But almost instantly she added with a laugh, "Oh, all right, go ahead.

I can't read this anyway. Why, it's frightful!" She came swiftly toward the piano and stood the big flat quires of score paper on the rack. "Show me how this goes," she commanded, but he pushed back a little with a gesture almost of fright.

"No," he protested sharply. "I can't. I can't begin to play that stuff."

She remained standing beside his shoulder, looking at the score.

"They're strange words," she said, and began reading them to herself, half aloud, haltingly.

"'Low hangs the moon. It rose late,
It is lagging—O I think it is heavy with love, with love.'"

"Walt Whitman," he told her. "They're all out of a poem called *Sea-Drift*."

She went on reading, now audibly, now with a mere silent movement of the lips, half puzzled, half entranced, and catching—despite her protest that she could not read the music,—some intimations of its intense strange beauty.

"' ...*do I not see my love fluttering out among the breakers?... Loud I call to you, my love ... Surely you must know who is here ... O rising stars! Perhaps the one I want so much will rise ... with some of you ... O trembling throat! Sound clearer through the atmosphere ...*'"

With a shake of the head, like one trying to stop the weaving of a spell, she turned the pages back to the beginning.

"This means Novelli," she said. "I'll get him. I'll get him this morning. He's the best accompanist in Chicago. We'll go to work on them and when we've got them presentable, I'll let you know and sing them to you. Where do you live?"

He got up for a paper and pencil and wrote out an address and a telephone number. She was still staring at that first page of the score when he brought it back to her.

"I've never heard any of those songs myself," he told her.

At that she looked around at him, looked steadily into his face for a moment and then her eyes filled with tears. She reached out both hands and took him by the shoulders. "Well, you're going to hear them this time, my dear," she said. As she moved away, she added in a more matter-of-fact tone, "Just as soon as we can work them up, in a few days perhaps. I'll let you know."

# CHAPTER III
# THE PEACE BASIS

There were four in their party but it was only with Alfred Baldwin that Mary Wollaston danced. The other man—Black his name was, and he came from Iowa City or Dubuque or thereabouts—devoted all his attention to Baldwin's wife. He was very rich, very much married—out in Iowa—and whenever he made his annual business trip to New York, he liked to have a real New York time. They had dined together at the Baldwins' apartment with a vague idea of going afterward to see a play of Baldwin's then drawing toward the close of a successful season's run. But dinner had been late and they had lingered too long over it to make this excursion worth while. It had amused both Mary and Christabel to discover Black's secret hope of being taken back-stage and introduced to the beautiful young star who was playing in the piece and taking her out to supper with them. He didn't know that Baldwin hated her with a perfect hatred and never got within speaking distance of her if he could help it.

So, by way of making up to the western visitor for his disappointment they taxied up-town about ten o'clock to the brightest, loudest and most fantastically expensive of New York's dancing restaurants. Once there, he took command of the party; confidently addressed the head waiter by his first name and began "opening wine" with a lavish hand. He was flirting in what he conceived to be quite a desperate and depraved manner with Christabel, and what enhanced his pleasure in this entertainment was that he did it all right under the nose of the husband, who obviously didn't mind a bit. He would talk eloquently when he got home, with carefully selected corroborative details, about the wickedness of New York.

Mary liked the Baldwins. Christabel was on the executive committee of their Fund and one of the best and steadiest and most sensible supporters it had. She was a real person. Baldwin, himself, whom she hadn't known so long nor so well and had regarded from afar as a rather formidable celebrity, proved on better acquaintance, though witty and sophisticated, to be as comfortable as an old glove. Altogether they were the nearest thing to friends that her long sojourn in New York had given her. She had sometimes thought rather wildly of putting them to the test and seeing whether they were real friends or not.

To-night, though, even they irritated her. She wished Christabel would snub that appalling bounder, Black, as he deserved. How could she go on playing up to him like that! As for Baldwin, she wished he would just dance with her and not talk. She supposed that the amount of alcohol they had consumed since seven o'clock had something to do with his verging upon the vein, the Broadway sentimental vein, that he had got started on and couldn't seem to let alone.

It wasn't new to Mary. Indeed it was a phenomenon familiarly associated in her mind with Forty-second Street restaurants and late hours and strong drink, particularly gin. The crocodile tear for the good woman who stayed at home; who didn't know; who never, please God! should know. The tribute to flower-like innocence—the paper flower-like innocence of the stage *ingenue*!

Baldy wasn't as bad as that, couldn't ever conceivably be as bad as that, no matter how much he had had to drink. Perhaps, if she had not been hypersensitive to-night,—in an impossible mood for any sort of party really—she might have failed to detect the familiar strain in his sensible, rather fatherly talk. As it was, she thought she did detect it and it made her want to scream—or swear!

There is one point to be urged in Baldy's defense that Mary never learned to allow for. Gin or no gin, the effect of contrast she presented to her surroundings in a place like this, her look of a seraphic visitor gone astray, would have given any one the impulse, at least, to rush to the rescue. To begin with, it was not possible to credit her with the twenty-five years she truly claimed; nineteen, in a soft colored evening frock like the one she had on to-night, was about what one would have guessed. Then, you never would have believed, short of discovering the fact yourself, how strong she was; her slenderness and the fine articulation of her joints made her look fragile. Her coloring helped the illusion along, the clear unsophisticated blue of her eyes, the pallor of her hair that the petals of a tea-rose could have got lost in,—it was, literally, just about the tint of unbleached linen— and the pearly translucence of her skin. If you got the opportunity to look close enough to see that there wasn't a grain of powder upon it, not even between the shoulder blades, it made you think of flower petals again. What clenched the effect was her healthy capacity for complete relaxation when no effort was required of her. She drooped a little and people thought she looked tired. She never could see herself like that and never made due allowance for the effect she produced, invariably upon strangers and not infrequently upon an old friend.

To-night, she lacked the name to label her mood by, rejecting rather fiercely the one that kept offering itself. You couldn't be homesick when home was the last place in the world you wanted to go back to—the place you were desperately marshaling reasons for staying away from.

It was the non-appearance of her brother, Rush, that had brought a lot of dispersed feelings to a focus. She had heard nothing later from him than the letter she referred to when she last wrote to her father. She had expected a cable and it hadn't come. She had this morning gone over to Hoboken to meet the transport he had said he expected to sail on, but having got down to the pier a little late, after the debarkation had begun, she could not be sure that she hadn't missed him. So she had gone back to her tiny flat in Waverly Place and had spent the rest of the day there, vainly hoping that he would turn up or at least that she should get some word of him. And sitting around like that for hours and hours she had, which was a silly thing to do, let her thoughts run wild over things—a thing—that there was simply no sense in thinking about at all.

It was an odd fact, which she had noted long before today, that anything connected with home, a letter from her father or her aunt, news of the doings of any of her Chicago friends (the birth of Olive Corbett's second baby, for example), any vivid projection of a bit of the pattern of the life into which she had once been woven, roused that nightmare memory. Or gave, rather, to a memory which normally did not trouble her much, the quality of a nightmare; a moment of paralyzed incredulity that it could have happened to her; a pang of clear horror that it really and truly had happened to her very self; to this Mary Wollaston who still lived in the very place where it had happened.

This afternoon, while she had sat awaiting from moment to moment the appearance of her brother, or at least the sound of his voice over the telephone, the pang had been prolonged into an agony. She had let herself drift into a fantastic speculation of a sort that was perfectly new. What if the boy who had shared that crazy adventure with her, himself an officer bound overseas, had fallen in with Rush, made friends with him, told him the story!

This was pure melodrama, she knew. There was, in any external sense, nothing to be feared. The thing had happened almost a year ago. It had had no consequences—except this inexplicable one that her brother's approach brought back the buried memory of it. Why should it cling like that? Like an acid that wouldn't wash off! She was not, as far as her mind went, ashamed of it. Never had been. But, waiving all the extenuating circumstances—which had really surrounded the act—admitting that it was a sin (this thing that she had done once and had, later, learned the impossibility of ever doing again), was it any worse than what her brother had probably done a score of times?

What was this brother of hers going to be like? It wasn't possible, of course, that she would find him the boy he had been five years ago, before he went to France—though from some of his letters one might have thought he hadn't changed a bit. Wasn't it likely that he'd turn out to be some one she could cling to a little; confide her perplexities to—some of them? Was there a chance that ripened, disillusioned, made gentle and wise by the alchemy of the furnace he had come through, he might prove to be the one person in the world to whom she could confide everything? That would make an end to her nightmare, she felt sure.

The question whether he was or was not going to turn out like that was one presently to be answered. Until she knew the answer she didn't want to think at all, least of all about those things which Baldy's talk to-night kept rousing echoes of.

"Oh, they all look good when they're far away," she said, picking that bit of comic supplement slang deliberately to annoy him. "I don't believe our grandfathers and grandmothers were always such models of decorum as they tried, when they had grown old, to make us think. And the simple primitive joys ... I believe an old-fashioned husking bee, if they had plenty of hard cider to go with it, was just as bad as this—coarser if not so vulgar. After all, most of these people will go virtuously home to bed pretty soon and you'd find them back at work to-morrow morning not any the worse, really, for this. It may be a rather poor sort of home they go to, but how do you know that the vine-covered cottage you have been talking about was any better?"

"Not to mention," he added, in humorous concurrence, "that there was probably typhoid in the well the old oaken bucket hung in. It seems odd to be convicted of sentimentality by an innocent babe like you. But if you had been looking at the party down at the end table behind you that I've had under my eye for ten minutes, perhaps you'd feel more as I do. No! don't turn around; they have been looking at us."

"Moralizing over us, perhaps," she suggested. "Thinking how wicked we probably were."

"No," he said, "I happen to know the girls. They live down in our part of town, just over in the Village, that is. They have been here six or eight years. One of them was quite a promising young illustrator once. And they're both well-bred—came obviously from good homes. And they've both gone, well—clean over the edge."

Somehow his innocent euphemism annoyed her. "You mean they are prostitutes?" she asked.

He frowned in protest at her employment of the word but assented unequivocally. He was used—as who is not—to hearing young women discuss outspokenly such topics but he couldn't forgive it from one who looked like Mary Wollaston.

"I have a hunch," he said, "that the two boys who are with them are officers out of uniform. I noticed that they looked the other way pretty carefully when that major who is sitting at the next table to ours came in."

"Let's dance again," she said. "I love this Hawaiian Moonlight thing."

He saw her take the opportunity that rising from the table gave her for a good square look at the party he had been talking about and some change in her manner made him say with quick concern, "What is it?"

But she ignored the question and stepped out upon the floor with him. They had danced half-way round the room when she said quietly, "One of the boys at that table is my brother Rush."

Baldwin said, "He has seen you, I think." He felt her give a sort of gasp before she replied but the words came steadily enough.

"Oh, yes, we saw each other at the same time."

He said nothing more, just went on dancing around the room with her in silence, taking care, without appearing to do so, to cut the corner where Rush was sitting, rather broadly. After two or three rounds of the floor, she flagged a little and without asking any questions, he led her back to their table. Luckily, Christabel and her Iowan had disappeared.

As soon as she was seated she asked him for a pencil and something she could write on—a card of his, the back of an old letter, anything. She wrote, "Won't you please come and ask me to dance?" and she slid it over to him. He read it and understood, picked up a busboy with his eye and despatched him with the folded scrap for delivery to Captain Wollaston at the end table.

Mary meanwhile had cradled her chin in her palms and closed her eyes. She had experienced so clear a premonition before she turned round to look at the party at the end table that one of those officers out of uniform would turn out to be Rush that the verification of it had the quality of something that happens in a dream. She felt a sharp incredulity that it could really be they, staring at each other across that restaurant. More than that, the brother she saw was not—in that first glance—the man she had been trying all day to make up her mind he would be. Not the new Rush with two palms to his *Croix de Guerre* and his American D.S.C.; and the scars in his soul from the experiences those decorations must represent; but the Rush she had said good-by to in the autumn of 1914 when he set out to be a freshman at Harvard, the kid brother she had counciled and occasionally admonished, in the vicarious exercise of her father's authority. And in his panic-stricken gaze at her, she had recognized his instinctive acceptance of that position. Exactly so would he have looked five interminable years ago if she had caught him in mischief.

Then, like the undertow of a big wave, the reaction caught her. It was intolerable that he should look at her like that. He who had earned his manhood and its privileges in the long death grapple with the grimmest of realities. Certainly she was not the one to cast the first stone at him. She must contrive somehow, at once, to make that clear to him. The urgency of the thing lay in her belief that the whole of their future relationship depended upon the removing of his misapprehension now—to-night.

She could not go to that table where he sat without seeming more than ever the school mistress in pursuit of a truant, but perhaps he would come to her if she put her request right. They had danced together quite a lot in the old days. She danced so well that not even her status of elder sister had prevented his enjoying the exercise of their combined accomplishment.

A horrible misgiving had attacked her when she had scribbled the note and closed her eyes, that the cocktails and the champagne she herself had consumed since seven o'clock might have clouded her judgment—if, indeed, they were not responsible for the whole nightmare. Would she be equal to following out the line she had set for herself?

But no trace of that misgiving was apparent to her when Rush, after a wait of only two or three minutes, appeared at her table. She greeted him with a smile and a Hello, nodded a fleeting farewell to Baldwin and slipped comfortably into her brother's arms out on the floor. They danced away without a word. There was the same quite beautiful accord between them that there had been in the old days, and the sense of this steadied her. They had gone all the way around the floor before she spoke.

"It is like old times, isn't it?" she said. "And it does seem good. You don't mind, do you,—for ten minutes?"

"Ten minutes?" he echoed dully.

She knew then, as she had indeed been aware from the first, that he was drunk and that only by the most painful effort, could he command his scattered wits at all. It made her want to cry that he should be trying so hard. She must not cry. That would be the final outrage. She must be very simple and clear. She must—*must* contrive to make him understand.

"Will you listen to me, dear, and do exactly what I ask you to? I want you to go back to your people and forget that you have seen me at all."

"I am going to take you home—out of this," he said laboriously.

"I'm going home soon, but not with you. I want you to go back to—to the girl you brought here. No, dear, listen. This is the only reason I sent for you. To tell you that I wasn't going to try to scold you. I don't mind a bit. I want to tell you that, so that when you come back to me to-morrow or next day or whenever your party is quite over, you won't feel that you have anything to try to explain or apologize for. Now take me back to my place and then go on to yours."

"I won't take you back to him," he said doggedly. "What do you think I am? I'm drunk, but not enough for that. I am going to take you home."

She tried to laugh but in spite of herself it was more like a sob.

"Rush, dear, don't be silly. I am perfectly all right—or would be if I hadn't drunk quite so much champagne. They'll take me home. His wife's here with him and they're old friends of mine. They know a lot of our friends in Chicago. Please, Rush...."

"Do you think I'd go back to that—" he managed to pull up on the edge of an ugly word—"back to those people, and leave you here? Is it your wrap on that chair? We'll stop and get it and then we'll go."

She could have wept with vexation over the way her scheme had gone awry but there was clearly nothing else to do. She retrieved her cloak, simply said good night to Christabel and the man named Black, leaving Baldy to explain things as he chose.

Five minutes later she gave a taxi driver the address of her flat and dropped back against the cushions beside her brother. Neither of them spoke a word during that fifteen-minute drive. Mary wept quietly most of the way—it didn't matter there in the dark. The thought of this splendid glorious brother of hers painfully endeavoring to drag himself back into a state of sobriety from his first wild caper after long wearing of the harness of discipline—an escapade she supposed that he must have been looking forward to for days—dragging himself back to protect her—oh, it was too hopeless! Should she ever be able to explain to him why she had sent for him, and that her intentions had been the opposite of those of the moralizing meddler he would take her for? If only she could make it up to him somehow. She would have liked to reach over and pull him down into her arms, mother him and tell him not to mind—there was something so intolerably pathetic about his effort to sit soberly straight—but she resisted this impulse savagely. The alcohol in her own veins was responsible for this. She could not quite trust herself not to go maudlin. So she froze herself tight and huddled away from him into her own corner.

She did not think beyond the address she had given to the chauffeur until they pulled up at her door. Then she turned to Rush and asked, "Where shall he take you? Are you staying at a hotel?"

"I am going to take you home," he said precisely.

She saw she did not dare to let him go. There was no telling what serious trouble he might get into, in his illicit civilian dress, if she turned him adrift now. So she said, simply, "Well, here we are. Come in."

She opened the street door with her latch-key, and punched on the hall lights. She dreaded the two flights of stairs, but with the help of the banister rail he negotiated them successfully enough. And then he was safely brought to anchor in her sitting-room. It was plain he had not the vaguest idea where he was.

"I'll make some coffee," she said. "That will—pull us both together. And it won't take a minute because it's all ready to make for breakfast."

She was not gone, indeed, much longer than that, but when she came back from her kitchenette he had dropped like a log upon her divan, submerged beyond all soundings. So she tugged him around into a more comfortable position, managed to divest him of his dinner-jacket and his waistcoat, unbuttoned his collar and shirt-band, took off his shoes, and covered him up with an eiderdown quilt. Then she kissed him—it was five years since she had done that—and went, herself, to bed.

At ten o'clock the next morning she sat behind her little breakfast table—it was daintily munitioned with a glass coffee machine, a grapefruit and a plate of toast—waiting, over *The Times*, for Rush to wake up. She looked more seraphic than ever, enveloped in a white turkish toweling bathrobe and with her hair in a braid. Her brother lay on the divan just as she had left him the night before. Presently the change in his breathing told her that he was struggling up out of the depths of sleep. She looked over at him and saw him blinking at the ceiling. When his gaze started round her way, she turned her attention to the busy little coffee machine which opportunely needed it.

It was a minute or two before he spoke. "Is that really you, Mary?"

She smiled affectionately at him and said, "Hello," adding with just an edge of good-humored mischief, "How do you feel?"

He turned abruptly away from her. "I feel loathsome," he said.

"Poor dear, of course you do. I'll tell you what to do. I've got a nice big bathroom in there. Go in and take a cold one." Then—"You've grown inches, Rush, since you went away but I believe you could still get into a suit of my pajamas—plain ones, not ruffly. Anyhow, I've another big bathrobe like this that you could roll up in. You'll be just in time for the coffee. You won't know yourself by then."

"I wish I didn't," he said morosely.

There wasn't much good arguing with that mood, she knew, so she waited a little.

"Is this where you live?" he asked. "You brought me here last night?"

"You brought me," she amended.

He frowned over that but didn't take it in. The next moment though he sat up suddenly and after a struggle with the giddiness this movement caused, asked, "Who else is here? Where's the other girl that lives with you?"

"She's not here now," Mary said. "We are all by ourselves."

He rose unsteadily to his feet. "I've got to get out of here quick. If anybody came in ..."

"Rush, dearest!" she entreated. "Don't be silly. Lie down again— Well, then take that easy chair. Nobody will come in." Then over his air of resolute remorse she cried, on the edge of tears herself, "Oh, *please* don't be so unhappy. Do let's settle down and be comfy together. I don't have to go to the office to-day. My job's just about played out. But nobody ever comes here to see me in the daytime. And it wouldn't matter if they did."

But this change of attitude was clearly beyond him. "I'll have to ask you to tell me what happened last night. You were there at that restaurant with friends of yours I suppose. I must have disgraced you up to the hilt with them. I should think you'd hate the sight of me."

"You didn't disgrace me at all," she contradicted, and now the tears did came into her eyes. "They knew I was expecting you and I told Mr. Baldwin who you were. You came up in the nicest way and asked me to dance and when we went away together there wasn't a thing—about you—that they could see. I was on the point of tears myself because my plan had gone wrong. But that would have seemed natural enough to them."

He frowned at the name Baldwin, as if he were trying to recover a memory. Now he felt vaguely in his trousers pocket and pulled out the crumpled visiting card that had her note scribbled on the back of it. "You haven't told me yet what happened," he said.

"Oh, I was afraid you wouldn't remember." She looked away from him as she said it and a little unwonted color crept into her cheeks.

"Afraid?" he questioned.

"I wanted you to understand," she said, "and now I'll have to tell you again. It was because I was trying so hard not to meddle that I did. I sent that little note to you just to get a chance to tell you not to mind my seeing you there with those others—not to let it spoil your party. I couldn't bear to have you come to me to-day, or to-morrow or whenever it was, feeling—well, ashamed you know, and explanatory. That's what I tried to tell you last night but couldn't make you understand. So I did, really, just exactly what I was meaning not to. Of course, I loved you for coming away and I love having you here like this, all to myself. But I didn't mean to—to spoil things for you."

He stared at her a moment in blank inapprehension; then a deep blush came burning into his face. "You didn't understand," he said thickly. "You didn't know what those girls were."

"Oh, Rush!" she cried. "Of course I did. I knew exactly what they were—better than you. I even knew who they were. They live not very far from here."

He paled and his look was frightened. "How did you know that?" he demanded. "How could you know a thing like that?"

"They've lived here in the Village for years," she said, summarizing Baldy without quoting him as her authority. "One of them used to be an illustrator—or something—before she went—over the edge. They're two of our celebrities. One can't go about, unless he's stone blind, without picking up things like that."

"You did know what she was, then," he persisted, doggedly pushing through something it was almost impossible for him to say, "and yet, knowing, you asked me to leave you alone and go back to her. You wanted me to do that?"

"I didn't want you to!" she cried. "I hated it, of course. But men—people—do things like that, and I could see how—natural it was that you wanted to. And if you wanted to, I didn't think it fair that it should be spoiled for you just because we happened to recognize each other. I didn't want you to hate me for having spoiled it. That's all."

She gave him the minute or two he evidently needed for turning this over in his mind. Then she turned her back on the window she had withdrawn to and began again.

"I used to be just a big sister to you, of course. Ever so superior, I guess, and a good bit of a prig. And all this time over there in France with nothing but my letters and that silly picture of me in the khaki frame, I suppose you have been thinking of me, well,—as a sort of nice angel. I'm not either, really. I don't want to be either.

"I want to be somebody you feel would understand anything; somebody you could tell anything to. So that it would work the other way as well. Because I've got to have somebody to tell things to,—troubles, and worries. And I've been hoping, ever since your letter came, that it would turn out to be you."

"What sort of troubles?" He shot the question in rather tensely.

There was a breathless moment before she answered, but she shook it off with a laugh and her manner lightened. "There's nothing to be so solemn about as all that. We don't want to wallow. We'll have some breakfast—only you go first and tub."

He was too young and healthy and clean-blooded to resist the effect upon his spirits which the cold water and the fresh white bathrobe and the hot strong coffee with real cream in it produced. And the gloomy, remorseful feeling, which he felt it his moral duty to maintain intact, simply leaked away. She noted the difference in him and half-way through their breakfast she left her chair and came round to him.

"Would you very much mind being kissed now?" she asked.

His answer, with a laugh, was to pull her down upon his knee and hug her up tight in his arms. They looked rather absurdly alike in those two white bathrobes, though this was an appearance neither of them was capable of observing. She disengaged herself presently from his embrace and went to find him some cigarettes, refraining from taking one herself from a feeling that he would probably like it better just then if she did not.

Back in her own place over her coffee and toast, she had no difficulty in launching him upon the tale of his own recent experiences. What the French were like now the war was over; and the Boche he had been living among in the Coblenz area;—the routine of his army life, the friends he made over there, and so on. Altogether she built him up immensely in his own esteem.

It was plain he liked having her for a younger sister instead of for an older one, listening so contentedly to his tales, ministering to his momentary wants, visibly wondering at and adoring him.

But she broke the spell when she asked him what he meant to do now.

He turned restlessly in his chair. "I don't know," he said. "I don't know what the deuce there is I can do. Certainly father's idea of my going back to college and then to medical school afterward, is just plain, rank nonsense. I'd be a doddering old man before I got through—thirty years old. I should think that even he would see that. It will have to be business, I suppose, but if any kind friend comes around and suggests that I begin at the bottom somewhere—Mr. Whitney, for instance, offering me a job at ten dollars a week in his bank—I'll kill him. I can't do that. I won't. At the end of about ten days, I'd run amuck. What I'd really like," he concluded, "for about a year would be just this." His gesture indicated the bathrobe, the easy chair and the dainty breakfast table. "This, all the morning and a ball-game in the afternoon. Lord, it will be good to see some real baseball again. We'll go to a lot of games this summer. What are the Sox going to be like this year?"

She discussed the topic expertly with him and with a perfectly genuine interest, at some length. "Oh, it would be fun," she finished with a little sigh, "only I shan't be there, you know. At least I don't think I shall." Then before he could ask her why not, she added in sharper focus, "I can't go home, Rush."

"Can't!" he exclaimed. "What do you mean by that?"

"Oh, nothing to make a fuss about," she said with a frown of irritation. "I wish you weren't so jumpy this morning,—or perhaps, it's I that am. All I meant was that home isn't a comfortable place for me and I won't go back there if I can help it—only I am afraid I can't. That's the trouble I wanted to talk to you about."

"I thought you liked the new stepmother," he said. "Hasn't she turned out well?—What am I supposed to call her, anyhow? I wanted to find out about that before I was right up against it."

"Call her?" Mary was a little taken back. "Why, anything you like, I should think. I've always called her Paula.—You weren't thinking of calling her mother, were you?"

"Well," he protested, "how should I know? After all, she is father's wife. And she must be fairly old."

"But, Rush, you've *seen* her!"

"Only that once, at the wedding. She was made up to look young then, of course. Painted and dyed and so on, I suppose. I felt so embarrassed and silly over the whole thing—being just a kid—that I hardly looked at her. And that was a long while ago."

Mary laughed at that, though she knew it would annoy him. "She never paints nor dyes nor anything, Ruddy. She doesn't have to. She's such a perfectly raving beauty without it. And she's more beautiful now than she was then. She really is young, you see. Hardly enough older than we are to matter, now that we're grown up."

She saw Rush digesting this idea of a beautiful young stepmother whom he was to be privileged to call—straight off—by her first name, with a certain satisfaction, so she waited—rather conscious that she was being patient—for him to come back from the digression of his own accord. Presently he did.

"What does she do that you don't like?"

"She does nothing that isn't perfectly nice, and good-tempered, and—respectable," Mary assured him, and added on a warmer note, "Oh, and she's really amiable and lovely. I was being a cat. But I am truly fond of her—when I have her to myself. It's when she's with father ..."

She broke off there, seeing that she could not make that clear to him (how could she since she would not state it in plain terms to herself?) and hurried on, "It's really father whom I don't get on with, any more. He worries about me and feels sorry for me and wants me to come home. But I'm nothing to him when I do come—but an embarrassment.—No, it isn't rot. He knows it himself and feels horrid about it and raises my allowance when I go away, though it was foolishly big already; and then, as soon as I'm back here he begins worrying again, and urging me to come home. He didn't insist as long as I was doing war work, but now that that's played out, I suppose he will.

"Oh, I know well enough what I ought to do. I ought to answer some advertisement for a typist—I can do that, but not stenography—and take a regular job. The sort you said you'd shoot Mr. Whitney for offering you. And then I ought to take a hall bedroom somewhere in the cross-town twenties and live on what I earned. That's the only thing I can see, and, Rush, I simply haven't the courage to do it. It seems as if I couldn't do it."

His lively horror at the bare suggestion of such a thing drew her into a half-hearted defense of the project. Numbers of the girls she knew down here who had been doing war work were going enthusiastically into things like that—or at least were announcing an invincible determination to do so.

Only they were cleverer than she at that sort of thing and could hope for better jobs. They were in luck. They liked it—looked forward to a life of it as one full of engaging possibilities. But to Mary it was nothing, she hardly pretended, but a forlorn last shift. If one couldn't draw nor write nor act nor develop some clever musical stunt, what else was there for a girl to do?

"Well, of course," said Rush, in a very mature philosophical way and lighting a cigarette pretty deliberately between the words,—"of course, what most girls do, is—marry somebody." Then he stole a look around at his sister to see how she had taken it.

There was a queer look that almost frightened him in her blue eyes. Her lips, which were trembling, seemed to be trying to smile.

"That's father's idea," she said raggedly. "He's as anxious now that I should marry somebody—anybody, as he was that I shouldn't five years ago—before he found Paula. You see I am so terribly—left on his hands."

There was, no doubt, something comical about the look of utter consternation she saw on her brother's face, but she should not have tried to laugh at him for a sob caught the laugh in the middle and swept away the last of her self-control. She flung herself down upon the divan and buried her face in one of the pillows. He had seen men cry like that but, oddly enough, never a woman. What he did though was perhaps as much to the point as anything he could have done. He sat down beside her and gathered her up tight in his arms and held her there without a word until the tempest had blown itself out. When the sobs had died away to nothing more than a tremulous catch in each indrawn breath, he let her go back among the pillows and turn so that she could look up at him. By that time the sweat had beaded out upon his forehead, and his hands, which had dropped down upon her shoulders, were trembling.

"Well," she asked unsteadily. "What do you think of me now?"

He wanted to bend down and kiss her but wisely he forbore. "It's easy to see what's the matter," he said. "This war business you have been doing has been too much for you. You're simply all in." Then happily he added, "I'd call you a case of shell-shock."

She rewarded that with a washed-out smile. "What's the treatment going to be?" she asked.

"Why," he said, "as soon as I'm done tucking you up properly in this eiderdown quilt, I'm going out to your icebox and try to find the makings of an egg-nog. Incidentally, I shall scramble up all the rest of the eggs I find and eat them myself. And then I'll find something dull to read to you until you go to sleep. When it's dark enough so that my evening clothes won't attract too much attention, I'll go back and get into uniform; then I'll buy two tickets for Chicago on the fast train to-morrow, and two tickets for a show to-night; and then I'll come back and take you out to dinner. Any criticisms on that program?"

"Not just for this minute," she said contentedly. "I don't know whether I'm going to Chicago with you, tomorrow, or not."

"That's all right," he said. "I know all about that." He added, "I hope the other girl won't mind—the one who lives here with you. What was her name?"

"Ethel Holland? Oh, she went over to France with the Y.M.C.A. just about a year ago. I've tried to find somebody to take her place, but there didn't seem to be any one I liked well enough. So I've been living alone."

She saw his face stiffen at that but his only comment was that that simplified matters.

# CHAPTER IV
# THE PICTURE PUZZLE

There was a good quarter of an hour beginning with the tear-blurred moment when Mary caught sight of her father looking for her and Rush down the railway station platform, during which the whole fabric of misgivings about her home-coming dissolved as dreams do when one wakes. It had not been a dream she knew, nor the mere concoction of her morbid fancy. He had not looked at her like this nor kissed her like this—not once since that fatal journey to Vienna five years ago. Had something happened between him and Paula that made the difference? Or was it her brother's presence, that, serving somehow to take off the edge, worked a mysterious catalysis?

When John, after standing off and gazing wordless for a moment at this new son of his, this man he had never seen, in his captain's uniform with bits of ribbon on the breast of it,—tried to say how proud he was and choked instead, it was for Mary that he reached out an unconscious, embracing arm, the emotion which would not go into words finding an outlet for itself that way.

When they got out to the motor and old Pete, once coachman, now chauffeur, his eyes gleaming over the way Rush had all but hugged him, said to her, "You home to stay, too, Miss Mary?" her father's hand which clasped her arm revealed the thrilling interest with which he awaited her answer to that question. The importunity of the red-cap with the luggage relieved her of the necessity for answering but the answer in her heart just then was "Yes."

It was with a wry self-scornful smile that she recalled, later that day, the emotions of the ride home. If at any time before they got to the house, her father had repeated the old servant's question, "Are you home to stay, Mary?" she would, she knew, have kissed the hand that she held clasped in hers, wept blissfully over it and told him she wanted never to go away again. She hadn't minded his not asking because she thought she knew quite surely why he had not. He was afraid to risk his momentary happiness upon her answer. And why had she not volunteered the assurance he wanted so eagerly and dared not ask for? The beastly answer to that question was that she had enjoyed the thrill of his uncertainty—a miserable sort of feline coquetry.

Well, it had been short-lived, that little triumph of hers. It had stopped against a blank wall just when the car stopped under the *ports cochère* of the Dearborn Avenue house. John's arm which had been around her was withdrawn and he looked with just a touch of ostentation at his watch. She knew before he spoke that when he did, his tone would ring flat. The old spell was broken. He was once more under the dominion of the newer, stronger one.

"I'm terribly late," he said. "I must drive straight along to the hospital. I'll see you to-night. We're having a few old friends in to dinner. Run along now. Your Aunt Lucile will be waiting for you."

His omission to mention Paula had been fairly palpable. Her reply, "All right, dad, till to-night, then. *Au 'voir*" had been, she knew, as brittle and sharp-edged as a bit of broken glass. It had cut him;—she had meant it to.

Well it served her right. Paula deserved to own the stronger spell. Paula's emotional channels were open and deep. No choking snags and sandbars, no perverse eddies in them. Look at her with Rush to-day! There was a situation that fairly bristled with opportunities for blundering. She might, with this grown-up son of her husband's whom she had hardly seen, have shown herself shy, embarrassed, at a loss how to take him. She might have tried to be archly maternal with him or elder-sisterly. But she played up none of these sentimental possibilities, seemed, indeed, serenely unaware of them. She treated him just as she had always treated Mary—as a contemporary. From the beginning she had no trouble making him talk. For one thing her acquaintance with France and Germany was intimate enough to enable her to ask him questions which he found it pleasantly stimulating to try to answer. As she felt her way to firmer ground with him, she allowed what was evidently a perfectly spontaneous affection to irradiate the look she turned upon him and to warm her lovely voice.

So she must have begun—as simply and irresistibly as that—in Vienna!

Mary tried hard to think of it as a highly skillful performance, but this was an attitude she could not maintain. It was not a performance at all; it was—just Paula, who, having taken her father away from her was now, inevitably, going to take her brother too. Not because she meant to—quite unconscious that she was doing any harm ("and of course she isn't, except to a cat like me")—that was the maddening, and at the same time, endearing thing about her.

For there was a broad impartiality about her spell that tugged at Mary even while she forlornly watched Rush yielding to it. And the way it affected Aunt Lucile was simply funny. She melted, visibly, like a fragment left on the curb by the iceman, whenever Paula—turned the current on. What made this the more striking was that Aunt Lucile's normal mood to-day impressed Mary as rather aggressively sell-contained. Was it just that Mary had forgotten how straight she sat and how precisely she moved about? Had she always had that discreet significant air, as if there were something she could talk about but didn't mean to—not on any account? Or was there something going on here at home that awaited—breathlessly awaited—discovery? Whatever it was, when Paula turned upon her it went, laughably;—only it would have been a pretty shaky sort of laugh.

It was after lunch that Paula electrified them by suggesting that they all go together to a matinée. That's an illustration of the power she had. To each of the three, to Lucile and to Mary as well as to the now infatuated Rush, she could make a commonplace scheme like that seem an irresistibly enticing adventure. Lucile recovered her balance first, but it was not until Nat had fetched the morning paper and they had discussed their choice of entertainments for two or three minutes that she said of course she couldn't go. She didn't know what she'd been thinking of. The number of things imperatively to be done or seen to in preparation for the party to-night would keep her busy all the afternoon.

Then Mary followed suit. If this was really going to be a party—she hadn't quite got this idea before—she'd have to spend the afternoon unpacking and putting her frocks in order or she wouldn't have anything to wear.

"Well," Paula said comfortably, "until they turn me on like a Victrola at nine o'clock or so, I've nothing to do with the party except not think about it." She made this observation at large, then turned on Rush. "You'll come with me, won't you, and keep me from getting frightened until tea-time?"

Rush would go—rather!—but he laughed at the word "frightened."

"I'm not joking," she said, and reaching out she covered his hand, which rested on the cloth, with one of hers.

He flushed instantly at that; then said to the others with slightly elaborated surprise, "It *is*, cold, for a fact."

"So is the other one," said Paula. "For that matter, so are my feet. And getting colder every minute. Come along or we'll be late."

Mary branded this as a bit of rather crude coquetry. It wasn't conceivable that a professional opera singer of Paula's experience could look forward with any sort of emotion to the mere singing of a few songs to a group of familiar friends. It occurred to her, too, that Paula had calculated on her refusal to go to the matinée as definitely as on Aunt Lucile's and for a moment she indulged the idea of changing her mind and going along with them just to frustrate this design. Only, of course, it wouldn't work that way. She couldn't keep Rush from being taken away from her by playing the spoil-sport. She couldn't keep him anyhow she supposed. She made a hasty, rather forlorn retreat to her own room as soon as the departing pair were safely out of the house.

That room of hers exerted now a rather curious effect upon her mood. It had been hers ever since her promotion from the nursery and it, like her brother's adjoining, had been kept unchanged, unoccupied during her long absence.

The furniture and the decoration of it had been her mother's last Christmas present. The first Mrs. Wollaston had lived under the influence of the late Victorian esthetes, and Mary's room looked as if it had been designed for Elaine the lily maid of Astolat, an effect which was heightened by a large brown picture in a broad brown frame of Watts' Sir Galahad. After her mother's death, that winter, Mary added a Botticelli Madonna, the one with the pomegranate, which she hung by itself on a wall panel. There was a narrow black oak table under it to carry a Fra Angelico triptych flanked by two tall candlesticks. It wasn't exactly a shrine, even if there was a crimson cushion conveniently disposed before it, and if Mary for a while said her prayers there instead of in the old childish way at her bedside, and if she genuflected when she passed it, that was her own affair.

Coming to it now, as to port after storms, with the intention almost openly avowed to herself of lying down upon the bed and, for an hour or two, feeling as sorry for herself as she could, she found an appalling strangeness about its very familiarity that pulled her up short. The abyss she stared into between herself and the Mary Wollaston whose image was so sharply evoked by the ridiculously unchanged paraphernalia of that Mary's life, turned her giddy. Even the face which looked back at her from the frame of that mirror seemed the other Mary's rather than her own.

From the doorway she stood, for a moment, staring. Then she managed a smile (it was the only possible attitude to take) at Sir Galahad, above the bed. The notion of flinging herself down for a self-pitying revel upon that bed,—the other Mary's virginal little narrow bed—had become unthinkable. The thing to do was to stop thinking. Quickly.

She stripped off her suit and blouse, slipped on a pongee kimono that she got out of her hand-bag, unlocked her trunk and began discharging its contents all about the room. She covered the chairs with them, the bed, the narrow table—that had never had anything upon it but that Fra Angelico triptych and the two candlesticks—the round table with the reading lamp, the writing desk in the corner, the floor. Then, a little out of breath, she paused.

Which among two or three possible frocks should she wear for the party to-night? What sort of party was it going to be anyhow? It was curious, considering the fact that they had done nothing but sit and talk all the morning, how vague her ideas about it were. Her father had said something out in the car about having a few old friends in for dinner. Paula was going to sing and professed herself frightened by the prospect. Also she had cited it as the reason for an unusually and almost strenuously unoccupied day. On the other hand it was keeping Aunt Lucile distractedly busy.

Was it the chance result of their preoccupation with other things that she had been given no more intelligible account of it, or was it something that all three of them, her father, Paula and Aunt Lucile, were walking round the edge of? The nub of some seriously trivial quarrel? Was that why Paula was so elaborately disengaged and Aunt Lucile so portentous? Was it even perhaps why her father had so abruptly fled this morning without coming into the house?

She treated this surmise kindly. It was something to think about anyhow; something to sharpen her wits upon, just as a cat stretches her claws in the nap of the drawing-room rug. She rescued from oblivion half a dozen remarks heard during the morning, whose significance had gone over her head, and tentatively fitted them together like bits of a picture puzzle. She hadn't enough to go on but she believed there was something there. And when a little later in the afternoon, she heard, along with a knock on her door, her aunt asking if she might come in, she gave her an enthusiastic welcome, scooped an armful of things out of a chair and cleared a sitting space for herself at the foot of the bed.

"Would this blue thing do for to-night?" she asked, "or isn't it enough of an affair? What sort of party is it anyhow?"

"Goodness knows," said Lucile. "Between your father and Paula I find it rather upsetting."

Mary had reached out negligently for her cigarette case, lighted one and letting it droop at a rather impossible angle, supported by the lightest pressure of her lips so that the smoke crept up over her face into her lashes and her hair, folded her hands demurely in her lap and waited for her aunt to go on. She was mischievously half aware of the disturbing effect of this sort of thing upon Lucile.

"What has there been between them?" Mary asked, when it became clear that her aunt needed prompting. "Between father and Paula, I mean. Not a row?"

Mary never used language like this except provocatively. It worked on her aunt as she had meant it to.

"There has been nothing between them," she said, "that requires a rowdy word like that to express. It has not been even a quarrel. But they have been for the last day or two, a little—at …"

"Outs?" Mary suggested.

This had been the word on Lucile's tongue. "At cross purposes," she amended and paused again. But Mary seeing that she was fairly launched waited, economically, meanwhile, inhaling all the smoke from her cigarette. "I suppose after all, it's quite natural," Lucile began, "that Paula should attract geniuses, since she's rather by way of being one herself."

Mary took the cigarette in her fingers so that she could speak a little more crisply than was possible around it. "Who is the genius she's attracting now? Doesn't father like him? And is he being not asked to the party? I'm sorry, aunt, I didn't mean to interrupt."

"He is being asked which, it appears, is what Paula objects to; only not until after dinner. That she insisted upon. Really," she went on, in response to her niece's perplexed frown, "I shall be much more intelligible If you'll let me begin at the beginning."

"Please do," said Mary. "Where did Paula find him?"

"I found him," said Miss Wollaston. "Paula discovered him a little later. I found him on a bench in the park and told him he might come to tune the drawing-room piano. Paula had him tune her piano instead and spent what must have been a rather mad day with him over it. He brought round some songs the next day for her to try and she and Portia Stanton's husband have been practising them with hardly any intermission since. The idea was that when they had 'got them up' as they say, the man,—March his name is, Anthony March, I think,—should be invited round to hear Paula sing them. Paula insists, absurdly it seems to me, that he never has heard a note of them himself; that he can't even play them upon the piano. How he could compose them without playing them on the piano first, is beyond me. But she is inclined to be a little emotional, I think, over the whole episode. Quite naturally—even Paula can't deny that—your father thought he would like to be present when the songs were sung and it was arranged that it should be this evening."

"She may not have been able to deny that it was natural," Mary observed, "but I'd bet she didn't like it."

"It's only fair to Paula to say," Miss Wollaston insisted, "that she did nothing to exhibit a feeling of that sort. But when, at John's suggestion, I spoke of the possibility of having in the Cravens and the Blakes,—the Cravens are very musical, you know—and Wallace Hood who would be really hurt if we left him out, Paula came nearer to being downright rude than she often allows herself to be. She said among other things that she didn't propose to have March subjected to a 'suffocating' affair like that. She said she wanted him free to interrupt as often as he liked and tell them how rotten they were. That was her phrase. When I observed that Mr. March didn't impress me as the sort of person who could conceivably wish to be rude as that she said he could no more remember to be polite when he heard those songs for the first time than she herself could sing them in corsets. She summed it up by saying that it wasn't going to be a polite affair and the fewer polite people there were, hanging about, the better. There was, naturally, nothing I could say to that."

"I should think not," Mary agreed, exhaling rather explosively an enormous cloud of smoke. "Poor Aunt Lucile!" Her commiseration didn't sound more than skin deep.

"The matter rested there," the elder woman went on, "until your father received Rush's telegram that you were coming to-day. Then he took matters into his own hands and gave me a list of the people he wanted asked. There are to be about a dozen besides ourselves at dinner and perhaps as many more are to come after."

"I can see Paula when you told her that," Mary reflected. "Or did you make dad tell her himself? Yes, of course you did! Only what I can't understand is why Paula didn't say, 'All right. Have your party, and I'll sing if you want me to. Only not—what's his name?—March's songs.' And have him all to herself, as she wanted him, later. That would have been mate in one move, I should think."

Then, at the fleeting look she caught in the act of vanishing from her aunt's face, she cried, "You mean she *did* say that? And that father turned to ice, the way he can and—made a point of it? You know it's serious, if he's done that."

With a vigor meant to compensate for a sad lack of conviction, Miss Wollaston protested against this chain of unwarranted assumptions. But she admitted, at last, that her own surmise accorded with that of her niece. John certainly had said to her at breakfast that he saw no reason for foregoing the musical feature of the evening simply because an audience was to be present to hear it. Paula's only comment had been a dispassionate prediction that it wouldn't work. It wouldn't be fair to say she sulked; her rather elaborate detachment had been too good-humored for that. Her statement, at lunch, that she was to be turned on like a Victrola at half past nine, was a fair sample.

"What's he like, this genius of hers?" Mary wanted to know. "Young and downy and helpless, I suppose. With a look as if he was just about to burst into tears. I met one like that last winter." She knew exactly how to get results out of her aunt.

"He's not in the least like that! If he had been I should never have brought him home, not even to tune the piano. He's quite a well behaved, sensible-appearing young man, a little over thirty, I should say. And he does speak nicely, though I think Paula exaggerates about that."

"Sensible or not, he's fallen wildly in love with her, of course," Mary observed. "The more so they are the more instantaneously they do it."

But this lead was one Miss Wollaston absolutely declined to follow. "If that clock's right," she exclaimed, gazing at a little traveling affair Mary had brought home with her, "I haven't another minute." It was not right, for it was still keeping New York time, but the diversion served. "Wallace Hood spoke of coming in to see you about tea-time," she said from the doorway. "I'm going to be to busy even to stop for a cup, so do be down if you can."

# CHAPTER V
# JOHN MAKES A POINT OF IT

Mary was warmly touched by the thought of Wallace's coming to see her in that special sort of way when he was certain of finding her at dinner an hour or two later. Her feelings about him were rather mixed but he dated back to the very earliest of her memories, and his kindly affectionate attitude toward her had never failed, even during those periods when she had treated him most detestably. Even as a little girl, she had been aware of his sentimental attachment to her mother and perhaps in an instinctive way had resented it, though her actual indictment against Wallace in those days had always been that he made her naughty; incited her by his perpetual assumption that she was the angelic little creature she looked, to one desperate misdemeanor after another, for which her father usually punished her. Mary had, superficially anyhow, her mother's looks along with her father's temper.

But for two years after Mrs. Wollaston's death, she and Wallace had been very good friends. She was grateful to him for treating her like a grown-up, for talking to her, as he often did, about her mother and how much she had meant to him. (She owed it, indeed, largely to Wallace that her memories of this sentimental, romantic, passionless lady with whom in life she had never been completely in sympathy, were as sweet and satisfactory as they were.) He had taken infinite pains with her, guiding her reading and her enjoyment of pictures in the paths of good taste. He took her to concerts sometimes, too, though at this point her docility ceased. She wouldn't be musical for anybody. He gave her much-needed advice in dealing with social matters which her sudden prematurity forced her to cope with. And with all this went a placidity which had no part at all in her relations with her father.

She got the idea, during this period, that he meant, when she was a little older, to ask her to marry him, and she sometimes speculated whether, if he did, she would. There would be something beautifully appropriate about it;—like the Professor's Love Story. Usually, though, she terminated the scene with a tender refusal.

She had long known, of course, how unreal all this was. Wallace had faded into complete invisibility at the time when she fell in love with Captain Burch and quarreled with her father about him. She couldn't remember afterward whether he had even been on the scene or not. But the savor of their friendship, though mild, was a pleasant one and there was none of her old acquaintances she'd rather have looked forward to to-day at tea-time in the drawing-room. She knew exactly what he would be like; just what they would say to each other. The only doubt in her mind was whether he'd bring her chocolates or daffodils.

She guessed wrong. It was a box of candied strawberries that he gave her as soon as their double hand-shake set him free. But nothing else came at once to the surface to falsify her prevision. She remembered how he liked his tea and was able to get an affectionate warmth into her voice, that sounded real though strangely enough it wasn't, in agreeing with him how like old times this was and how good it seemed to be home. Then came the joy of having Rush back again, and the war, and the Peace Conference, — only we weren't going to talk about things like that. And then Alan Seeger, Rupert Brooke, Conningsby Dawson.

But oddly enough, she felt herself going back to still older times, to the abominable little girl who had yielded to irresistible desires such as making faces at him and rubbing the nap of his silk hat the wrong way. She repressed, vigorously, this lawless vein. She was determined for this one day to be just as nice as he tried, so hard, to think she was. But with this resolution occupying her mind the talk presently ran rather thin, her contribution to it for whole minutes drying up entirely. It was after a rather blank silence that he said he supposed Paula was lying down, resting for to-night's performance. His inflection struck Mary as a little too casual and reminded her that it was his first mention of her stepmother's name. This roused her attention.

"Oh, Paula's off playing with Rush," she said. "I believe they went to a matinée."

He exclaimed at that, over Paula's stores of energy and her reckless ways of spending them. He said she gave him the impression of being absolutely tireless, superimposing a high speed society existence which John Wollaston and he, in relays, could hardly keep up with, upon the heavy routine of work in her studio. He illustrated this with a schedule of her activities during the last three days. "Oh, yes," he threw in, in parenthesis, "I'm as much in the family as ever. When your father can't do escort duty, they call on me." He added in conclusion that he was glad she had already made a start toward getting acquainted with Rush.

Was this relief, Mary wondered—at learning that she was not at this moment engaged less domestically somewhere with Anthony March? But she doubted whether this was a good guess. If he did feel any such relief, it was not, at all events, from a personal jealousy; for the illuminating conviction had come over her that Wallace could not possibly be one of Paula's conquests. A man still capable of cherishing as the most beautiful event of his life, that sentimental platonic friendship he had enjoyed with her mother, would be immune against Paula's spells.

She wondered if he wasn't a little afraid of Paula. If he did not, in his heart, actually dislike her. But if this were true, why did he willingly devote so many of his hours to squiring her about, substituting for her husband? (She told herself, as one discovering a great truth, that a substitute was exactly what Heaven had ordained Wallace Hood to be.) She kept him going about Paula easily enough, as a sort of obbligato to these meditations and her name was on Wallace's lips when John Wollaston came into the room.

"Where is she?" he asked Mary. "I hoped I'd find her resting for to-night." Evidently he had been up to her room to see. The relief was plainly legible in his face when he got Mary's answer.

"She and Rush, eh," he said. "I'm glad they've made a start together, but they ought to be back by now. They drove, didn't they?"

She couldn't inform him as to that and by way of getting him to come to anchor, offered him his tea.

"Oh, I'll wait for the others," he said. "They can't be much later than this.—I'm glad she's taken a vacation from those songs," he went on presently from the fireplace. "She told me last night she'd been working all day with Novelli over them. Only sent him home about half an hour before it was time for her to dress for dinner. Do you suppose,"—this to Wallace—"that they're as wonderful as she thinks they are?"

It was obvious to Mary that Hood's reply was calculated to soothe; his attitude was indulgent. He talked to Mary about March as just another of Paula's delightful extravagances. March's indignant refusal, at first, to tune the Circassian grand, his trick of sitting on the floor under Paula's piano while she played for him, his forgetting to be paid, though he had not, in all probability, a cent in his pockets, were exhibited as whimsicalities, such as Wallace's favorite author, J.M. Barrie, might have invented. It was just like Paula to take him up as she had done, to work away for days at his songs, proclaiming the wonder of them all the while. "We're all hoping, of course," he concluded, "that when she's finished with them to-night, she'll sing us some of the old familiar music we really love."

The neat finality of all this, produced, momentarily, the effect of ranging Mary on the other side, with Paula and her musician. But just at this point, she lost her character of disinterested spectator, for Wallace, having put March back in his box and laid him deliberately on the shelf, abruptly produced, by way of diversion, another piece of goods altogether.

"I hope Mary's come home to stay," he said to John. "We can't let her go away again, can we?"

Afterward, she was able to see that it was a natural enough thing for him to have said. It would never have occurred to him, pleasant, harmless sentimentalist that he was, that John's second marriage might be a disturbing factor in his relation with Mary and that the question so cheerfully asked as an escape from the more serious matter that he had been talking about, struck straight into a ganglion of nerves.

But at the time, no such excuse for him presented itself. She stared for a moment, breathless, paled a little and locked her teeth so that they shouldn't chatter; then, a wave of bright anger relaxed her stiffened muscles. She did not look at her father but was aware that he was fixedly not looking at her.

"I don't know whether I am going to stay or not," she said casually enough. "There isn't any particular reason why I should, unless I can find something to do. You haven't a job for me, have you?"

"A job?" Wallace gasped.

"In your office," she explained. "Filing and typing, or running the mimeograph. It seems to be a choice between something like that and—millinery."

"That's an extravagant idea," her father said, trying for, but not quite able to manage, a tone that matched hers. "Good lord, Wallace, don't sit there looking as if you thought she meant it!"

"You do look perfectly—consternated," she said with a pretty good laugh. "Never mind; I shan't do anything outrageous for a week or two. Oh, here they come. Will you ring, dad? I want some more hot water."

Rush came into the drawing-room alone, Paula having lingered a moment, probably before the mirror in the hall. Mere professional instinct for arranging entrances for herself, Mary surmised this to be. And she may have been right for Paula was not one of those women who are forever making minute readjustments before a glass. But when she came in, just after Wallace Hood had accomplished his welcome of the returned soldier, it was hard to believe that she was concerned about the effect she produced upon the group about the tea-table. She didn't, indeed, altogether join it, gave them a collective nod of greeting with a faint but special smile for her husband on the end of it and then deliberately seated herself with a "No, don't bother; this is all right," at the end of the little sofa that stood in the curve of the grand piano, rather in the background.

When Mary asked her how she wanted her tea, she said she didn't think she'd have any; and certainly no cakes. No, not even one of Wallace's candied strawberries. There was an exchange of glances between her and Rush over this.

"They have been having tea by themselves, those two," Mary remarked.

"No," said Rush, "not what you could call tea."

Paula smiled vaguely but didn't throw the ball back, did not happen, it appeared, to care to talk about anything. Presently the chatter among the rest of them renewed itself.

Only it would have amused an invisible spectator to note how those three Wollastons, blonde, dolichocephalic, high-strung, magnetically susceptible, responded, as strips of gold-leaf to the static electricity about a well rubbed amber rod, to the influence that emanated from that silent figure on the sofa. Rush, in and out of his chair a dozen times, to flip the ash from his cigarette, to light one for Mary, to hand the strawberries round again, was tugging at his moorings like a captive balloon. When he answered a question it was with the air of interrupting an inaudible tune he was whistling. John still planted before the fireplace, taking, automatically, a small part in the talk just as he went through the minimum of business with his tea, seemed capable of only one significant action, which he repeated at short, irregular intervals. He turned his head enough to enable him to see into a mirror which gave him a reflection of his wife's face; then turned away again, like one waiting for some sort of reassurance and not getting it. Mary, muscularly relaxed, indeed, drooping over the tea-table, had visible about her, nevertheless, a sort of supernormal alertness. Every time her father looked into the mirror she glanced at him, and she rippled, like still water, at all of her brother's sudden movements.

As for Wallace Hood, one look at him sitting there, as unresponsive to the spell as the cup from which he was sipping its third replenishment of tea, would have explained his domestication in that household;—the necessity, in fact, for domesticating among them some one who was always buoyantly upon the surface, whose talk, in comfortably rounded sentences, flowed along with a mild approximation to wit, whose sentiments were never barbed with passion;—who was, to sum him up in one embracing word, appropriate.

Mary, in addition to feeling repentant over her outbreak just before Paula came in, experienced a sort of gratitude to him for being able to sit squarely facing the sofa, untroubled by the absent thoughtful face and the figure a little languorously disposed that confronted him. His bright generalities were addressed to her as much as to the rest of them; his smile asked the same response from her and nothing more.

Nothing short of an explosion that shattered all their surfaces at once could have got a single vibration out of him. By that same token, when the explosion did occur, he was the most helpless person there, the only one of them who could really be called panic-stricken.

John had, at last, crossed the room and seated himself beside his wife. He spoke to her in a low voice but her full-throated reply was audible everywhere in the room.

"No, I'm not tired and I really don't want any tea. I've gone slack on purpose because that's how I want to be till nine o'clock. I've just eaten an enormous oyster stew with Rush. That's what we waited for."

John frowned. "My dear, you'll have ruined your appetite for dinner."

"I hope so," she said, "because I'm not to have any."

At that, from the other two men, there began an expostulatory—"No dinner!" "You don't mean …!" but it was silenced by John's crisp—"You're planning not to come down to dinner, then?"

"Oh, I'll come down," said Paula, "and I'll sit. But I don't mean to eat anything. Unless you think that will be too much like a—what is it?—skeleton at the feast."

"I think it would seem somewhat-exaggerated," he said.

"Well," Paula retorted, drawing the rest of the room into it again just as Wallace was making a gallant effort to start a subsidiary conversation to serve as a screen, "that's because you haven't heard those songs. If there's a singer in the world who'd dare—cut loose with them right after eating the sort of dinner Lucile will have to-night for Mary and Rush, I'd like to see him try it."

"I didn't mean to imply that they were not difficult. I dare say they are all but impossible. But it does seem to me that you are taking the occasion of singing them—a little too—emotionally."

The tone he was trying for was meant to have nothing in it—for other ears than hers, at least, beyond mere good-humored remonstrance. But her reply tore all pretense aside. She let him have it straight.

"You're the one who's being emotional about it," she said.

The blood leaped into his face at that but he did not reply.

"Look here, John," she went on—and her big voice swept away the polite convention that the others were not listening, "I've told you that this won't work and you must see now that that's true. There's still time to call up March and tell him that it's to-morrow instead of to-day. Because of Rush and Mary. Won't you let me do that?"

It is just possible that if he had been alone with her, he might have acknowledged the issue, might have admitted that this new composer whose works she had been so absorbed in, frightened him, figured in his mind as the present manifestation of a force that was trying to take her away from him. And having let her see that, he could safely enough have said, "Have your own way about it. You know what will work and what won't. Only make it as easy for me as you can." But in the presence of his children—it was they, rather than Wallace, that he minded—he was at once evasive and domineering.

"I thought we'd already disposed of that suggestion," he said. "If the situation is as it has been made to appear to me there is not the smallest reason why March should be put off; why Mary and Rush and the friends we have asked in to meet them, shouldn't be permitted to hear his songs; or why I shouldn't myself. I think we'll consider that settled."

Paula rose all in one piece. "Very well," she said—to the audience, "it is settled. Also it's settled that I shall not come down to dinner. As for what people will think, I'll leave that to you. You can make any explanation you like. But I shall sing those songs to March—and for him—for all they're worth. I don't care who else is there or whether they like it or not.—A lot of patronizing amateurs! Bring them up to the music room about nine o'clock, if you like. I'll be there."

She left behind her, in that Victorian drawing-room, a silence that tingled.

# CHAPTER VI
# STRINGENDO

A crisis of this sort was just what the Wollastons needed to tune them up. The four of them, for Lucile had to be counted in, met the enemy—which is to say their arriving guests—with an unbroken front. They explained Paula's non-appearance with good-humored unconcern. She was afraid if she sat down to Lucile's dinner that she would forget her duty and eat it and find herself fatally incapacitated for cutting loose on Mr. March's songs afterward. They must be rather remarkable songs that required to be approached in so Spartan a manner. Well, Paula assured us that they were. The family declined all responsibility in the matter, not having themselves heard a note of them, but if you wanted to you might ask Mr. Novelli, over there. He'd been working over them with Paula for days. As for the composer, he was as much a mystery as his songs. He wasn't coming to the dinner but was expected to appear from somewhere afterward.

Novelli, as it happened, was not very productive of information. Half an hour before the dinner, his wife had telephoned Lucile to ask if he might bring a guest of his own, a certain Monsieur LaChaise, who was one of the conductors at the Metropolitan and was to have the direction of the summer opera out here at Ravinia this year. Portia added with the falsely deprecatory air of a mother apologizing for a child's prank, that Pietro had in fact, already invited him to the dinner and had only just informed her of the fact. Lucile had assured her, of course, that this addition to the company would cause not the slightest inconvenience, served on the contrary to bring it up to the number that had originally been counted upon.

When LaChaise arrived the discovery that he talked no English at all beyond a few rudimentary phrases, a fact which normally would have seemed calamitous, was now merely treated as an added feature of the evening. He and Novelli were in the midst of an animated discussion when they arrived. They stuck together in the drawing-room as if locked in the same pair of handcuffs and seating arrangements were hastily revised so that they might go on talking in untroubled mutual absorption straight through the dinner. Rush being placed handily by, where he could come to the rescue in case of need.

It was only the extremest surface of Mary sitting at the head of the table in Paula's place (which once had been her own) that was engaged with her unforeseen duties as hostess. And yet in a way, the whole of her consciousness had been drawn to the surface. The strong interior excitement that had been burning in her during all this day of her home-coming, the rising conviction that life at home might turn out to be something very different indeed from the thing that it had, down in New York, looked like, the blend of foreboding with anticipation that accompanied it, and finally a sense of the imminence of something important, not quite to be accounted for by the quarrel between her father and his wife,—all this emotional reaction found its outlet during the long dinner in a quite unusual vivacity. Her sphere of influence spread down the table until it embraced a full half the length of it on both sides and those just beyond the reach of it, aware that they were missing something, listened but distractedly to the talk of their more remote partners. And while she was doing all this she managed with her left hand, as it were, to, keep going a vivid little confidential flirtation with the Stannard boy, Graham, a neighbor and a contemporary of hers just back from service on a destroyer.

The thing that stimulated her to all this was a consciousness of her father's intense awareness of her. She had been deliberately evasive of him since his quarrel with Paula. What he wanted of her she knew as well as if he had expressed the need of it in so many words. He had turned to her for it as soon as Paula had gone up-stairs and Rush had accompanied the thoroughly demoralized Wallace into the hall. She had found a certain hard satisfaction in denying it to him, in not nestling up into the arms that happened, for the moment, to be vacant of Paula. This was so imperative an instinct that she had not even reproached herself for it, though she supposed she would later.

The sense that something in some way or other decisive was going to happen to-night, quickened her pulse as she mounted, along with the last of their guests to the music room, in response to Paula's message that Mr. March had come and that the "rehearsal" was about to begin. She looked about eagerly for a man who might be March but could not discover him anywhere. Was he, perhaps, she absurdly wondered, sitting once more under the piano?

Novelli drooped over the keyboard. LaChaise was half hidden in a deep chair in one of the dormers. Paula, her back to the little audience, stood talking to Novelli. Mary allowed herself a faint smile over the expression in those faces that Paula wouldn't look at. The half-concealed impatience, the anticipatory boredom, showed through so unfaltering a determination to do and express to the end the precisely correct thing. Even her father's anger looked out through a mask like that.

LaChaise, from his corner said something in French that Mary didn't catch. Novelli straightened his back. And in that instant before a note was sounded, Mary's excitement mounted higher. The absorption of those three musicians, the intensity of their preoccupation, told her that the something she had expected was going to happen—now. But she did not know that it was going to happen to her.

Long ago the family had acquiesced in Mary's assertion that she was not in the least musical and in her stubborn refusal to "take" anything, even the most elementary course of lessons on the piano. She had been allowed to grow up in an ignorance almost unique in these days, of the whole mystery of musical notation and phraseology, an ignorance that might be reckoned the equivalent of a special talent.

Later, indeed, she had made the discovery—or what would have been a discovery if she had fully admitted it to herself—that music sometimes exerted a special power over her emotions. Whether it was a certain sort of music that created the mood or a certain sort of mood that was capable of responding to music, she had never seriously inquired. The critical jargon of the wiseacres always irritated her. She supposed it meant something because they seemed intelligible to each other but she rather enjoyed indulging the presumption that it did not. When she went to concerts, she liked to go alone, or at least to be let alone, to sit back passively and allow the variegated tissue of sound to envelop her spirit as it would. If it bored her, as it frequently did, there was no harm done, no pretense to make. If, as more rarely happened, it stole somehow into complete possession, floated her away upon strange voyages, she was at least immune from analysis and inquisition afterward.

So it was with no critical expectancy that she listened when Novelli began to play; indeed, in the active sense, she did not listen at all. She forgot to be amused by the composed faces about her; she forgot, presently, whose music it was and whose voice she heard. What she felt was a disentanglement, an emergence into more open, wider spaces,—cold ethereal spaces. It seemed, though, that it was her own mood the music fitted into, rather than the other way about.

She heard the talk that followed the polite rustle of applause at the first intermission, without being irritated by it, without even listening to what it meant, though here and there a phrase registered itself upon her ear. Henry Craven's "Very modern, of course. No tonality at all, not a cadence in it," and Charlotte Avery's "No form either. And hardly to be called a song. A tone poem, really, with a part written into it for the voice."

The music began again, and now was given ungrudging credit for the recreation of her mood. Only its admitted beauty created a longing which it did not serve to satisfy. The cold open sky with its mysterious interstellar spaces, the flow of the black devouring clouds, the reemergence of the immortal Pleiades, remote, inhuman, unaware, brought no tranquillity but only a forlorn human loneliness.

On that note it ended, but Paula, with a nod to Novelli, directed him to go straight on to the love song. The two do not form a sequence in the poem; indeed the love song occurs very early in it and the Burial of the Stars comes afterward, nearly at the end. But I think, as March did, that Paula's instinct was sound in using the unearthly Schubert-like beauty of the Burial of the Stars as a prelude to the purely human passion of the love song.

It is, I suppose, one of the supreme lyric expressions in the English language of the passion of love. Furthermore, Whitman's free unmetered swing, the glorious length of his stride, fell in with March's rhythmic idiom as though they had been born under the same star.

The result is one of those happy marriages so rare as to be almost unique, in which the emotional power of a great song is enhanced by its musical setting, and where, conversely, a great piece of lyric music gains rather than loses by its words.

March did not use the whole poem. His setting begins on the line "Low hangs the moon," and ends with the "Hither, my love! Here I am! Here!" Why he elected not to go on with it, I don't know. Possibly, because his own impulse was spent before Whitman's; possibly, because he did not wish to impose the darker melancholy of the latter stanzas upon the clear ecstasy of that last call.

It lost something, of course, from the inadequacy of the piano transcription, for it was conceived and written orchestrally. Paula, too, has given finer performances of it;—indeed, she sang it better a little later that same evening. But spurred as she was by the knowledge that the composer was listening to it and by her determination to win a victory for it, she flung herself into it with all the power and passion she had.

I doubt whether any other auditor ever is more completely overwhelmed by it than Mary was. It was so utterly her own, the cry of it so verily the unacknowledged cry of her own heart, that the successive stanzas buried themselves in it like unerring arrows. The intensity of its climax was more poignant, more nearly intolerable, than anything in all the music she had ever heard. Limp, wet, breathless, trembling all over, she sat for a matter of minutes after that last ineffable yearning note had died away.

There was a certain variety in the emotions of the rest of the audience, but they met on common ground in the feeling of not knowing where to look or what to say. Their individualities submerged in a great crowd, they might—most of them—have allowed themselves to be carried away, especially if they'd come in the expectation—founded on the experience of other audiences—that they would be carried away. But to sit like this, all very much aware of each other while a woman they knew, the wife of a man they had long known, proclaimed a naked passion like that, was simply painful. What they didn't know you see—there was no program to tell them—was whether the thing was inspired or merely dreadful, and when it was over they sat in stony despair, waiting, like the children of Israel, for a sign.

It was LaChaise who broke the spell by crossing the room and unceremoniously displacing Novelli at the piano. He turned back to the beginning of the score and began reading it, at first silently, then humming unintelligible orchestral parts as he was able to infer them from the transcription; finally with noisy outbursts upon the piano, to which din Novelli contributed with one hand reached down over the conductor's shoulder. Paula standing in the curve of the instrument, her elbows on the lid, followed them from her copy of the score. It got to the audience that an alert attitude of attention was no longer required of them. That in fact, so far as the three musicians were concerned, nothing was required of them, not even silence. As an audience they ceased to exist. They were dissolved once more into their social elements and began a little feverishly to talk.

The realization broke over Mary with the intensity of panic that some one of them might speak to her. She rose blindly and slipped out into the hall, but even there she did not feel safe. Some of them, any of them, might follow her. She wanted to hide. There was a small room adjoining the studio—it had been the nurse's bedroom when the other had been the nursery—and its door now stood ajar. She slipped within and closed it very softly behind her.

Here in the grateful half-dark she was safe enough although the door into the studio was also part way open. There was nothing in here but lumber—an old settee, a bookcase full of discarded volumes from the library and an overflow of Paula's music. No one would think of looking for her in here.

But as she turned her back upon the door that she had just closed, she saw that some one was here, a man in khaki sitting on the edge of that old settee, leaning forward a little, his hands clasped between his knees. She had come in so quietly he had not heard her.

It seemed to her afterward that she must have had two simultaneous and contradictory ideas as to who he was. She knew,—she must have known, instantly—that he was Anthony March, but his uniform suggested Rush and drew her over toward him just as though she had actually believed him to be her brother. And then as he became aware of her and glanced up, Paula in the other room began singing the last song over again, her great broad voice submerging the buzz of talk like the tide rushing in over a flat. Without a word Mary dropped down beside him on the settee.

In the middle of a phrase the music stopped.

"A vous le tour!" they heard LaChaise say to Novelli. "Je ne suis pas assez pianiste. Maintenant! Recommencons, n'est-ce-pas?"

The song resumed. March's frame stiffened.

"Oh night! do I not see my love fluttering out among the
breakers?
What is that little black thing I see there in the white?"

"Now then," March whispered. "Quicker! My God, can't they pick it up?" Like an echo came LaChaise's "Plus vite! *Stringendo*, jusque au bout!" and with a gasp the composer greeted the quickened tempo. Then as the song swept to its first tempestuous climax he clutched Mary's arm. "That's it," he cried. "Can't you see that's it?"

"Loud! loud! loud!
Loud I call to you, my love!
High and clear I shoot my voice over the waves,
Surely you must know who is here, is here,
You must know who I am, my love."

He let go her arm. The song went on.

"Low-hanging moon!
What is that dusky spot in your brown yellow?
O it is the shape, the shape of my mate!
Oh moon, do not keep me from her any longer."

From there, without interruption it swept along to the end.

It was during the ecstatic pianissimo just before the final section that their hands clasped. Which of them first sought the contact neither of them knew but they sat linked like that, tingling, breathless during the lines:—

"… somewhere I believe I heard my mate responding to me,
So faint I must be still, be still to listen,
But not altogether still, for then she might not come immediately to
me."

On the last "Hither, my love! Here I am! Here!" the clasp tightened, convulsively. But it was not until the circuit was broken that the spark really leaped across the gap.

There was no applause in the other room when the song ended for the second time, but it won a clear half minute of breathless silence before the eddies of talk began again. During that tight-stretched moment the pair upon the settee, their hands just unclasped, sat motionless, fully aware of each other for the first time, almost unendurably aware, thrilling with the just-arrived sense of the amazing intimacy of the experience they had shared. Neither of them was innocent but neither had ever known so complete a fusion of his identity with another as this which the spell of his music had produced.

They sat side by side but not very close, not so close that there was contact anywhere between them and neither made any move to resume it. Both were trembling uncontrollably and each knew that the other was.

The hum of talk in the other room rose louder and finally became articulate in Charlotte Avery's crisp, "Good night, my dear Paula, we've had a most interesting evening. I shall hope to hear more of your discovery. And see him too sometime if you make up your mind to exhibit him."

March started from his seat at that. "Don't make any noise," Mary whispered, rising too, and laying a detaining hand on him. "Nobody will come in here. They'll all go now. We must wait."

He obeyed tractably enough, only turned toward her now and gazed at her with undissimulated intensity; not, though, as if speculating who she might be, rather as if wondering whether she were really there.

"Don't you want them to find you, either?" he asked.

"N-not after that," she stammered; and added instantly, "We mustn't talk."

So silent once more, they waited while the late audience defiled in irregular, slow moving groups down the hall toward the stairs. Mary distinguished her father's voice, her brother's, her aunt's, all taking valiantly just the right social note. They were covering the retreat in good order. And she heard Portia Stanton taking her husband home. But the music room was not yet deserted. There were sounds of relaxation in there, the striking of a match, the sound of a heavy body—that of LaChaise, probably—dropping into an easy chair.

"And now," Mary heard him say to Paula—"Now fetch out your composer. Where have you had him hidden all this while?"

"He's in there. I was just waiting until they were really gone. I'll get him now, though. No, sit still; I'd rather, myself."

March, however, didn't move; not even when they could hear Paula coming toward the door. He stood gazing thoughtfully at Mary, his eyes luminous in the dark. It occurred to her that the conversation in the other room had been in French and that he had not understood it.

"Oh, go—quickly!" she had just time to breathe. Then she crowded back, close against the partition wall. The door opened that way, so that when Paula flung it wide it screened her a little.

The singer stood there, a golden glowing thing in the light she had brought in with her. "Where are you?" she asked. Then she came up to March and took him by the arms. "Was it good?" she asked. "Was it—a little—as you meant it to sound?"

When he did not speak, she laughed,—a rich low laugh that had a hint of tears in it, pulled him up to her and kissed his cheek. "You don't have to answer, my dear," she said. "Come in and hear what LaChaise has got to say about it."

Without effort, irresistibly, she swept him along with her into the music room.

Mary, when they were gone, let herself out by the other door as softly as she had come in. She fled down one flight of the stairs and a moment later had locked the door of her own room behind her. She switched on the light, gave a ragged laugh at Sir Galahad; then lay down, just as she was, on the little white bed, her face in the pillow, and cried.

# CHAPTER VII
# NO THOROUGHFARE

It was hours later, well along toward one o'clock in the morning when Rush coming into his room saw a light under the door communicating with his sister's and, knocking, was told he might come in.

He found her in bed for the night, reclining against a stack of pillows as if she had been reading, but from the way she blinked at the softened light from the lamp on her night table, it appeared that she had switched it on only when she heard him coming. She might have been crying though she looked composed enough now;—symmetrically composed, indeed, a braid over each shoulder, her hands folded, her legs straight down the middle of the bed making a single ridge that terminated in a little peak where her feet stuck up (the way heroines lie, it occurred to Rush, in the last act of grand operas, when they are dead) and this effect was enhanced by the new-laundered whiteness of the sheet, neatly folded back over the blankets and the untumbled pillows.

"You always look so nice and clean," he told her, and, forbearing to sit on the edge of the bed as a pat of her hand invited him to, pulled up a chair instead. It was going to be a real talk, not just a casual good-night chat.

"We were wondering what had become of you," he said. "Poor Graham was worried."

"Graham!" But she did not follow that up. "I decided we'd had temperament enough for one evening," she explained in a matter-of-fact tone, "so when I saw I was going to explode I came away quietly and did it in here. By the time it was over I thought I might as well go to bed."

"It doesn't look as if you'd exploded very violently," he observed.

"Oh, I've cleared away the ruins," she said. "I hate reminders of a mess."

It was like her exquisiteness to do that and it tightened his throat to think about it. He'd have liked to make sure what the cause of the explosion had been, but thought he'd better wait a while for that. All he ventured in the way of sympathetic approbation was to reach out and pat the ridge that extended down the middle of the bed. "It certainly has been one devil of an evening," he said.

"I suppose it has," she agreed, thoughtfully. Then, noticing that this had rather thrown him off his stride, she went on, "Tell me all that's been happening since I ran away. How did Paula act when it was over?"

"I haven't seen her," he said. "She never came down at all. Of course it must have been—well, in a way, a devil of an evening for her, too. Though I can't believe our being there cramped her style very much in singing those songs. If it did, I'd hate to think what she would have done if we hadn't been. I hope March liked his own stuff. He was there all the while, you know. She must have had him tucked away in that little old room of Annie's that opened off the nursery. Somewhere anyhow, because long after every one else had gone, he came down-stairs with the Frenchman. I got one surprise just then all right. He's a private soldier, did you know that? Just a plain doughboy."

"Overseas?" Mary asked.

"As far as Bordeaux, with the Eighty-sixth. Saxaphone player with one of the artillery bands. In a way I'm rather glad of it. That that's what he turns out to be, I mean."

"Why?" Mary made the word rather crisply.

"Oh, well," Rush explained uncomfortably, "you know what it had begun to look like. Paula quarreling with father about him and not going down to dinner; and—cutting loose like that over his music. But of course there couldn't be anything of that sort—with a chap like that."

"What is the lowest military rank," Mary inquired, "that you think Paula could fall in love with?"

The satirical import of her question was not lost upon him but he held his ground. "It may sound snobbish but it's true just the same," he insisted. "A doughboy's a doughboy, and Paula wouldn't get mixed up with one—any more than you would."

There was a silence after that.

"His music didn't sound to me like doughboy music," Mary observed at last. "Nor his going to Walt Whitman to get the words."

"Was that Walt Whitman? It sounded to me as if he was making it up as he went along." He had the grace to grin at himself over that admission, however. "Oh, well," he concluded, "Paula's all right anyhow. I think she's—wonderful, myself. Only poor old dad! He is a peach, Mary. It's funny how differently I remember him. He acted like one real sport to-night."

"Afterward, you mean." Mary, it seemed, would not have characterized her father's behavior earlier in the evening in just that way. "Tell me all about it. Only reach me a cigarette first."

He obeyed the latter injunction with an air of protest. "It's the only thing you do that I wish you didn't," he said.

"Why? Do you think it's bad for me?"

He wouldn't commit himself by answering that. The retort it offered her was obvious. "It doesn't seem like you," he explained.

"Very well," she said, taking a light from his match, "then I shall go on just to keep you reminded that I'm not plaster of Paris. I like to have somebody around who doesn't think that."

"Father doesn't," Rush asserted, and got so eager a look of inquiry from her that he regretted having nothing very substantial to satisfy it with. "Oh, down there in the hall," he said, "after everybody but March and the Frenchman had gone. Aunt Lucile began fussing about you. She was rather up in the air, anyway. She'd done the nonchalant, all right, — overdone it a bit in fact — as long as there was any one around to play up to. But when we had got rid of the Novellis — they were the last — she did a balloon ascension. She had a fit or two in general and then came round to wondering about you. Wanted to know when we'd last seen you — what *could* have happened to you, — that sort of thing. I'd been having a little talk with Graham so I supposed I knew. But of course I said nothing about that."

He was looking rather fixedly away from her and so missed her frown of incomprehension. "Well, but father?" she asked.

It had been coming over him that what his father had said was not just what he wanted to report to Mary. Not while she felt about him as she had confessed, down there in New York, she did. But he had let himself in for it.

"Why, it wasn't much," he said; "just that nothing could have happened to you; that you wouldn't 'fall off anything and break.' What you said about plaster of Paris made me think of it. He was only trying to get Aunt Lucile quieted down."

"While he had Paula on his mind, he didn't want to be bothered about me. That's natural enough, of course." Her dry brittle tone was anything but reassuring. Still without looking at her, he hurried on.

"Well, it *is* natural that he should be worried about Paula. I know how I'd feel about a thing like that. It was rather weird while we waited after Aunt Lucile went up to bed for those two to come down. Old Nat was fussing around the drawing-room, shutting up and putting things to rights.

Dad sent him to bed, too, told him we'd do the locking up ourselves. I got the idea that he was expecting Paula to come sailing down, with March, you know, and perhaps didn't want any one around. So I made a bluff of going to bed myself. But he told me to stick; said we'd settle down and have a smoke presently. I don't know how long it was before we heard LaChaise and March coming but it seemed a deuce of a while.

"Dad was right on the job then, calm as a May morning. He introduced March and me and said something polite about his music, never a word about his having been hiding all the evening.

"Then LaChaise spoke to dad in French. Said there was some business he wanted to talk with him about and that he'd like an appointment. I wasn't sure that dad quite got him so I crashed in and interpreted.

"Dad reached out and took hold of me, as if he was sort of glad that I was there, and told me to tell Mr. LaChaise that we had plenty of time right now, and if there was anything to discuss the sooner we got at it, the better.

"I handed that on in French—I tried not to lose any of the kick out of it—and while I was doing that March made a move to go.

"Dad told him not to. I wish you could have been there. I remember he said after inviting him to stay, 'I imagine you are as much concerned in this as any one.' It didn't faze March though. He said that he didn't believe that what Mr. LaChaise had to say concerned him. Then he made a stiff little bow for good night and went off down the hall to get his hat. Oh, that wasn't like a doughboy, I'll admit. I went to the door with him and we made a little conversation there for a minute or two just to—take off the edge. That's when I found out where he'd been.

"Father had taken LaChaise into the drawing-room when I got back but I don't believe either of them had said three words. They were waiting for me. Dad led off by asking what he thought of March, and LaChaise told him, though you could see that wasn't what was on his mind. He said March had a very strong and original talent and that he believed he had operas in him. There was one about finished that he was going to look at to-morrow. Then he pulled up short and said it was Paula he wanted to talk about.

"Dad caught that all right without waiting for me to translate it. What he wanted to get at, right at the jump off, was whether Paula knew LaChaise had come down to talk about her. Was he to consider Mr. LaChaise her emissary? I took a chance on *émissaire* for that and it worked all right.

"Well, the Frenchman said, as cool as you please, that he was. Said he wouldn't have ventured to intrude otherwise:—and dad froze to ice right there. But LaChaise went on and spoke his piece just the same. He said he'd

Mary Wollaston | 71

come to-night to verify the enthusiastic reports he had heard of her singing but that she had outdone them all. He said the voice itself was unusual, of great power and of beautiful quality, adequate in range for anything that could be expected of her. But he said that was only the beginning of it. The important things were that she was a real musician in the first place and a woman with real passions in the second.

"I didn't know whether to translate that to dad or to shut the Frenchman up myself right there. I would have liked to take a punch at him. But, of course, you're nothing but a part of the machinery when you are interpreting, so I handed it on, without looking at dad. All he said was, 'We'll get to the point, if you please, Monsieur.'

"LaChaise understood that without waiting for me. He said he had had no hesitation in offering Paula a contract to sing the leading dramatic soprano rôles at Ravinia this summer and that he had told her if it worked anywhere near as well as he expected it to there was no doubt of her getting a good Metropolitan engagement next season. He finished up by saying he had had to ask her to make a decision as soon as possible because he was at that moment negotiating with some one else who couldn't be put off very long.

"Dad asked then whether Paula had given him an answer to-night. LaChaise told him she had accepted—subject to his obtaining dad's consent. Then he finished up with a full-dress bow. 'That is the point you have asked me to come to, Monsieur,' he said.

"Dad never said a word for a minute. You could see it must have been ghastly for him. I guess LaChaise must have seen it himself, for he went on and tried to soften it down a bit. Said he didn't want to seem to *brusqué* the affair. All he wanted to ask dad to-night was that he should agree to consider the matter, bearing in mind that a real artist like *madame*, his wife, couldn't be kept shut up in a brass tower indefinitely.

"Dad cut him off rather short on that. He said that from a legal or business point of view, which was all that could possibly concern LaChaise, his consent wasn't necessary. If his wife signed a contract he would put no obstacles in the way of her fulfilling it. Beyond that he had obviously nothing to say.

"Well, that was about all. They both put on all the trimmings saying good night to each other and LaChaise thanked me very handsomely for interpreting. I chucked him into his overcoat and let him out the front door.—And bolted it after him, you bet! Lord, but I hated to go back to dad after that.

"I needn't have worried though. When we sat down for our smoke in the library, it was exactly as if nothing had happened. I'd have been tearing my hair but old dad…. He certainly is a peach."

Rush paused there for some comment from her and when she made none, looked around at her. Her hands were lightly clasped across her breast, her eyelids nearly closed. Save for her barely perceptible breathing, she lay dead still.

"Have I talked you to sleep?" he asked.

"No," she said, "I was thinking what a mixed-up thing life is. The way you can't help liking and admiring the people you wish you could hate and hating and hurting the ones you love." Then her eyes came open with a smile and she held out a hand toward him. "You don't have to answer that. It's the sort of silly thing people say when they have been drinking gin. What I was really wondering was whether there will be anything about Mr. March's opera in that contract Paula signs with LaChaise?"

This startled him. "I never thought of that," he answered. "Do you suppose that's it? Oh, it can't be! She wouldn't chuck dad for that doughboy piano tuner. Not Paula!"

"Oh, no," said Mary. "She wouldn't do that. It wouldn't look to her like that, anyhow. She's got enough, don't you see, for everybody; for dad and—and the doughboy as well. Father wouldn't have any less, if he could just make up his mind that he didn't have to have it all. And as for the other, why, it might be the greatest thing that could possibly happen to him;—being in love with Paula and writing operas for her and having her sing them the way she sang those songs to-night. I suppose that's what a genius needs. And you couldn't blame her exactly. At least there always have been people like that and the world hasn't blamed them—no matter how moral it pretends to be. It's the other sort of people, the ones who won't take anything unless they can have it all and who can't give anything unless they can give it all—those that haven't but one thing to give—that are—no good."

He didn't more than half understand her, which was fortunate, since he was rather horrified as it was. He put it down broadly as the same sort of nervous crisis that he had encountered in New York, a sort of hypersensitiveness due to the strain of war work—the thing he had amused her by speaking of as shell-shock.

"I think perhaps I know what has upset you to-night," he said uncomfortably. "At least Graham told me about it."

Mary Wollaston | 73

She looked at him with a puzzled frown. It was the third time that he had brought up the Stannard boy's name. What in the world...?

"He's terribly distressed about it," Rush went on. In his embarrassment he wasn't looking at her and she composed her face. "He didn't mean to shock you or—or offend you. He says he gave you reason enough to be offended, but only because you didn't understand. He says he has always— cared for you a lot. He said he thought you were the most—well, about the most perfect thing in the world. Only to-night he said he got carried off his feet and went further than he had any right to. And he simply can't bear to have you think that he meant anything—disrespectful. He felt he had to apologize to you before he went home, but you didn't come down so finally he told me about it and made me promise that I'd tell you to-night. Of course, I don't know what he did," Rush concluded, "but I can tell you this. Graham Stannard's a white man; they don't make them whiter than that."

Her reply, although it was unequivocally to the effect that it was all right—Graham needn't worry—failed, altogether, to reassure him. Was this, after all, he wondered, what she had exploded about? She prevented further inquiry, however, by an abrupt change of the subject, demanding to be told what it was that he and his father, all these hours, had been talking about.

He took up the topic with unforced enthusiasm. He had been surprised and deeply touched over the discovery that his father did not require to be argued out of the project either to send him back to Harvard or to start him in at the bottom in Martin Whitney's bank. "If he'd just been through it all himself, he couldn't have understood any better how I feel about it."

"Did you tell him about the farm?" Mary asked.

This was an idea of Graham's which she and Rush had been developing with him during the half hour in the drawing-room before they had gone down to dinner. Young Stannard, during his two years on a destroyer, had conceived an extraordinary longing for Mother Earth, and had filled in his dream in tolerably complete detail. What he wanted was an out-of-door life which should not altogether deprive him of the pleasures of an urban existence; and he accomplished this paradox by premising a farm within convenient motoring distance of Chicago, on one of the hard roads. Somewhere in the dairy belt, out Elgin way perhaps. You could have wonderful week-end house parties in a place like that, even in winter, with skiing and skating for amusements, and in summer it would be simply gorgeous. And, of course, one could always run into town for the night if there was anything particular to come for.

Mary had volunteered to keep house for them and they had talked a lot of amusing nonsense as to what her duties should be. Graham, too, had a kid sister, only seventeen, who fitted admirably into the picture. She loved the country, simply lived in riding breeches and rode like a man—a sight better than most men—and drove a car like a young devil. There was nothing, in fact, she couldn't do.

Graham was altogether serious about it. He had been scouting around during the fortnight since his return and had his eyes on two or three places that might do. There was one four-hundred-acre property that was altogether desirable, ideal in fact, except for the one painful particular that the cost of it was just about twice as much as Graham's father was willing to run to. But if Rush would go in with him they need seek no further. The thing was as good as settled.

"I did talk to father about it," Rush now told Mary. "The thing is a real idea. Graham and I talked seriously about it while we were smoking before we went up-stairs. The scheme is to run a dairy, hog and poultry combination on a manufacturing basis and then sell our whole product direct to two or three customers in town, one or two of the clubs—perhaps a hotel. Deliver by motor truck every day, you see, and leave the middleman out entirely. It's the only way to beat the game. Father saw it like a shot. He said it would take a lot of money, of course, but he thought he could manage my share."

Mary relaxed just perceptibly deeper in the pillows and her eyelids drooped again. "It's getting awfully late," Rush said; "don't you want to go to sleep?" But he needed no urging to go on when she asked him to tell her all about it, and for another half hour he elaborated the plan.

He was still breezing along on the full tide of the idea, when, happening to glance at her little traveling clock, he pulled himself up short, took away her extra pillows, switched off her night lamp and ordered her to go to sleep at once. Her apparent docility did not altogether satisfy him and two or three times during the hour before he himself fell asleep, he sat up to look under the door and see whether she had turned the light on again.

He was right about that, of course. The enforced calm Mary had imposed upon herself as a penance for the tempest of emotion she had indulged—she had lain without moving, hardly a finger, from the time she remade that bed and crept back into it until hearing Rush coming she switched on the light—had had a sort of hypnotic effect upon her. So long as her body did not move, it ceased to exist altogether and set her spirit free, like a pale-winged luna moth from its chrysalis to adventure into the night. The light it kept fluttering back to was that blinding experience with March while the music of his song had surged through her and her hand had been crushed in his.

Rush's coming in had brought her back to that tired still body of hers again; his voice soothed, his presence comforted her; at his occasional touch she was able to relax. (If only there were some one who loved her, who would hold her tight—tight—) She hoped he would go on talking to her; on and on. Because while he talked she could manage to stop thinking—by the squirrel-like process of storing away all the ideas he was suggesting to her for consideration later.

But when the respite was over and she lay back in the dark again, she made no effort to deny admission to the thoughts that came crowding so thickly. She must think; she must, before the ordeal of the next breakfast table, have taken thought. She must have decided if not what she should do, at least what she could hope for. She was much clearer and saner for the little interlude with Rush.

Suppose in the first place;—suppose that Paula's rebellion was serious. Suppose the Tower of Brass violated and the Princess carried away by the *jinn* or upon the magic carpet—whichever it was—to a world where none of them could follow her. Suppose John Wollaston bereft again. Would not Mary's old place be hers once more? Would not everything be just as it had been during those two years before her father went to Vienna?

But some instinct in her revolted utterly at that. It was an instinct that she could not completely reason out. But she knew that if such a calamity befell, her old place would not exist or would be intolerable if it did.

Suppose again:—suppose that Paula's rebellion could be somehow frustrated. Would it be possible to save Paula for her father by saving March from Paula? In plain words, by diverting him from Paula to herself.

That was a disgustingly vulgar way of putting it. But wasn't it what she meant? And if she couldn't be honest with her own thoughts.... Well then, were her powers of attraction great enough, even if they were consciously exerted to the utmost, to outpull Paula's with a musician, with a man whose songs she could sing as she had sung to-night?

That moment in Annie's old bedroom off the nursery supplied concretely enough the answer to her question. They had been soul to soul in there, they two. There was no language to describe the intimacy of it, except perhaps the hackneyed phrases of the wedding service which had lost all their meaning. And while they had stood together in the half dark, Paula had opened the door, bringing the light in with her. She had taken him confidently in her strong hands and kissed him and led him away without one hesitating backward thought.

And the truth seemed clear enough, incandescent, now she looked back at it, that it was Paula who had possessed him all along. That moment which she had called her own had been Paula's. Mary had got it because she had happened to come in and sit down beside him. She had, as it were, picked his pocket. She stood convicted the moment the rightful owner appeared. That was how much her chance of "saving" March from Paula amounted to.

What a hypocrite she had been to use that phrase even in her thoughts. Save him from Paula, indeed! Paula could give him, even if she gave only the half loaf, all he needed. She could inspire his genius, float it along on the broad current of her own energy. Compared to that, what could Mary give? What would it, her one possible gift, amount to?

She pulled herself up short. Wallowing again! No more of that. She'd leave March alone, and on that resolution she'd stop thinking about him. She'd think about Rush and Graham and the farm.

Graham! They didn't come, Rush had said, any whiter than that. Probably he was right about it. It was a wonderful quality, that sort of whiteness. What was it he had done (she didn't even remember!) that had caused him such bitter self-reproach? You couldn't help liking him. It ought not to be hard to fall sufficiently in love with him. And out on a farm... A farmer's wife certainly had enough to do to keep her from growing restless. With a lot of children, four to half a dozen,—no one could call that a worthless life.

And it was practicable. With an even break in the luck, she could accomplish the whole of it. A man like Graham she could make happy. Her one gift would be enough for him; all he'd want. What was it he had told Rush to-night? That he had always thought her the most perfect...

At that, appallingly, she was seized in the cold grip of an unforeseen realization. She couldn't marry a boy like that—she couldn't marry any man who regarded her like that—without first telling him what she was; what she was not! She would have to make clear to him—there was simply no escape from that—the nature of the thing that had happened in that tiny flat in New York where she had lived alone so long.

It was possible, of course, oh, more than that, probable even, that after hearing the story he would still want to marry her. That he might regard her, no matter what she said, as having been wronged; her innocence, though once taken advantage of by a scoundrel, intact. His love would be reenforced by pity. He'd think of nothing, in the stress of that moment, but the desire to protect her, to provide a fortress for her.

But would she dare, on these terms, marry him, or any other man for that matter, no matter how ardently he professed forgiveness? It wouldn't be until after the marriage was an accomplished thing, its first desires satisfied, its first tension relaxed, that the story of her adventure would begin to loom black and thunderous over the horizon of his mind. (Who was the man? How could it have happened? In what mood of madness could she have done such a thing? Might it ever,—when might it not—happen again?) No! Marriage was difficult enough without being handicapped additionally by a perennial misgiving like that. No thoroughfare again!

She started once more around the circle, but one can not keep at that sort of thing forever. About sunrise she fell asleep.

# CHAPTER VIII
# THE DUMB PRINCESS

None of his own family knew quite what to make of Anthony March. All of them but his mother disapproved of him, on more or less mutually contradictory grounds. Disapproved of him more than they did of one another, though he occupied a sort of middle ground between them. It is a possible explanation to the paradox that each of them regarded him as a potential ally and so spent more time trying to change his ways, scolding at him, pointing out his derelictions and lost opportunities, than it was worth while spending on the others who were hopeless.

I shall be a little more intelligible, perhaps, if I tell you briefly who they were. The father, David March, and Eveline, his wife, were New Englanders. They both came, as a matter of fact, from within ten miles of Glastonbury, Connecticut, though they didn't discover this fact until after they'd met a number of times in the social and religious activities of the Moody Institute. The lives of both had been woven in the somber colors of Evangelical religion. With him this ran close to fanaticism and served as an outlet for a very intense emotional life. She was not highly energized enough to go to extremes in anything, but she acquiesced in all his beliefs and practises, made him in short, a perfectly dutiful wife according to the Miltonian precept, "He for God only, she for God in him."

Back in New England she probably would not have married him for she was a cut or more above him socially, the played-out end of a very fine line, as her beautiful speech would have made evident to any sensitive ear. But in Chicago, the disheveled, terrifying Chicago of the roaring eighties, to all intents and purposes alone, clinging precariously to a school-teacher's job which she had no special equipment for, she put up only the weakest resistance to David March's determination that she should be his wife.

He was a skilled artisan, a stringer and chipper in a piano factory (chipping, if you care to be told, is the tuning a piano gets before its action is put in). One would hardly have predicted then, considering the man's energy and intelligence, that he would remain just that, go on working at the same bench for thirty-five years. But, as I have said, his energy found its main outlet in emotional religion.

Their first child, born in 1886, was a girl whom they named Sarah. Anthony came two years later and for twelve years there were no more. Then came the late baby, whom they appropriately named Benjamin and allowed a somewhat milder bringing up than the iron rule the elder ones had been subjected to.

It was the dearest wish of David's life to make a preacher of Anthony and he must have got by way of answers to his prayers, signs which reconciled him to the sheer impossibility of this project. The boy's passion for music manifested itself very early and with this David compromised by training him for the higher reaches of his own craft. He got employment for Anthony in the piano factory for a year or two after his graduation from high school and then sent him on for a liberal two years in a school in Boston where the best possible instruction in piano tuning was to be had.

Sarah was half-way through high school when her brother Benjamin was born and for two years after she graduated, her mother's ill health, the familiar breakdown of the middle forties, kept her at home. Then she defied her father and took a job in a down-town office. What he objected to, of course, was not her going to work but the use she made of the independence with which self-support provided her. The quarrel never came to a real break though often enough it looked like doing so, and except for the brief period of her marriage Sarah always lived at home.

When Anthony came back from Boston, he revolted, too. He had not been a prodigal; indeed, during his second year in the East, he had in one way or another, earned his own living and he had learned even beyond his father's hopes to tune pianos. But he did it at an incredibly small expense in time and energy. What his heart went into during those two years was the study of musical theory and composition, and, thanks to a special aptitude which rose to the pitch of genius, he managed to make the comparatively meager training he could get in so short a time, suffice to give him the technical equipment he needed.

He came home armed, too, with a discovery. The discovery that a man not enslaved by a possessive sense, a man whose self-respect is not dependent upon the number of things he owns, a man able therefore to thumb his nose at all the maxims of success, occupies really a very strong position.

He didn't like the factory, though he gave it what he considered a fair trial. He didn't like the way they tuned pianos in a factory. The dead level of mechanical perfection which they insisted upon was a stupid affront to his ear. And, of course, the strict regimentation of life at home, the, once more, dead level of the plateau upon which life was supposed to be lived, was distasteful to one with a streak of the nomad and the adventurer in him.

Thanks to his discovery he was able to construct an alternative to a life like that. A skillful piano tuner could earn what money he needed anywhere and could earn enough in a diligent week to set him free, his simple wants provided for, for the rest of the month.

But even a wanderer needs a base, a point of departure for his wanderings, and his father's house could not be made to serve that purpose, so Anthony domiciled himself, after a long quest, in the half story above a little grocery just off North LaSalle Street and not far from the river.

It happened when Anthony had been living there a year or more that the grocer, with whom he was on the friendliest of terms, got, temporarily, into straits at precisely the time that Anthony had three hundred dollars. He had won a prize of that amount offered by a society for the encouragement of literature for the minor orchestral instruments, with a concerto for the French horn. The grocer offered his note for it, but Anthony thought of something better. He bought his room. It was to be his to live in, rent free, for as long as time endured.

He took a childlike pleasure in this lair of his. It accumulated his miscellaneous treasures like a small boy's pocket. He made a mystery of it. He never gave it as his address. Not even his family knew where it was, nor, more than vaguely, of its existence. The address he had given Paula was the one he gave every one else, his father's house out on the northwest side, just off Fullerton Avenue. This room, in a sense seldom attained, was his own. When he came back from France, the day Lucile saw him sitting on the bench in the park, he found it exactly — save for a heavy coating of dust — as he had left it, in 1917, when he went down to Camp Grant.

A good philosophy, so John Wollaston with a touch of envy had admitted — if you can make it work. Where it breaks down with most young men who set out so valiantly with it, is the point where one sees the only girl in the world and recognizes the imperious necessity of winning her, of holding out lures for her, of surrounding her, once won, with the setting her superlative worth demands. That this did not happen to Anthony March was due to the fact that the young woman he — not so much saw as gradually perceived, was his sister Sarah's friend, Jennie MacArthur.

Independence had been forced upon Jennie so early that she never was called upon to decide whether she liked it or not. She had an inquiring mind — perhaps experimental would be the better word for it — abundant self-confidence and a good stiff backbone. It was easy to make the mistake of thinking her hard. She was not a pretty woman, with her sandy hair and rather striking freckles, but she was well formed, she dressed always with that crisp cleanliness which is the extravagant standard of young women who work in good offices, and her voice had an attractive timbre.

To Sarah March (who, having fought for independence, was a little at a loss what to do with it) Jennie's experience and her rather interesting range of friends were a Godsend. It was at one of Jennie's parties in the tiny pair of rooms where she lived alone that Sarah met Walter Davis, a mechanical draftsman by day and an ardent young Socialist by night, whom she afterward married.

On the other hand, the home which Sarah was sometimes rather dubious about the advantage of possessing, was to Jennie a delightful place to be a familiar visitor in. She liked old David, who was a surprisingly charming person when he had no authority over you, she liked Mrs. March, she adored little Ben—young Ben he was now rapidly growing up to be—and finally, she began taking an interest which eventually outweighed all the rest, in the family black sheep, Anthony.

The intimacy between them which began around the time of Sarah's marriage continued intermittently for nearly four years. It had not, indeed, been definitely broken off when he went into the army.

When the attraction faded as it had definitely begun to do some months before he went to Camp Grant, it left their friendship unimpaired, enriched on the contrary. He could talk to her more easily, confide his thoughts to her more freely than to any one else he knew.

This ability to be confided in and depended upon was one of her special talents. She had emerged, years before, from the crowded stenographers' room in a big engineering concern into the private office of the chief. He was an erratic genius, brilliant, irritable, exacting, tireless, all but impossible to maintain any consistent relation with but one of bitter enmity. He had about made up his mind that a fresh stenographer every morning was all he could hope for, when Jennie became his Scheherazade. By the time the war broke out she was as indispensable to him as his hands. He had made her an officer of the company and paid her a salary of six thousand dollars a year, but she went on remembering his engagements, writing his letters and soothing the outraged feelings of his clients just as she had done in humbler days. She was, in the good, old-fashioned sense, his better half. Her amusement was the stock market and she played it cannily and with considerable success with his rather diabolic encouragement.

She was in New York when March got home, and he saw her for the first time since his return at his father's house on a Sunday morning more than a fortnight after the evening at the Wollastons' when Paula had sung his songs.

It was his first appearance anywhere since the afternoon in Novelli's studio when he had shown his opera to La Chaise and Paula. It had been agreed among them that with certain important changes, it would make an admirable vehicle for Paula's return to the operatic stage, and being a small affair from the producer's point of view, involving only one interior set, would be practicable for production during the summer at Ravinia in case the project for Paula's singing there went through. March had agreed to the changes and withdrawn into his stronghold over the grocery store with a determination not more than to come up for air until he had worried the thing into the shape they wanted.

He didn't know it was Sunday—having attributed the peacefulness he found pervading Fullerton Avenue to his own good conscience, a purely subjective phenomenon—until in the parlor of his father's house the sight of his brother Ben at the piano playing a soundless tune upon the tops of the keys, brought it home to him. When he inquired for the rest of the family, he learned that they were up-stairs getting ready for church.

"I hope," he said, with a grin at his younger brother, "that you aren't suffering from that old hebdomadal sore throat of yours."

"No, it's all right," Ben said, declining though to be amused. "I've got a gentleman's agreement with Sarah. Every other Sunday. Father's well enough satisfied now if he gets one of us. When they're all gone, I can slip out and buy a Sunday paper—jazz up the piano—have a regular orgy. Every other Sunday! Gee, but it's fierce!"

"It's pathetic," March said. "Poor father! I don't suppose there's any help for it."

What struck him was the pitiful futility of his father's persistence in trying to impose his ways, his beliefs, his will, upon one so rapidly growing into full independence. The only sanction he had was a tradition daily becoming more fragile. He was in for the bitterness of another disappointment. That was what there was no help for.

Naturally young Ben didn't interpret it this way. "You're a nice one to talk like that," he said resentfully. "You've always done whatever you pleased."

"There's nothing to prevent you from doing the same thing if you look at it that way," Anthony observed. "You've got a job a man could live on, haven't you?"

"Live on? Fifteen dollars a week?"

And it may be admitted that Ben's sense of outrage had some foundation. Years ago he had made up his small young mind that he would never work in the factory and he settled the question by getting himself a job in one of the piano salesrooms on Wabash Avenue. He wasn't precisely a salesman yet, he might perhaps have been spoken of by an unkind person as an office boy. But it was essential that he look like a salesman and act like a salesman, even in the matter of going to lunch. Some day soon, he was going to succeed in completing a sale before some one else came around and took it out of his hands, and he could then strike for a regular commission.

In the meantime with shoes and socks and shirts and neckties costing what they did, the suggestion that his salary was adequate to provide a bachelor's independence was fantastic and infuriating.

"Yes," he grumbled, "if I wanted to live in a rat hole and look like a tramp."

"My rat hole isn't so bad to live in," Anthony said, "but I'd be sorry to think I looked like a tramp. Do I, for a fact? I haven't had this suit on since I went into the army but I thought it looked all right."

"Oh, there's a big rip in the back of the shoulder where the padding is sticking through and your cuffs are frayed and your necktie's got a hole worn plumb through it where the wing of your collar rubs. You don't look like a tramp, of course, because you look clean and decent. It would be all right if you had to be like that. Only it's all so darned unnecessary. You could make good money if you'd only live like a regular person. Every day or two, somebody telephones to know if you aren't home and if there isn't some way we can get word to you, and it's kind of humiliating to have to say there isn't;—that we don't know where you are, haven't seen you for a week,—things like that. Of course, it's none of my business, but I'm trying to pull out of this. I'd like to be somebody someday and it would be a darn sight easier if you were trying to pull the same way instead of queering us all the time."

"Yes, I know," Anthony said thoughtfully. "But then there's Sarah on the other hand who can't forgive me for not putting on a red necktie and going Bolshevik. She'd have me put in my time trying to upset the bourgeois applecart altogether."

Ben grinned. "You ought to have heard her go on about the limousine that came and left a note for you the other day. Lady inside, chauffeur in a big fur coat. He came up to the door and asked whether you were home and left the note when Sarah said you weren't. Last Thursday, I think that was, just before supper. It's over there on the mantel, I guess. Sarah's afraid you're going to turn into a little brother of the rich."

"You tell Sarah," Anthony said off the top of his mind, the rest of it obviously engaged with the note,—"you tell Sarah there's nothing capitalistic about this. This is from her Doctor Wollaston's wife. Certainly he earns his living if anybody does."

"Do they want their piano tuned again?" Ben asked.

"They don't mention it. They want to know if I'll come to lunch to-day. I'm going to telephone to see if the invitation has expired."

"Good lord!" said Ben, "what have you got to wear? You can't go looking like that!" He meant to go into particulars when his brother came back from the telephone. But by that time he had something of nearer concern to himself to think about. Anthony found him staring out the window with an expression of the liveliest dismay.

"Oh, look who's here!" he said. "Can you beat it?"

Anthony looked and saw a little Ford coupé pulling up to the curb in front of the house; looked more closely at the person at the wheel and blinked.

"Jennie MacArthur! I thought she was still in New York. But what's she doing in that car?"

"Oh, she bought it last fall," Ben said. "She's getting rich. But can't you see what it means? She's coming around to see Sarah and that'll give Sarah an excuse for staying home from church. And that means that *I'll* have to go."

"Don't worry about that," Anthony said, catching up his hat. "I'll head her off. Tell mother I'll be around to-night."

He intercepted Jennie at the car door, caught both her hands and pressed them tight, pushed her back into her seat as he did so, climbed in and sat down beside her. "I'm supposed to be saving Ben from the horrible fate of getting dragged to church when it's really Sarah's Sunday," he said. "If you'll just drive me around the corner, I'll explain."

But she prevented him with a little laugh when he would have begun. "This is good enough for me. I don't want any explanation."

"It's pretty good," he agreed. "Stop a minute now we're safely around the corner and let me have a look at you."

She obeyed him, literally, pulling up to the curb again, accorded him the look he wanted and took, meanwhile, one of her own at him. Neither of them, however, seemed to find just the phrase in which to announce the result of this scrutiny. She started on again presently and he relaxed against the cushion. "This is more like being home again than anything that's happened yet," he said. "Are we to have a real visit?"

She was free till lunch she told him, and he, after saying "Well, that's something," admitted his own engagement. "However, that's the best part of two hours. The thing is not to waste any of it."

Naturally enough they wasted a good deal of it. They talked about the little car they were riding in, how she had learned to drive, why she had bought it; how Mr. Ferris, her boss, had said he wouldn't be any good for the day after coming down-town in a tight jammed elevated train and how, having tried the new method of transportation she had agreed with him; how it was as easy to run as a typewriter.

A few minutes more of that, she thought, and she'd begin telling Ford jokes, so she wrenched around to a new subject and asked him how much he'd seen of France; what he thought of the French; how long he'd been home; and what it seemed like to be in civilian clothes again;—topics upon which he enlarged as well as he could. She had driven meanwhile, north to Diversey Boulevard and had then turned west, around the ring. They were out in the middle of Garfield Park when she said after a hard, tight silence, "Isn't this perfectly ghastly?"

"It's awful," he agreed. "I don't know what's the matter with us—or whose fault it is. But I certainly didn't mean to get started like this."

"I expect that's it," she told him. "Haven't you been trying to treat me just exactly right? Make me feel perfectly comfortable? Haven't you been—being tactful, with all your might, ever since we started? Because I have."

"Well, then, for heaven's sake," he said, "let's quit! Quit trying so infernally hard, I mean. It's too nice a morning to spoil. You know, if the sun manages to come out, as it's trying to, it will be a very handsome April day."

"I don't think talking about the weather is much of an improvement," she commented. "Tony, let's give it up, for to-day I mean. We'll try again sometime from a fresh start. This is perfectly hopeless."

He tried to pretend that she didn't mean it but she made it clear even with a touch of asperity that she did. "Oh, all right," he growled and reached for the handle to the door.

"Don't be silly," she commanded. "I'm not going to leave you out here in the wilds of Garfield Park. Where do you want to go? Is it too early for your lunch?"

"Mrs. Wollaston told me to come at one," he said. "You aren't supposed to be ahead of time for a thing like that, are you? Anyhow, I've got to go back to my room first."

She caught up the name. "Sarah told me about your going there. First to tune the piano and then the evening when she sang your songs. Sarah's quite eloquent about it."

"Yes, poor Sarah, I know. Ben was quoting her this morning. However, that won't make the least difference with what I'm going to do."

"What are you going to do?" she asked.

"Why, I suppose," he said, "that I'm going to do what people speak of as settling down. What they mean by that is taking an interest in consequences—more of an interest in what things lead to than in what they are. Well, that's what I'm at now."

"That's a change, all right, for you," she said.

He agreed with her. "I knew when it happened," he added. "It happened when I heard Paula Carresford sing one of my songs. Do you remember the story that used to be in the school reader about the tiger that tasted blood and ate up the princess? You know, Jennie, it's practically true that up to that night I'd never heard any of my music at all—except mutilated fragments of it as I played it myself. And I'll tell you it was a staggering experience. The queerest experience I ever had in my life, too. I'll tell you about that sometime. But I changed right there, just the way the tiger did. I don't happen to want a fur overcoat nor an automobile nor an apartment on the Drive. I honestly don't want them. They aren't a part of my dreams— never were. But I do want to hear my own music. I want to hear it done for all it's worth. I want to hear orchestras play it and singers as good as Paula Carresford sing it. And in order to do that I've got to look ahead a little. I've got to stop doing always exactly as I damned please. I've got to do things because somebody besides myself wants them done."

"Have you got something like that to do to-day—with an eye to the consequences?" she asked.

He looked sharply around at her. She was very intent on her driving just then. "That's a remarkably good guess in a way," he said. "I dread going to that house to lunch. A month ago I'd have refused—or pretended I hadn't got the invitation until too late. And I'd have pretended to myself that it was because I didn't care to play the social game; didn't want to take on obligations of a kind I couldn't meet. But now I've told Mrs. Wollaston I'd come, I know the real reason why I don't want to.

"I said just now I didn't want a fur overcoat nor an automobile, and that's eighty percent true. And yet, there's a crawly little snob inside me that's in a panic right now because I haven't got proper clothes to wear and because I'm going to have to sit down in front of a lot of funny shaped forks that I don't know the special uses of.

"Oh, there's more to it than that of course. It's rather a cross-grained situation. Wollaston doesn't like me. He thinks I'm responsible for his wife's having kicked over the traces and signed up to sing at Ravinia this summer. In a way, I suppose I am. She's planning to use that opera of mine, you remember, — *The Outcry* we called it — for a novelty, provided they like the way I've padded up her part. The big rôle in it is really for the baritone, of course. That's what I've been slaving over for the last two weeks. If she makes a hit with it, she'll take it to the Metropolitan next winter. Of course, there's no reason in God's world why she shouldn't do that if she can get away with it. She hasn't any children to look after; she told me she didn't even keep house for her husband. All the same he regards me as a sort of potential homewrecker."

"You can't quite blame him for that, can you?" Jennie suggested. "If you began reading a story about a beautiful young opera singer who left her husband to go back on the stage again and sing an opera by a musical genius she'd discovered, wouldn't you expect them to fall in love with each other?"

"That shows what nonsense stories are," he said. "That couldn't happen to us in a thousand years. She's beautiful, and kindly, and affectionate. She's got temperament enough to blow the cork out of any bottle you tried to hold it down in. But I couldn't fall in love with her if I tried. It doesn't happen on that basis. Besides which, it's my belief that she's altogether in love with her husband. All the same, she's taken me up. She means to push me for all she's worth and let her husband like it or lump it as he pleases. She's got some plans, I don't know just what, for showing me off to one or two of the 'right' people to-day. You can imagine what it will be like, can't you?"

"I should think it would be rather good fun — that sort of game," she commented.

"That's where the forks come in," he said. "And not having a proper coat. That sort of social skill is the suit of armor those people wear. I've got to go back to my room and sew up the rip Ben told me about and trim my cuffs and try to tie my necktie so that the worn-out spots won't show-and make them do."

It was but a few minutes later—they had been silent ones—that she stopped her car in front of the little grocery store where the rickety outside stair led up to his door.

"I'll come in with you and sew up the rip in your coat," she said.

She wouldn't have made that offer, indeed would hardly have driven him up to his own door, if she had not been a young woman with steady nerves and a level head, and an abundant confidence in both. Because that dingy little wooden building with its outside stair to his attic, was the nucleus of memories that had by no means lost their poignancy. It was not, after all, so many years ago that she had mounted that stair for the first time, and it couldn't be considered strange that her heart quickened a little as she climbed it now.

The room startled her by being so utterly unchanged. Not only the major articles in it; the stove, the iron bed, the deal table he wrote at, the carpenter's bench, the half invented musical typewriter that he had once attempted to convert an old square piano into, the hollow-backed easy chair,—but the quite minor and casual trifles as well. On top of the set of home-made shelves that served for his music and his books was a sort of still-life composed of a meerschaum pipe with a broken stem and an empty goblet of pressed glass, standing upon a yellow paper-covered copy of Anatole France's *Thaïs*, that had been just like that the last time she was here. She had stuck a bunch of sweet peas she was wearing into that goblet. It made an uncannily short bridge to the past, a trivial reminder like that.

Evidently he felt it, too. Perhaps he had followed her glance toward that dusty shelf corner. Because, a moment after he had shut the door behind them, opened a window and taken a look at the fire, he came hesitantly and a little awkwardly up to her and took her by the shoulders as if to draw her into an embrace. He was very gentle about it.

Also he was ludicrously tentative. If she'd wanted to let herself go she could have laughed rather hysterically about that. She disengaged herself from his hands, decisively, indeed, yet without any air of pique.

"Oh, no, my dear," she said. "Take off your coat and let me get to work. Where's your sewing kit?"

He produced it instantly (the room was not in real disorder; it only looked like that to one who did not understand its system), gave her his coat, wandered restlessly about for a few minutes and presently came to rest at the deal table where he had spent the greater part of the last fortnight, turning over, discontentedly, the sheets of score paper he had left there.

Over her sewing she let her mind run free, forgetting this present Sunday with its problems, mixing a pleasant amalgam of the past. She wasn't heartbroken, you know, hardly regretful. She had life about as she wanted it. She never had been in love with March in the accepted meaning of the phrase—she had never even thought she was—and it is altogether probable that if she had found him eager to resume the old relation, she would have felt a certain reluctance about taking it up again. Life changed with the years and some of its old urgencies quieted down—for the time anyhow. Still the night when she had worn those sweet peas remained a fragrant memory. She was recalled to the present by the violent gesture he made over the score on his work table.

"This damned thing is rotten," he said with angry conviction. "I knew it,—I knew it while I wrote it. It may be what they want, but it's rotten. Straight into the stove is where it ought to go."

"Is that what you're writing for Mrs. Wollaston?" she asked.

He nodded. "I was trying to make up my mind whether to take this with me to-day or not. If she's the musician I think she is, she'll tell me to carry it out to the ash can."

"Well, that will be better than putting it in the stove yourself," she observed, going back with an air of placidity to her sewing, "because then you'll know it's bad and if you burn it up now, you won't. You haven't even heard it."

"I heard it before I wrote it," he argued. "I hear it again when I read it. That's a silly argument. Of course I know it."

"You said a little while ago that you'd never heard any of your music until Mrs. Wollaston sang those songs. They sounded better than you thought they would."

"That's different," he protested. "I knew they were good, damned good. Only I didn't quite realize how good they were. I suppose I won't realize until I hear her sing this how rotten it is. But I don't need to. I know well enough right now."

He went on turning the pages back and forth with gloomy violence, reading a passage here and another there and failing to get the faintest ray of comfort out of any of it, even out of the old soiled quires which belonged obviously to the original score.

"Is it all bad?" she asked. "Or just the new part."

"The whole thing," he grunted.

"That's that Belgian thing, isn't it?"

"That's the one."

"Well," she pointed out to him, "you thought that was good once. If it all looks alike to you this morning, perhaps what you've just been writing is as good as that, and it's just your mood to-day that makes it look rotten."

He closed the score and slapped his hand down upon it with a gesture of dismissal. Then he rose and leaned back against the edge of the table. "That's good logic, my dear," he conceded, "but it doesn't cover the ground. The old stuff was good in a way. I really meant it and felt it and I managed to get it down on paper. And the new stuff is like it, in that it's a damned clever imitation of it. I had to do it that way because I couldn't get back into the old mood. I'm sick of atrocities and horrors—everything that's got the name of war in it, even though I was never under fire myself. Well, writing the imitation has made me hate the thing I was trying to imitate. I stuck at it for the reason I told you this morning. But, good God, when it results in stuff like this...! Jennie, what shall I do about it? Shall I take this thing now and chuck it into the stove and then tell La Chaise and Mrs. Wollaston to go to the devil? Or shall I tuck it under my arm like a good little boy and see if I can get away with it?"

She looked at him thoughtfully. "What is the new thing you want to write?" she asked.

He smiled. "You're a wonder, Jennie," he said. "There is a new thing. I'm simply swamped in it. It won't let me alone. It's been driving me pretty nearly crazy. That's why it's been such perfect hell sticking to this other thing. Jennie, it's another opera. A big one, full size. A romantic fairy opera. I haven't got it in order yet. It isn't fit to talk about. But it's about a princess, a little blue-eyed, pale-haired princess, who is under a spell. She's dumb. She's dumb except in the presence of her true lover. Do you see? They are trying to cure her and they can't. But mysteriously in the night they hear her singing. Her lover is with her, and they try to solve the mystery. Maybe they kill him, I don't know. Or maybe they make him faithless to her. I don't know whether there is a fairy story like that or whether I just made it up. And I haven't worked it out at all. I haven't any words for it, no book, nor anything. But I tell you it comes in waves, whole scenes from it. I'd like a hundred hands to write it down with. I'd like to take one header into it and never come up. And meanwhile I'm slugging away at that other damned thing because Mrs. Wollaston and LaChaise want it,—because it's the main chance."

She asked why he didn't tell them about the new idea and get them to adopt it instead, but he greeted this suggestion with an impatient laugh.

"It would be absolutely impossible for Ravinia in the first place," he said. "The thing would need as big a production as, oh, *Pelléas and Melisande*. And then this woman could never sing it. She isn't the type. This is different altogether from anything she could do. Oh, no, it's quite hopeless until after I've succeeded with something else. But, oh, my God, Jennie, if you could hear it!"

She had finished her repairs on his coat and rising now held it up to him. While he was groping for the sleeves, she asked quietly, "Who is the princess, Tony? The dumb little princess with the blue eyes."

For a second he stood just as he was, like one suddenly frozen, then he settled into his coat, walked over to his work chair and dropped into it, leaning forward and propping up his head with his hands. "Yes," he said. "In a way, perhaps, there is some one. That's what I was going to tell you about. She came in as quiet as a little ghost, just as Mrs. Wollaston was beginning to sing and she sat down beside me without a word. And somehow while we listened, we—we were the same person. I can't make you understand that. It never happened to me before, nothing in the least like it, nothing so—intimate. I felt that song go vibrating right through her. She didn't speak at all, even after it was over, except to say that we mustn't talk—while we were waiting for the people in the other room to go away. And then Mrs. Wollaston came and got me. She didn't see her at all. She had disappeared somehow by that time."

He stopped but Jennie, it seemed, had nothing to say just then. She turned away to her outdoor wrap but she laid it down again and stood still when he went on.

"You don't want to run away with the idea that I'm in love with her," he said. "That isn't it. That's particularly—not it. I haven't an idea who she is nor any intention of trying to find out. Even if I knew the way to begin getting acquainted with her, I'm inclined to think I'd avoid it. But as an abstraction—no, that's not what I mean—as a symbol of what I'll find waiting for me whenever I get down to the core of things ... I've got a sort of—superstition if I don't do anything to—to break the spell, you know, that sometime she'll come back just the way she came that night."

With a little exaggeration of the significance of the act, she put on the coat she had crossed the room to get. He got up and came over to help her but he stopped with a sudden clenching of the hands, and a wave of color in his face as he saw the look in hers. At that she came swiftly to meet him, pulled him up in a tight embrace and kissed him.

"Good luck, my dear," she said. "I must be running and so must you. I'd take you with me only we go different ways. Carry your score along to the Wollastons. That's the first step to the princess, I guess."

# CHAPTER IX
# IN HARNESS

The episode upon which March had built the opera he called *The Outcry*, was one that was current during the autumn of 1914. A certain Belgian town had been burnt and it had been officially explained that this was done because the German officer who was billeted upon the burgomaster had been shot. The story was that the burgomaster's son shot him because he had raped his sister. The thing got complete possession of March's mind. At first just the horror of it and later its dramatic and musical possibilities. He saw, in orchestral terms, the sodden revelry in that staid house—with its endless cellars of Burgundy. He saw the tight-drawn terror in the girl's room where she lay in bed. He saw the room lighted fitfully by the play of searchlights over the city; the sinister entrance from a little balcony through the French widow, of the officer in uniform, his shadow flung ahead of him by the beam of the searchlight. He saw the man, blood—as well as wine—drunk, garrulous and fanatic with the megalomania of the conquering invader. He saw the man's intention made clear from the first, but the execution of it luxuriously postponed. Safely postponed because of the terrified girl's acceptance of his assurance that if anything happened to him, if a hand were raised against him, her father and a dozen more hostages would be shot and the town burned to the ground. Then came the girl's irrepressible outcry when he first touched her; the brother's knock at the door; her frantic effort to reassure him frustrated by the officer's drunken laugh; the forcing of the door and the fight half in the dark; the killing of the girl and then of her ravisher.

The thing that wouldn't let March alone, that forced him into the undertaking, was the declaration of the brutal philosophy of the conqueror made by the officer while he gloated over the girl who was to be his prey; the chance to put into musical terms that paranoiac delusion of world conquest. One recognized in it, vaguely, some of 'Wagner's themes and some of Straus', distorted and grown monstrous.

The thing had haunted March, as I have said, and he had tried to find somebody who would write him the book, the indispensable preliminary to his getting to work. Failing here, he had audaciously made up his mind to write it himself. It was not his first attempt to do, in the mere light of nature, a thing commonly supposed to be impossible except at the end of painful instruction. He had once experimented at painting in oils, he had tried his hand at the stylus, he had made a few figurines in modeling-wax. He wrote his play, then, by the simple process of building first with painstaking accuracy, a model of his stage, the girl's room in that burgomaster's house with the French windows giving upon the little balcony. He modeled the furniture in plastiscene. He bought three little dolls to represent his characters. And then he reported what he saw happening in that room; what his characters did and what they said. By the time he had finished this work, the music was all in his head. He couldn't write it down fast enough.

It had been one of the great experiences of his life, writing that opera. Jennie's reminder that he had once believed it good, was a conservative statement. LaChaise and Paula were deeply impressed by the power, both of its music and its drama and saw possibilities in it for a sensational success. The drawback, fatal unless it could be overcome, lay in the fact that the dominant rôle in it was that of the baritone. Dramatically the soprano's part was good enough, but there was nowhere near enough for her to sing. There was no reason though, they both asserted, and sent March away from their conference at least half convinced, why the girl's part could not be greatly amplified. There were various expedients;—a preliminary scene between the girl and her brother; an apostrophe to an absent lover; a prayer. Also instead of being frozen into terror-stricken silence by her ravisher's monstrous purpose, she could just as well be represented as making a desperate resistance. She could plead with him, denounce him; attempt to take advantage of his drunkenness and trick him. It could be made as good a woman's part as the big act of *Tosca*.

March had assented to all this and gone to work.

Paula did not tell him, as he had gloomily prophesied to Jennie, to take the new first scene he brought her that Sunday out to the ash can. And, indeed, it sounded so much better when they read it over together, that he was for the moment reassured. But her attitude toward the opera was different from the one she had taken toward the group of Whitman songs, and this difference grew more marked at their subsequent sessions over it. There had been about the songs the glamour of discovery. One does not hasten to apply the assayer's acid to treasure trove. And, too, it was an altruistic impulse which had prompted her to take up the songs.

There aren't many people who can travel steadily, or very far, on that motivation, and Paula was not one of them. From the moment when she took the plunge, ignored—all but defied—her husband's wishes, and signed the

Ravinia contract, she ceased to be concerned for anything, broadly speaking, but her own success. March's opera, then, was not, to her, the expression of his genius but a potential vehicle for hers. She was acutely critical of it. She knew what she wanted and it was not thinkable that she should put up with anything less.

She was not aware of this change of attitude. She was blessed with a vigorous non-analytical mind that asked no awkward questions, suggested no paralyzing doubts. The best thing that could possibly happen to March's opera was that it should be made to fit her; that it should demand precisely all her resources and nothing that was beyond them. Obviously, since it was going to be her opera, a thing she was going to wear.

Had she been, as many eminent persons in her profession are, a mere bundle of insensate egotisms complicated by a voice, she would have driven March to flat rebellion in a week, all his good resolutions notwithstanding. What made it tolerable was that she had a good musical intelligence of her own, and a real dramatic sense. He could recognize, what she wanted as an intelligible thing, consistent with itself. Only, it was not his thing-not the thing he saw. By reason of its very consistency it was never the thing he saw.

"She wouldn't do it that way," he would protest.

"I would," Paula would tell him. "I wouldn't lie there, whimpering."

He was always arguing with her—wrangling, it almost came to, sometimes—in defense of his own conception. For a sample:

"Look at what she is; a burgomaster's daughter. That means prosperous, narrow-minded, middle-class people. She's convent-bred, devout. She's still young or she'd be married. She's altogether without experience. She's frightened just as a child would be over what's going on in the house. And the prayer she says when she goes to bed would be just the nice little prayer a child would say, an Our Father or a Hail Mary, whatever it might be. As simple as possible, on the surface, but with an undertone of overmastering terror. The sort of Promethean defiance you're talking about would be inconceivable to a child like that."

"I suppose it would, to most of them," she admitted, "but this one's going to be different. After all, it's the exceptional ones that usually have operas written about them. I don't believe all the dancers in Alexandria were like Thais, nor all the gipsy cigar-makers in Seville like Carmen. I don't believe many little Japanese girls would feel about Pinkerton the way Cio Cio San did. Why can't our Dolores be an exception, too?"

The only answer he could make to that was that it spoiled the other figure, reduced him from a sort of cosmic monster to the mere custom-made grand-opera villain.

"What if it does?" she retorted. "This isn't being written for Scotti or Vanni Marcoux. It's being written for me." That was the tonic chord they always came back to. It was Paula's opera.

March presently began to feel, too, that he was growing to be nothing more than Paula's composer. It was important to the success of their enterprise that his reputation should be intensively exploited among the rich and influential who figured as patrons of the Ravinia season. She went at the task of building it as ruthlessly as she remodeled his opera.

Her demands upon him were explicit. In the first place he was to bring her all his music, early as well as late, trivial as well as important, in order that she might select from it what, if anything, might be exploited at once. She had promised to give a recital just before Easter, in aid of one of the local charities—it was one that boasted an important list of patronesses—and if she could make an exclusive program of his songs she would like to do so. Then, while it was too late to get any of his compositions performed by the orchestra this season, it would be a good thing to get Mr. Stock to read something in the hope of his taking it for next year. An announcement, even a mere unofficial intimation, that Anthony March (whose opera ... and so on)—was to be represented on the symphony programs next season, would help a lot.

What dismayed him most was her insistence—she was clear as a bell about this—that he himself get up the accompaniments to some of the simpler of his songs so that when she took him out to meet people who wanted to hear a sample of his music then and there, they could manage, between them, some sort of compliance. He nearly got angry, but decided to laugh instead, over her demand that he be waiting, back stage, when she gave her recital of his songs (which she did with great success) to come out at the end and take his bow in his now discarded uniform. It was the only reference she ever made to his shabby appearance.

(It was steadily growing shabbier, too, since she left him hardly any time at all for tuning pianos. She would have been utterly horrified had she known what tiny sums he was living on from week to week. And it never occurred to her when she suggested that a certain score of his ought to be copied, that he could not afford to take it out to a professional copyist and so sat up nights doing it himself. He did it rather easily, to be sure, since it was one of the numerous things at which he had earned a living.)

There was only one of her many demands that he persistently refused to comply with. And she took this refusal rather hard; acted more hurt than angry about it, to be sure, but came back to it again and again. When she discovered that he made no pretense of living at his father's house, she asked for his real address so that she could always be sure of getting at him when she wanted him. This he would not give her. If he did, he said, it would only result in his staying away from there and doing his work somewhere else. It was one of his simple necessities to know that he couldn't be got at. He would make every possible concession. Would go, or telephone, at punctiliously regular and brief intervals, to his father's house to learn whether she had sent for him, but give up the secrecy of his lair he would not. It wasn't possible.

I think she compensated herself for this refusal by sending for him sometimes when she did not really need him, just to be on the safe side, and, on the same basis, engaged his attendance ahead from day to day. Anyhow, she occupied, in one way or another, practically the whole of his time; and the dumb little blue-eyed princess knocked at his door in vain. Only in those hours when sheer fatigue had sent him to bed had she any opportunity of visiting him. Sometimes she made white nights for him by haunting those hours, refusing to go away; sometimes, by not coming at all, she filled him with terror lest she had gone for good—would not come back even when he was ready for her. When that panic was upon him he hated Paula with a devouring hatred.

Of the human original of his blue-eyed princess, he saw during those weeks, nothing. On that first Sunday when he lunched at the house he heard them speak of a member of the family, a daughter of John Wollaston, named Mary, who had been living in New York and had recently returned but was not lunching at home that day. He got the idea then that she might be the girl who had so mysteriously come in and sat beside him while Paula sang; and without any evidence whatever to support this surmise, it became a settled conviction. But an odd shrinking, almost superstitious, as he had confessed to Jennie, from doing anything that might break the spell kept him from asking any questions.

During the first week of his almost daily visits to the house, he got repeated intimations of her, a glimpse once through an open door on the third floor into a room that struck him as being, probably, hers. The impression, once more, when he was coming down from the music room that this was the door which he had just heard softly shut as if some one, the princess herself, of course, who had stood listening to the music for a while, had withdrawn there when she heard his step on the stairs. Once on the settee in the hall he saw a riding crop and a small beaver hat that he felt a curious certainty belonged to her and once out of a confusion of young voices in the drawing-room, and a dance tune going on the Victrola, he heard some one call out her name, hers he was sure though he didn't hear her answer. Perhaps she had answered without speaking. The dumb princess again.

Then suddenly even these faint hints of her presence ceased, and he remarked their absence with a troubled wonder until one day Paula volunteered the statement that Mary had gone away on a visit for a month or two, out to Wyoming, where a great friend of hers, Olive Corbett, and her husband had a ranch.

By asking a few intelligent questions, he could have found out a lot more about her from Paula for she was disposed to talk freely enough about the family life she was so oddly enclosed in, and their perpetual quarrels about the opera never carried over into their breathing spells. In the long hours of their almost daily sessions the occasional rests made up quite a total and March accumulated a lot of information about Paula herself.

Indeed it was not quite as idle as that sounds. Paula talked to him thirstily, gave him somehow the impression that she had had no one for a good many years with whom she could converse without reservation in her own idiom.

She came, he learned, of a Virginia family which had migrated during her early childhood to California. It was obvious that they were well-bred, but equally so that they were not very competent. The victims, he judged, of a lot of played-out southern ideas and traditions. They were still living and March allowed himself to guess that they were one of the minor reasons why Doctor John had to earn a lot of money.

Paula with her splendid physique and gorgeous voice must have looked to them like the family hope. They had managed at considerable sacrifice to send her abroad, but evidently without any idea of the time and the money it takes to erect even the most promising material into a genuine success. After a year or two, she had been abandoned to make her way as best she could.

Even now that they were safely consigned to the past, Paula could not talk about the shifts and hardships of that time with any relish. The discouragements must have sunk in pretty deep. She hinted—it was not the sort of topic she could discourse candidly about—that the blackest of those discouragements had come from the amorous advances of men who had it in their power to open opportunities to her but wanted a *quid pro quo*.

He asked her in that connection whether during those hard times she had never felt inclined to fall in love on her own account.

"I never cared a snap of my fingers for any man," she said with obvious sincerity, "until I saw John."

This slowness of her erotic development surprised him rather until he evoked the explanation that her energies had been concentrated upon her musical ambition. Music, since she was a real musician, had been a genuine emotional outlet for her.

March speculated rather actively upon the relation between Paula and her husband. There was no dark room in the composer's mind. He was the other pole from Aunt Lucile. All human problems set his mind at work. He was not widely read in the literature of psychology and he had a rough working theory which he regarded as his own, a dynamic theory. People got started off in life with a certain amount of energy. It varied immensely between individuals, of course, but one couldn't alter the total of his own. Upon that store you ran until you were spent. What channels this stream of energy cut for itself was partly a matter of luck, partly one of self-determination. The important fact was that there was only so much and that what went down one way did not also go down another. It might be a hundred rivulets or one river, it couldn't be both. This philosophy was largely responsible for the ordering of his own life, for his doing without possessions, for the most part without friends, for his keeping the brake set so tightly upon his sex impulses.

John must have come into Paula's life, he reflected, at a time when the musical outlet to her energies had been dammed up. Her main stream, like that of the Mississippi, had cut a new channel for itself. Had there been, he wondered, some similar obstruction in the main channel of John Wollaston's emotional life? Anyhow, there was no doubt that for the five years since this cataclysm had occurred, the course of true love had run smooth and deep. But suppose now that, through LaChaise's intervention, Paula's musical career was again opened to her, would the current turn that way? Would John be left stranded? Had Paula herself any misgivings to this effect?

That she was deeply troubled about her present relation with John and in general about John himself, would have been plain to a less penetrating eye than Anthony's. There was no open quarrel between them. Wollaston dropped into the music room sometimes, late in the afternoon, to ask how the opera was getting along. His manner to March on these occasions was one of, perhaps, slightly overwrought politeness, but the intention of it did not seem hostile. Toward Paula he presented the image of humorous, affectionate concern, the standard behavior of the perfect husband.

It was Paula, on these occasions, who gave the show away, betraying by a self-conscious eagerness to make him welcome, the fact that he was not. She made the mistake of telling him he looked tired and worried, facts too glaringly true to be bandied about in the presence of a stranger. He looked to March as if he were approaching the elastic limit of complete exhaustion. That it looked pretty much like that to Paula herself was made evident from the way she once spoke about him, her eyes full of tears, after he had left the room.

"He's working so insanely hard," she said. "Nights as well as days. I don't believe he's had five hours' consecutive sleep this week."

When March wanted to know why he did it, she hesitated, but gave him, at last, a candid answer. No one else would have answered it at all.

"I don't think it can be because he feels he has to," she said. "To earn the money, I mean. Of course, he's been buying a big farm, half of it, for Rush. But he said the other day that if I needed any extra money for this"—she nodded toward the score on the piano—"I was to let him know. Of course, he isn't happy about it and I suppose it makes him take things harder."

Naturally enough, March agreed with her here. John Wollaston was clearly a member of the gold coast class. It wasn't thinkable that his financial difficulties could be real. The unreality of them was, of course, the measure of the genuineness of his fear of losing Paula,—of seeing the main current of her life shift once more to its old channel. Did Paula see that, March wondered? What was it she foresaw?

He got a partial answer one day in the course of one of their quarrels about the opera. He had unguardedly given expression to his growing despondency about it.

"This thing can't go," he had said. "It's getting more lifeless from week to week. We're draining all the blood out of it and this stuff we're putting in is sawdust."

She whipped round upon him in a sudden tempest. "It's got to go," she said. "It's got to be made to go. If what you're putting into it is sawdust, take it out. Put some heart into it."

He had been staring gloomily at the score. Now he turned away from it. "That's what I don't seem able to do," he said.

She came up and took him by the shoulders so violently that it might almost be said she shook him. "You can't let go like that. It's too late. Everything I've got in the world is mixed up in it." She must have read his unspoken thought there for she went on, "Oh, I suppose you'd say I'd still have John if I did fail. Well, I wouldn't. He's mixed up in it, too. He'd never forgive me if I failed. It's the fear I'll fail and make myself look cheap and ridiculous that makes him hate it so. Well, I'm not going to. Make up your mind to that!"

Later, when he was leaving, under a promise to improve some of the passages they had been arguing about, she reverted to this aspect of the matter and added something. "John can see what a failure would mean. But what the other thing—the big real success—would mean to both of us, he hasn't the faintest idea of. He won't till I get it."

"He's a famous person, himself, of course," March observed, not without a gleam of mischief.

She echoed the word quite blankly, and he went on to amplify.

"That European Medical Commission that was out here a few weeks ago attended some of his clinics in a body. I don't suppose there's a first-class hospital anywhere in this country or in Europe where his name isn't known. That operation he did on Sarah turned out to be a classic, you know. He used a new technique in it which has become standard since."

But it seemed to him that she still looked incredulous when he went away, incapable of really digesting that idea at all. No, he wouldn't have bet much on the chance that any great success of hers could reunite them. The love life that they had been enjoying this last five years hadn't thrown out any radicles to bind them together—children for instance.

March wondered why there had been no children. He was not inclined to accept the obvious explanation that she hadn't wanted any. She had spoken once of her childlessness in a tone that didn't quite square with that explanation. Nor had she said it quite as she would, had she felt that her husband shared equally in her disappointment. It was all very intangible, of course, just the way she inflected the sentence, "You see, I haven't any children." Was it John that didn't want them? Well, he had two of his own, of course. Had he shrunk from having this new passion of his domesticated? And then he was a gynecologist. Was he, perhaps, afraid for her? That explanation had a sort of plausibility about it for Anthony March. If that were true, his caution had only brought him face to face with a greater risk. March felt sorry for John Wollaston.

But it quite truly never occurred to him to hold himself in the smallest degree responsible for the husband's troubles. To a man with a better developed possessive sense, it might have occurred that he was poaching in another's preserves. When a husband made it plain that he chose to keep a particularly rare and valuable possession such as a wife like Paula must be considered, in the tower of brass LaChaise had talked about, it became the duty of every other well-disposed male to take pains to leave no keys, rope ladders or files lying about by which she might effect her escape. But a consideration of this sort would not even have been intelligible to March, let alone troublesome.

# CHAPTER X
# AN INTERVENTION

Mary could not have described the thing there was about old Nat's manner of going by her door that led her to halt him and inquire what he was up to. One sees, sometimes, one of his children gliding very innocently along toward the nearest way out with an effect of held breath that prompts investigation. In this sixty-year old child, upon whom the terror of John Wollaston's desperate illness lay more visibly than on any other member of the household, this look of gusto was especially striking. Mary's question was prompted by no more serious an impulse than to share with him a momentary escape from the all-enveloping misery.

But she found old Nat unwilling to share his source of satisfaction with her. He protested, indeed, with an air of deeply aggrieved innocence, that nothing of the sort existed. A man was waiting now in the lower hall who had come to make the customary inquiries. Nat had conveyed them to Paula and was returning with her answer. This was so flagrantly disingenuous that Mary smiled.

"Who is the man?" she asked.

The old servant shuffled his feet. "It's that good-for-nothing piano tuner, Miss Mary," he told her reluctantly. "I reckon you don't know much about him. He's been coming around a lot since you've been away. He's been sticking to Miss Paula like a leech, right up to the day your father got sick. Then he didn't come any more and I thought we were done with him. But he came back to-day and asked me if Miss Paula was up in the music room. He'd have gone right straight up to that room where Doctor John is fighting for his life if I hadn't stopped him."

"Did you tell him father was ill?" she asked, and was astonished at the flare of passion this evoked from him.

"It ain't no business of his, Miss Mary," he said grimly. "Nothing about this family is any business of his." Then as if anxious to prevent the significance of that from reaching her, he hurried on. "He was so sure Miss Paula wanted to see him, I told him if he'd wait, I'd inform her that he was here. I've done told her and she said he was to go away. She couldn't be bothered with him. And then she said to me with tears in her eyes, 'I wish I'd never seen him, Nat.' Those were her words, Miss Mary. 'I wish my eyes had never beheld him!' That's what she said to me not a minute ago. I'm going down to fix him so she'll never see him again."

"You needn't go down," Mary said decisively. "I'll see him myself."

She had got home that morning summoned by a telegram, one of those carefully composed encouraging telegrams that are a simple distillate of despair. During the three days it had taken to accomplish her journey from the ranch, she had gradually relinquished all hope of finding her father alive. Rush, who met the train, had reassured her. It was a bad case of double pneumonia. They were expecting the crisis within twenty-four hours. The doctors gave him an even chance, but the boy was more confident. "They don't know dad," he said. "He isn't going to die."

On the way back to the house he had outlined the facts for her. His father had driven out to the farm in his open roadster a week ago Sunday to see how he and Graham were getting on—driven out alone, though he had spoken the night before, over the telephone, of bringing Paula with him. For some reason that hadn't come off. Dad had seemed well enough, then, though rather tired and dispirited. The day had begun as if it meant to be fine, for a change, but it had turned off cold again and begun to rain while they were walking over the place. His father, he was afraid, had got pretty wet. When they got back to the farm-house they found a telephone message urgently summoning him to town, and he had driven away, in the open car, without changing.

Rush had meant to telephone but had neglected this—they were terribly busy, of course, trying to get things done without any labor to do them with. He had come home Wednesday, on a promise to Graham's kid sister that he would attend a school dance of hers. He had dressed at home but not dined there and had seen nothing of his father until very late, about two o'clock in the morning, when he noticed a light in his room as he passed on the way to his own.

"I don't know why I stopped," he said. "He was talking and his voice didn't sound natural, not as if he was telephoning nor talking to any one in the room, either. He was trying to telephone—to the hospital to send an ambulance for him. He hadn't any breath at all, even then, and the thermometer he'd been taking his temperature with read a hundred and four."

"But—the *hospital*?"

"I know," Rush agreed. "It's pretty rum. He stuck to it. Wanted to be got straight out of the house without rousing anybody. He was a little bit delirious, of course. I agreed to it to pacify him, but I telephoned straight to Doctor Darby and he told me not to do anything till he got around. It wasn't more than ten minutes before he came. Paula had roused by that time, and she persuaded Darby against the hospital. She suggested the music room herself and as soon as he saw it he said it was just the place. They've got a regular hospital rigged up for him there and two men nurses. But the main person on the job is Paula herself. The two men keep watch and watch, but she's there practically all the time. They say she hasn't slept in more than half-hour snatches since that first night. She won't let any of us come near him—and Darby backs her up. The doctors are all crazy about her. Say it'll be her doing if dad pulls through. Well—she'd better make it!"

There wasn't time to explore the meaning of that last remark for they were then pulling up at the door. She laid it aside for future reference, however. She was so fortunate as to meet Doctor Darby on the stairs and so to get at once the latest and most authoritative report.

He brightened at the sight of her but she thought he didn't look very hopeful. He said though, that he believed her father was going to get well. "Medically, he hasn't more than an even chance. He hasn't much fight in him somehow. But that stepmother of yours means to pull him through. She doesn't mean to be beaten and I don't believe she will be. I've never seen the equal of her. It shows they're born, not made. She's never had, your aunt assures me, any nursing experience whatever."

Mary thought she detected a twinkle in Darby's eye over this mention of Aunt Lucile, but it was gone before she could make sure.

"You're to go up and see him for five minutes," he went on. "Paula's keeping a look-out for you. He mustn't be allowed to talk, of course, but she wants him to know you're back. She has an idea, and she's probably right, that he is worrying about you."

"What is there that I can do?" she asked. "To help, I mean."

"Hope," he told her bluntly. "Pray if you can. Cheer up your aunt a bit, if possible; she's in despair. Only don't try to take away any of her occupations. That's about all."

"In other words, nothing," she commented.

"Well, none of us can do much more than that," he said, "excepting always, Paula."

It was not until she had spent that heart-tearing five minutes at her father's bedside, while she talked cheerful little encouraging futilities in a voice dry with the effort she had to make to keep it from breaking, that she saw her aunt—and felt grateful for Doctor Darby's warning. Mary had never thought of Lucile before as an old woman, but she seemed more than that now,—broken and, literally, in despair—of her brother's life. And beyond this there was a bitterness which Mary could not, at first, account for.

"Paula, I hear, has allowed you to see him. For five minutes! Well, that is more than she has allowed me. Or any of us. It was a chance for showing off, I suppose, that was more than she could resist."

"I was a little afraid it might be that," Mary admitted. "Afraid of finding her—carefully costumed for the part, you know. But she wasn't. She didn't come into the room with me at all; just told me not to show I was shocked by the way he looked and not to let him talk. And she seemed glad I was back; not for me but because it might help him. It seems a miracle that he's still alive, after almost a week of that, and I guess it is she who has done it. They all say so."

"Men!" the old woman cried fiercely. "All men! The two nurses as well. There's something about her that makes idiots of all of them. She knows it. And she revels in it. It's the breath of life to her. She has played fast and loose with your father's happiness for it. And now she's playing with his life as well. And feeling, all the while, that it is a very noble repentance!"

"Repentance for what?" Mary asked. "Rush said something like that. I thought, before I went away, that father was getting reconciled to the Ravinia idea. Do you think it was worrying about ..."

"No, I don't," Lucile interrupted shortly. "Your father was exposed, soaking wet, to a cold north wind, while he was driving forty miles in an open car. That's the reason he took pneumonia. And it's the only reason. I don't know what Rush may have been saying to you, but I've known your father ever since he was born, and I can tell you that Paula might have gone on making a fool of herself to the end of time without his dying of it. He was—fond of her, I will admit. But he had a life of his own that she knows nothing about. He was too proud to tell her about it, and she hadn't wit enough to see it for herself. That's the truth, and this emotional sprawl she's indulging in now doesn't change it.—Meanwhile, she is adding to her collection five new men!"

"I don't believe," said Mary quietly, "that there is one of them she knows exists. Or wouldn't poison," she added with a smile, "to improve father's chance of getting well."

This won a nod of grim assent. "There are plenty of them. She could replace them easily enough. But her hunger for their worship is insatiable. For a while your father's—infatuation satisfied her. She may have tried to pull herself up to his level. I dare say she did. But even at that time she could not abide Wallace Hood, though he was kindness itself to her, simply because he kept his head. Unfortunately, this poor young musician was not able to keep his."

It seemed to Mary, even when allowance was made for the bitterness of the desperate old woman, who then went on for the better part of an hour with her bill of particulars, that this must be true. Paula must have lost her head, at any rate. What Mary herself had seen the beginning of, must have gone on at an accelerated speed until it was beyond all bounds. There had been few hours when March might not come to the house and none to which he did not stay. There were whole days when Paula was hardly out of his company. She took him about with her to people's houses. She talked about him when she went alone. Those who had at first not known what to think, at last had come to believe that there was only one thing they could.

"I tried to suggest to her, quite early, before it had gone so far, that she was in danger of being misunderstood. It only made her furious. And John was hardly less so when I mentioned to him that I had spoken to her. He would see nothing; kept a face of granite through it all."

"Aunt Lucile," Mary asked, after a little silence, "do you think she has really been—unfaithful to father?"

Miss Wollaston hesitated. "Should you consider the conduct I have described, to be an example of fidelity?"

"I mean, in the divorce court sense," Mary persisted.

"That," her aunt said, more nearly in her old manner than anything that Mary had yet seen—"that is a matter upon which I have no opinion."

It was a possibility that Mary had contemplated as early as that first night of all, when Paula, having sung his song, had come herself to find him in Annie's old bedroom where she had him hidden and with a broken laugh had pulled him up in her arms and kissed him, unaware that she was not alone with him. One kiss, as an isolated phenomenon, didn't mean much, Mary allowed, but when a man and a woman who were going to be left alone together a lot, started off that way, they were likely to—get somewhere. And where the man was the composer of that love song and the woman the singer of it, it was almost a foregone conclusion that they would.

But this was not the conclusion that she had come to when she stopped old Nat on his way down-stairs to turn March out of the house. The evidence, Rush's and Aunt Lucile's, might seem to point that way but it didn't, somehow, make a convincing picture. I think, though, that in any case, she would have gone down to see him.

He had found himself a seat on a black oak settee in the hall around the corner of the stairs and his attitude, when she came upon him, was very like what it had been the other time, bent forward a little, his hands between his knees, as if he were braced for something.

"Mrs. Wollaston won't be able to see you to-day," she said. He sprang to his feet and she added instantly, "I'm her stepdaughter, Mary Wollaston. Won't you come in?" Without waiting for an answer, she turned and led the way into the drawing-room.

So far it had been rehearsed, on her way down-stairs, even to the chair in the bow window which she indicated, having seated herself, for him to sit down in. She had up to that point an extraordinarily buoyant sense of self-possession. This left her for one panicky instant when she felt him looking at her a little incredulously as if, once more, he wondered whether she were really there.

"I think, perhaps, you haven't heard of father's illness," she began—not just as she had expected to. "Or did you come to ask about him?"

"No," he said. "I hadn't heard. Is it—yes, of course it must be—serious. I'm sorry."

She was struck by the instantaneous change in his manner. From being, part of him, anyhow, a little remote—wool-gathering would have been Aunt Lucile's term—he was, vividly, here. It wasn't possible to doubt the reality of his concern. As a consequence, when she began informing him of the state of things she found herself pulled away, more and more, from the impersonal phraseology of a medical bulletin. She told how the attack had come on; how they had put up a bed for him in the music room, where there was the most air, and begun what it was evident from the first would be a life-and-death struggle; she quoted what Rush had told her when he met the train. "I agree with Rush," she concluded. "They let me see him, for a few minutes, this morning, just so he'd know that I had come back. Yet it isn't possible not to believe that he will get well."

When she had squeezed away the tears that had dimmed her eyes, she saw that his own were bright with them. "He's more than just a great man," he said gravely. Then, after a moment's silence, "If there's anything I can do… It would be a great privilege to be of service to him. As errand boy, any sort of helper. I had some hospital experience at Bordeaux."

It was, on the face of it, just such an offer as any kindly disposed inquirer would have made. Such as Wallace Hood, for example, had, in fact, made, only rather more eloquently less than an hour ago. But Mary's impulse was not to answer as she had answered Wallace with a mere polite acknowledgment of helpless good intentions. In fact, she could find, for the moment, no words in which to answer him at all.

He said then, "I mustn't keep you."

Even in response to that she made no movement of release. "There's nothing, even for me to do," she said, and felt from the look this drew from him that he must, incredibly, have caught from her some inkling of what her admission really meant.

He did not repeat his move to go, nor speak, and there was silence between them for, perhaps, the better part of a minute. It was terminated, startlingly, for her, by her brother's appearance in the doorway. He had on his raincoat and carried his hat and an umbrella in his hands.

"Mary, I'm just going out" … he began, then broke off short, stared, and came on into the room. March rose, but Mary, after one glance at Rush's face, sat back a little more deeply in her seat. Rush ignored her altogether.

"My sister has been away during the last few weeks," he said to March. It had, oddly, the effect of a set speech. "If she had not been, I'm sure she would have told you, as I do now …" He stumbled there, evidently from the sudden blighting sense that he was talking like an actor—or an ass. "This isn't the time for you to come here," he went on. "This house isn't the place for you to come. When my father's well enough to take matters into his own hands again, he'll do as he sees fit. For the present you will have to consider that I'm acting for him."

Mary's eyes during the whole of that speech never wavered from March's face. There was nothing in it at all at first but clear astonishment, but presently there came a look of troubled concern that gave her an impulse to smile. Evidently it disconcerted her brother heavily for at the end of an appalling silence, not long enough however, to allow March to get his wits together for a reply, Rush turned about abruptly and strode from the room. A moment later they heard the house door close behind him.

The two in the drawing-room were left looking at each other. Then, "Please sit down again," she said.

# CHAPTER XI
# NOT COLLECTABLE

The effect of Rush's interruption was rather that of a thunderclap, hardly more. Recalling it, Mary remembered having looked again into March's face as the street door banged shut to see whether he was laughing. She herself was sharply aware of the comic effect of her brother's kicking himself out of the house instead of his intended victim, but she could not easily have forgiven a sign of such awareness from March.

He had betrayed none, had tried, she thought—his amazement and concern had rendered him pretty near inarticulate—to tell her what the look in his face had already made evident even to Rush; his innocence not only of any amorous intent toward Paula but even of the possibility that any one could have interpreted the relation between them in that way. He might have managed some such repudiation as that had she not cut across his effort with an apology for her brother.

It had been a terrible week for them all, she said. Especially for Rush and for his Aunt Lucile, who had been here from the beginning. Even the few hours since her own return this morning had been enough to teach her how nearly unendurable that sort of helplessness was.

It must have been in this connection that he told her what had not got round to her before, the case of his sister Sarah whom they had watched as one condemned to death until John Wollaston came and saved her. "He simply wouldn't be denied," March said. "He was all alone; even his colleagues didn't agree with him. And my father, having decided that she was going to die and that this must, therefore, be the will of God, didn't think it ought to be tampered with.

"I remember your father said to him, 'Man, the will of God this morning is waiting to express itself in the skill of my hands,' and it didn't sound like blasphemy either. He carried father off in his apron, just as he was, to the hospital and I went along. I scraped an acquaintance afterward with one of the students who had been there in the theatre watching him operate and got him to tell me about it. They felt it was a historic occasion even at the time; cheered him at the end of it. And that sort of virtuosity does seem worthier of cheers than any scraping of horsehair over cat-gut could ever come to. I wonder how many lives there are to-day that owe themselves altogether to him just as my sister does.—How many children who never could have been born at all except for his skill and courage. Because, of course, courage is half of it."

Upon Mary the effect of this new portrait of her father was electrifying; eventually was more than that—revolutionary. These few words of March's served, I think, in the troubled, turbid emotional relation she had got into with her father, as a clarifying precipitant.

But that process was slower; the immediate effect attached to March himself. The present wonder was that it should have been he, a stranger, equipped with only the meagerest chances for observation, who, turning his straying search-light beam upon the dearest person to her in the world, should thus have illuminated him anew. Even after he had gone it was the man rather than the things he had said that she thought about.

Amazingly, he had guessed—she was sure she had given him no hint— at the part Paula was playing in their domestic drama. It had come pat upon what he had told her of the lives her father had plucked from the hand of death, the ironic, "he saved others, himself he can not save," hanging unspoken in their thoughts.

"Paula will be fighting for his life," he said. "Magnificently. That must be one of your hopes."

She had confirmed this with details. She got the notion, perhaps from nothing more than his rather thoughtful smile, that he comprehended the whole thing, even down to Aunt Lucile. Though wasn't there a phrase of his,—"these uninhibited people, when it comes to getting things *done* ..." that slanted that way? Did that mean that he was one of the other sort? Wasn't your ability to recognize the absence of a quality or a disability in any one else, proof enough that you had it yourself? It would never, certainly, occur to Paula to think of any one as "uninhibited."

But the opposed adjective didn't fit him. She couldn't see him at all as a person tangled, helpless, in webs of his own spinning;—neither the man who had written that love song nor the man who had sat down in his chair again after Rush had slammed the door.

He wasn't even shy but he was, except for that moment when a vivid concern over John Wollaston's illness brought him back, oddly remote, detached. He might have been a Martian, when in response to her leading he discussed Paula with her; how good a musician she was; how splendidly equipped physically and temperamentally for an operatic career. "She has abandoned all that now, I suppose," he said. "Everything that goes with it. She would wish, if she ever gave us a thought, that LaChaise and I had never been born."

Mary would have tried to deny this but that the quality and tone of his voice told her that he really knew it and that, miraculously, he didn't care. She had exclaimed with a sincerity struck out of her by amazement, "I don't see how you know that."

"Paula's a conqueror," he had answered simply, "a—compeller. It's her instinct to compel. That's what makes her the artist she is. Without her voice she might have been a tamer of wild beasts. And, of course, a great audience that has paid extravagantly for its pleasure is a wild beast, that will purr if she compels it, snarl at her if she doesn't manage to. She's been hissed, howled at. And that's the possibility that makes cheers intoxicating. Left too long without something to conquer, she feels in a vacuum, smothered. Well, she's got something now; the greatest thing in the world to her,—her husband's life. She's flung off the other thing like a cloak."

Without, at the moment, any sense of its being an extraordinary question, Mary asked, "Are you glad? That she has forgotten you, I mean."

She was not able, thinking it over afterward, to recall anything that could have served as a cue for so far-fetched a supposition as that. It could have sprung from nothing more palpable than the contrast suggested between Paula, the compeller, the *dompteuse*, and the man who had just been so describing her. He was so very thin; he was, if one looked closely, rather shabby, and beyond that, it had struck her that a haggard air there was about him was the product of an advanced stage of fatigue,—or hunger. But that of course, was absurd. Anyhow, not even the sound of her question startled her.

Nor did it him. There was something apologetic about his smile. "It *is* a reprieve," he admitted. "I left her a week ago," he went on to explain,—"it must have been the day Doctor Wollaston fell ill—on a promise not to come back until I had got this opera of mine into the shape she wants. I came back to-day to tell her that it can't be done—not by me. I have tried my utmost and it isn't enough. I haven't improved it even from her point of view let alone from mine. She isn't an easy person to come to with a confession of failure."

"She's spoiling it," Mary said. "Why do you let her?"

But March dissented from that. "If we agree that the thing's an opera— and of course that's what it is if it's anything—then what she wants it made over into is better than what I wrote. She's trying to put the Puccini throb into it. She's trying to make better drama out of it. LaChaise agrees with her.

He said at the beginning that I relied too much on the orchestra and didn't give the singers enough to do. And, of course, it's easy to see that what a woman like Paula said or did would be more important to an audience than anything that an oboe could possibly say. When I'm with her, she— galvanizes me into a sort of belief that I can accomplish the thing she wants, but when I go off alone and try to do it...." He blinked and shook his head. "It has been a first-class nightmare, for a fact, this last week."

But Mary demanded again. "Why do you let her?"

"I made a good resolution a while ago," he said. "It was—it was the night she sang those Whitman songs. You see I've never been tied to anything; harnessed, you know. Somehow, I've managed to do without. But I've had to do without hearing, except in my own head, any of the music I've written. There was an old tin trunk full of it, on paper, that looked as if it was never going to be anywhere else. Well, I came to a sort of conviction after I went away from here that night, that those two facts were cause and effect; that unless I submitted to be harnessed I never would hear any of it. And it seemed that night that I couldn't manage to do without hearing it. Keats was wrong about that, you know,—about unheard melodies being sweeter. They can come to be clear torment. So I decided I'd begin going in harness. I suppose it was rather naive of me to think that I could, all at once, make a change like that. Anyhow, I found I couldn't go on with this. I brought it around to-day,—it's out there in the hall—to turn it over to Paula to do with as she liked. That's why it was so—incredible, when you came down the stairs instead."

He sprang up then to go, so abruptly that he gave her the impression of having abandoned in the middle, the sentence he was speaking. This time, however, rising instantly, she released him and in a moment he was gone. There had been a word from him about her father, the expression of "confident hopes" for his recovery, and on her part some attempt, not successfully brought off she feared, to assure him of his welcome when he came again. She didn't shake hands with him and decided afterward that it must have been he who had avoided it.

She was glad to have him go so quickly. She wanted him to go so that she could think about him. It was with a rather buoyant movement that she crossed the room to the piano bench and very lightly with her finger-tips began stroking the keys, the cool smooth keys with their orderly arrangement of blacks and whites, from which it was possible to weave such infinitely various patterns, such mysterious tissue.

A smile touched her lips over the memory of the picture her fancy had painted the night Paula sang his songs, the sentimental notion of Paula's inspiring him with an occasional facile caress to the writing of other love songs. She might have been a boarding-school girl to have thought of that. She smiled, too, though a little more tenderly, over his own attempt—naive he had called it—to go in harness, like a park hack, submissive to Paula's rein and spur. Pegasus at the plow again. She smiled in clear self-derision over her contemplated project of saving him from Paula. He didn't need saving from anybody. He was one of those spirits that couldn't be tied. Not even his own best effort of submission could avail to keep the harness on his back.

It was most curious how comfortable she had been with him. During the miserable month she had spent at home before she went to Wyoming with the Corbetts, she had dreaded a second encounter with March and had consciously avoided one. To meet and be introduced as the strangers they were supposed by the rest of the family to be, to elaborate the pretense that this was what they were—they who had shared those flaming moments while Paula sang!—would be ridiculous and disgusting. But anything else, any attempt to go on from where they had left off was unthinkable. In the privacy of her imagination she had worked the thing out in half a dozen ways, all equally distressing.

She had not made good her resolution to quit thinking about him. She was not able and did not even attempt to dismiss her adventure with him as a mere regrettable folly to be forgotten as soon as possible. It had often come back to her during sleepless hours of the long nights and had always been made welcome. She didn't wish it defaced as she had felt it necessarily must be by the painful anti-climax of a second meeting.

The impulse upon which she had taken him out of old Nat's hands was perhaps a little surprising now she looked back on it, but it had not astonished her at the time. Of course, there, there was something concretely to be done, an injustice to be averted from a possibly innocent head. She doubted though if it had been pure altruism.

Whatever its nature, the result of it had been altogether happy. She *was* glad she had come down to see him. There need be no misgiving now about the quality of their future encounters, were there to be any such. They were on solid ground with each other.

How had that been brought about? How had they managed to talk to each other for anyway fifteen or twenty minutes without either a reference to their adventure or a palpable avoidance of it? It wasn't her doing. From the moment when she got to the end of the lines she had rehearsed coming down the stairs, the lead had been in his hands. Indeed, to the latter part of the talk, what she had contributed was no more than a question or two so flagrantly personal that they reminded her in review of some of her childish indiscretions with Wallace Hood. How had he managed it?

He hadn't been tactful. She acquitted him altogether of that. She couldn't have endured tact this afternoon from anybody. Of course, the mere expressiveness of his face helped a lot. The look he had turned on Rush for example, that had stopped that nerve-racked boy in full career. Or the look he gave her when he first learned of her father's illness. That sudden coming back from whatever his own preoccupation might have been to a vivid concern for her father.

Well, there, at last, it was. That was his quality. A genius for more than forgetting himself, for stepping clean out of himself into some one else's shoes. Wasn't that just a long way of saying imagination? He had illuminated her father for her and in so doing had given her a ray of real comfort. He had interpreted Paula—in terms how different from those employed by Aunt Lucile! He had comprehended Rush without one momentary flaw of resentment. Last of all, he had quite simply and without one vitiating trace of self-pity, explained himself, luminously, so that it was as if she had known him all her life.

One thing, to be sure, she didn't in the least understand—the very last thing he had said. "That's why it was so incredible when you came down the stairs instead." That had been to her, a complete non sequitur, an enigma. But she was content to leave it at that.

Such a man, of course, could never—belong to anybody. He was not collectable. There would always be about him, for everybody, some last enigma, some room to which no one would be given the key. But there was a virtue even in the fringe of him, the hem of his garment.

Was she getting sentimental? No, she was not. Indeed, precisely what his little visit had done for her was to effect her release from a tangle of taut-drawn sentimentalities. She hadn't felt as free as this, as comfortable with herself, since she came home with Rush from New York.

She had no assurance that he'd come to the house again of his own accord or that Paula would send for him. But she was in no mood to distress herself just now, even with that possibility.

She crossed the room and got herself a cigarette, and with it alight she returned to her contemplation of the piano keyboard. She didn't move nor speak when she heard Rush come in but she kept an eye on the drawing-room door and when presently he entered, she greeted him with a smile of good-humored mockery. He had something that looked like a battered school atlas in his hand.

"What do you suppose this is?" he asked. "It was lying on the bench in the hall."

She held out a hand for it and together they opened it on the lid of the piano and investigated.

"It's the manuscript of his opera," she said. "He brought it around to leave with Paula. To tell her he had done with it. He's been trying to spoil it for her but he can't."

"I suppose I made an infernal fool of myself," he remarked, after a little silence.

She blew, for answer, an impudent smoke ring up into his face.

He continued grumpily to cover his relief that she had not been more painfully explicit,—"I suppose I shall have to make up some sort of damned apology to him."

"I don't know," she said. "That's as you like. I don't believe he'd insist upon it. He understood well enough."

He looked at her intently. "Has there been any better news from father since I went out?" he asked.

She shook her head. "Except that there's been none. Every hour now that we aren't sent for counts. What made you think there might have been?"

He said he didn't know. She looked a little more cheerful somehow, less—tragic. Evidently her visit to the Corbetts had done her good.

His eye fell once more on the manuscript. "Did he go off and forget that?" he asked. "Or did he mean to leave it for Paula? And what shall we do with it,—hand it over to her or send it back?"

Thoughtfully Mary straightened the sheets and closed the cover. "I'll take care of it for him," she said.

# CHAPTER XII
# HICKORY HILL

Pneumonia, for all it is characterized by what is called a crisis, has no single stride to recovery, no critical moment when one who has been in peril passes to safety. Steinmetz and Darby were determined that Mary and all the household should understand this fully. She had waylaid them in the hall as they were leaving the house together—this was seventy-two hours or so after Anthony March's call—and demanded the good news she was sure they had for her. There was a look about them and a tone in their voices that were perfectly new.

They would not be persuaded to say that her father was out of danger. There was very little left of him. His heart had been over-strained and this abnormal effect was now, in due course, transferred to the kidneys. All sorts of deadly sequellae were lying in ambush.

But the more discouraging they were, the more she beamed upon them. She walked along with them to the door, slipping her arm inside Doctor Darby's as she did so. "If you only knew," she said, "what a wonderful thing it is to have the doctors stop being encouraging and try to frighten you, instead. Because that means you really do think he's getting well."

"The balance of probability has swung to that side," Steinmetz admitted in his rather affected staccato. "At all events he's out of my beat." His beat was the respiratory tract and his treatment the last word in vaccines and serums.

She held Darby back a little. "Must we go on feeling," she asked, "that anything could happen any minute? Or—well, could Rush go back to the farm? Graham Stannard has gone to New York, I think, they're partners, you know, so he must be rather badly wanted. And this waiting is hard for him."

Rush could go, of course, Darby assured her. "For that matter," he went on with a quick glance at her, "why don't you go with him? Take your aunt along, too. For a few days, at least. You couldn't do better."

She demurred to this on the ground that it didn't seem fair to Paula. If there was a period of Arcadian retirement down on the books for anybody, it was Paula who was entitled to it.

But Paula, as Darby pointed out, wouldn't take it in the first place, and, surprisingly, didn't need it in the second. "She told me just now that she'd slept eighteen hours out of the last twenty-four and was ready for anything. She looked it, too."

He understood very well her irrepressible shrug of exasperation at that and interrupted her attempt to explain it. "It's another breed of animal altogether," he said. "And at that, I'd rather have had her job than yours. You're looking first rate, anyhow. But your aunt, if she isn't to break up badly, had better be carried off somewhere." He glanced around toward Steinmetz who had withdrawn out of ear-shot. "There are some toxins, you know," he added, "that are even beyond him and his microscopes."

Mary had meant to broach this project at dinner but changed her mind and waited until Aunt Lucile had withdrawn and she and Rush were left alone over their coffee cups for a smoke.

"Poor Aunt Lucile! She has aged years in the last three weeks. And it shows more, now the nightmare is over, than it did before."

"Is it over? Really?" he asked.

"Well, we don't need miracles any more for him. Just ordinary good care and good luck. Yes, I'd say the nightmare was over."

"Leaving us free," he commented, "to go back to our own."

"You can go back to the farm, anyhow," she said. "I asked Doctor Darby, especially, and he said so. He wants me to go along with you and take Aunt Lucile. Just for a week or so. Is there any sort of place with a roof over it where we could stay?"

He said, "I guess that could be managed." But his tone was so absent and somber that she looked at him in sharp concern.

"You didn't mean that the farm was your nightmare, did you?" she asked. "Has something gone terribly wrong out there?"

"Things have gone just the way I suppose anybody but a fool would have known they would. Not worse than that, I guess."

He got up then and went over to the sideboard, coming back with a decanter of old brandy and a pair of big English glasses. She declined hers as unobtrusively as possible, just with a word and a faint shake of the head. But it was enough to make him look at her.

"You didn't drink anything at dinner, either, did you?" he asked.

She flushed as she said, "I don't think I'm drinking, at all, just now."

"Being an example to anybody?" he asked suspiciously.

She smiled at that and patted his hand. "Oh, no, my dear. I've enough to do to be an example to myself. I liked the way it was out at the Corbetts'. They've gone bone-dry. And,—oh, please don't think that I'm a prig—I am a little better without it—just now, anyway. Tell me what's gone wrong at the farm."

"This is wonderful stuff," he said, cupping the fragile glass in his two hands and inhaling the bouquet from the precious liquor in the bottom of it. "It's good for nightmares, at any rate." After a sip or two, he attempted to answer her question.

"Oh, I suppose we'll come out all right, eventually. Of course, we've got to. But I wish Martin Whitney had done one thing or the other; either shown a little real confidence and enthusiasm in the thing or else stepped on it and refused to lend father the money."

"Lend?" Mary asked. "Did he have to borrow it?"

He dealt rather impatiently with that question. "You don't keep sixty or eighty thousand dollars lying around loose in a checking account," he said. "Of course, he had to borrow it. But he borrowed it of Whitney, worse luck—and Whitney being an old friend, pulls a long face over it whenever we find we need a little more than the original figures showed. That's enough to give any one cold feet right there.

"Graham's father is rich, of course, but he's tighter than the bark on a tree. He's gone his limit and he won't stand for anything more. He can't see that a farm like that is nothing but a factory and that you can't run it for any profit that's worth while without the very best possible equipment. He wanted us to pike along with scrub stock and the old tools and buildings that were on the place and pay for improvements out of our profits. Of course, the answer to that was that there wouldn't be any profits. A grade cow these days simply can't earn her keep with the price of feed and labor what it is. We didn't figure the cost of tools and modern buildings high enough—there *was* such a devil of a lot of necessary things that we didn't figure on at all—and the consequence was that we didn't put a big enough mortgage on the place. Nowhere near what it would stand. And now that we want to put a second one on, Mr. Stannard howls like a wolf."

The mere sound of the word mortgage made Mary's heart sink. She looked so woebegone that Rush went on hastily.

"Oh, that'll come out in the wash. It's nothing to worry about really, because even on the basis of a bigger investment than we had any idea of making when we went in, it figures a peach of a profit. There's no getting away from that. That's not the thing about it that's driving Graham and me to drink."

He stopped on that phrase, not liking the sound of it, and in doubt about asking her not to take it literally. She saw all that as plainly as if she had been looking through an open window into his mind. He took another deliberate sip of the brandy, instead, and then went on.

"Why, it's the way things don't happen; the way we can't get anything done."

He did not see the sympathetic hand she stretched out to him; went back to the big brandy glass instead, for another long luxurious inhalation and a small sip or two. "It's partly our own fault, of course," he went on, presently. "We've made some fool mistakes. But it isn't our mistakes that are going to beat us, it's the damned bull-headed incompetence of the so-called labor we've got to deal with."

He ruminated over that in silence for a minute or two. "They talk about the inefficiency of the army," he exclaimed, "but I've been four years in two armies and I'll say that if what we've found out at Hickory Hill is a fair sample of civilian efficiency, I'll take the army way every time. There are days when I feel as if I'd like to quit; — go out West and get a job roping steers for Bob Corbett, even if he is bone-dry."

She thought if he played any longer with that brandy glass she must cry out, but he drained it this time and pushed it away. With an effort of will she relaxed her tight muscles.

"I suppose I must have looked to you like a hopeless slacker," he said, "or you wouldn't have asked Darby to send me back to work. No, — I didn't mean to put it that way. I look like one to myself, that's all, when I stop to think. Only you don't know how it has felt, this last six weeks, to go on getting tighter and tighter in your head until you feel as if you were going to burst. I went out and got drunk, once, — just plain, deliberately boiled — in order to let off steam. It did me good, too, for the time being."

She didn't look shocked at that as he had expected her to — gave him only a rather wry smile and a comprehending nod. "We're all alike; that's the trouble with us," she said. "But you will take us out to Hickory Hill, won't you? Aunt Lucile and I. I'll promise we won't be in the way nor make you any more work."

She saw he was hesitating and added, "At that, perhaps, I may be some good. I could cook anyhow and I suppose I could be taught to milk a cow and run a Ford."

He laughed at that, then said a little uncomfortably that this wasn't what he had been thinking about. "I suppose you're counting on Graham's being in New York. He isn't. At least, he telegraphed me that he'd be back at Hickory Hill to-morrow morning. I knew you'd been rather keeping away from him and I thought perhaps..."

"No, that's all right." She said it casually enough, but it drew a keen look of inquiry from him, nevertheless. "Oh, nothing," she went on. "I mean I haven't made up with him. Of course, I never quarreled with him as far as that went. Only it's what I meant when I said just now that we were all alike, father and you and I. We all get so ridiculously—tight about things. Well, I've managed to let off steam myself."

He patted her hand approvingly. "That trip to Wyoming did you a lot of good," he observed.—"Or something did."

"They're wonderfully easy people to live with, Olive and Bob," she said. "They're immensely in love with each other I suppose, but without somehow being offensive about it. And they have such a lot of fun. Olive has a piebald cayuse, that she's taught all the *haute ecole* tricks. He does the statuesque poses and all the high action things just as seriously as a thoroughbred and he's so short and homely and in such deadly earnest about it that you can hardly bear it. You laugh yourself into stitches but you want to cry too. And Bob says he's going to train a mule the same way. If he ever does that pair will be worth a million dollars to any circus.—Well, we'll be doing things like that out at Hickory Hill some day. Because there is such a thing as fun left in the world."

"We'll have some of it this week," he agreed, and in this rather light-headed spirit they arranged details.

The only building at Hickory Hill that had been designed for human habitation was the farm-house and it was at present fully occupied and rather more by a camp cook and his assistant, the farm manager and half a dozen hands. The partners themselves slept in a tent. There was also a cook tent near the house where three meals a day were prepared for everybody, including the carpenters, masons, concrete men and well diggers who were working on the new buildings. They drove out in Fords from two or three near-by towns in time for breakfast and didn't go home till after supper. The wagon shed of the old horse barn served as a mess hall.

There were some beds, though, two or three spare ones, Rush was sure, that had never been used. Given a day's start on his guests, he would promise some sort of building which, if they would refrain from inquiring too closely into its past, should serve to house them.

"A wood-shed," she suggested helpfully, "or a nicely swept-out hennery. Even a former cow stable, at a pinch. Only not a pig-pen."

"If our new hog-house were only finished, you could be absolutely palatial in it. But I think I can do better than any of those. You leave that to me.—Only, how about Aunt Lucile? She's—essential to the scheme, I suppose. Can you deliver her?"

"She'll come if it's put to her right,—as a sporting proposition. She really is a good sport you know, the dear old thing. You leave her to me."

"Lord, I feel a lot better than I did when I sat down to dinner," he told her when they parted for the night, and left her reflecting on the folly of making mountains out of mole-hills.

# CHAPTER XIII
## LOW HANGS THE MOON

He broke his promise to be waiting for them Friday morning at the farm. It was Graham who caught sight of their car, as it stopped in front of the farm-house, and came plunging down the bank to greet them and explain how unavoidable it had been that Rush should go to Elgin.

He was somewhat flushed and a little out of breath but he seemed, after the first uncomfortable minute, collected enough. He mounted the running-board and directed the chauffeur to drive on across the bridge and fork to the right with the main road up to a small nondescript building on the far side of it.

It was a part of the farm, he explained, indicating the wilderness off to the left,—a part of what must once have been a big apple orchard. Indeed, exploring it yesterday for the first time, he had found a surprising number of old trees, which, choked as they were with undergrowth, looked as if they were still bearing fruit. The building, which they had never even entered until yesterday, had served as a sorting and packing house for the crop, though the old part of it—paradoxically the upper part—appeared to have been built as a dwelling by some pioneer settler. A second story had been added underneath by digging out the bank.

It stood well back from the road, a grass grown lane with a turning circle leading to it. It had what had once been a loading platform, wagon high, instead of a veranda. The lower story, a single room which they peered into through a crack in a warped unhinged door, seemed unpromising enough, a dark cobwebby place, cumbered with wooden chutes from the floor above by which, Graham explained, they rolled the apples down into barrels after they had been sorted up-stairs. A carpenter had been busy most of the morning, he added, flooring over the traps from which these chutes led down.

Mary, though, fairly cried out with delight, and even Miss Wollaston beamed appreciation when, Graham, having led them up the bank and around to the back of the building, ushered them in, at the ground level up here, to the upper story of the building. There was a fireplace in the north end of it with twin brick erections on either side which they thought must have been used for drying apples. The opposite end, partitioned off, still housed a cider mill and press, but they had contrived, he said, a makeshift bedroom out of it.

Along the east side of the room were three pairs of casement windows which commanded a view of the greater part of the farm; across the road, across Hickory Creek, across the long reach of the lower pasture and the seemingly limitless stretches of new plowed fields. The clump of farm buildings, old and new, was in the middle of the picture. Over to the left not quite a mile away, behind what looked like nothing more than a fold in the earth (the creek again, Graham explained. It swung an arc of two hundred degrees or so, about the main body of their tillable land) rose the heavily wooded slopes of Hickory Hill.

"We were surprised at this place," he said, "when we opened it up yesterday. It's the best view on the farm. It will be a fine place to build a real country house, some day, if we ever make money enough to do that."

"It is a real country house already," Mary told him briskly. "You two, living in a tent with a lovely old place like this just waiting for you! Wait until Aunt Lucile and I have had a day at it and you'll see."

He looked as if he believed her. Indeed, he looked unutterable things, contemplating her, there in that mellow old room,—wrinkling her nose a little and declaring that she could still smell apples. But all he said was that he supposed the roof leaked, but it couldn't be very bad because everything seemed quite decently dry and not at all musty. He added that he must be getting back to work, but that an odd-job man, capable more or less of anything, was at her disposal for as long as she wanted him.

She went with him to the door when he made his rather precipitate departure and stood, after she had waved him a temporary farewell, gazing up at the soft sun-bathed slope with its aisles of gnarled trees. She smiled at the sight of a decrepit long-handled wooden pump. She took a long breath of the smell of the month of May. Then she turned, with Aunt Lucile, to such practical matters as bedding, brooms and tea-kettles.

There was more to do than a first look had led them to suppose, and their schemes grew ambitious, besides, as they advanced with them, so that, for all the Briarean prodigies of Bill, the odd-job man, they went to bed dog tired at nine o'clock that night with their labors not more than half complete. They slept—Mary did, anyhow, the deepest sleep she had known in years.

She waked at an unearthly—a heavenly hour. The thin ether-cool air was quivering with the dissonance of bird calls; the low sun had laid great slow-moving oblongs of reddish gilt upon the brown walls of the big room.

(She had left her aunt in undivided possession of the extemporized bed-chamber.) She rose and opened the door and looked out into the orchard. But what her eye came to rest upon was the old wooden pump.

It was a triumph of faith over skepticism, that pump. Graham had contemned it utterly, hardly allowing, even, that it was picturesque, but Bill, the odd-job man had, with her encouragement, spent a patient hour over it and in the teeth of scientific probability, lo, it had given forth streams of water as clear as any that had ever miraculously been smitten out of a rock. The partners had forbidden her to drink any of it except boiled, until it had been analyzed.

She looked about. She had the world to herself. So she carried her rubber tub, her sponge and a bath-towel out to the warped wooden platform and bathed *en plein air,* water and sun together. She came in, deliciously shuddering, lighted a fire, already laid, of shavings and sticks, put the kettle on to boil and dressed. She felt—new born that morning.

This sensation made the undercurrent of a long fully filled day. She almost never had time to look at it but she knew it was there. It enabled her to take with equanimity the unlooked-for arrival (so far as she and her aunt were concerned) of Graham's young torn-boy sister, Sylvia. It made it possible for her to say, "Why, yes, of course! I'd love to," when Graham, along in the afternoon asked her if she wouldn't go for a walk over the farm with him. They spent more than an hour at it, sitting, a part of the time, side by side atop the gate into the upper pasture, yet not even then had the comfortable sense of pleasant companionship with him taken fright. It was a security that resided, she knew, wholly in herself.

He was holding himself, obviously, on a very tight rein, and it was quite conceivable that before her visit ended, he would bolt. There was a moment, indeed—when he came with Rush to supper at the apple house and got his first look at the transformation she had wrought in it—when that possibility must have been in the minds of every one who saw his face.

She had dramatized the result of her two days' labor innocent of any intention to produce an effect like that. The partners when they came dropping in from time to time had, learned nothing of her plans, seen none of their accomplishments, so to-night the old-fashioned settle which Bill had knocked together from lumber in the packing room and she had stained, two of the sorting tables, fitted into the corners beside the fireplace to make a dais, the conversion of another into a capital dining table by the simple expedient of lengthening its legs, the rag rug, discovered in the village, during a flying trip with Sylvia this morning in her car and ravished from the church fair it had been intended for, the sacks of sheeting Aunt Lucile had been sewing industriously all day, covered with burlaps and stuffed with hay to serve as cushions, the cheese-cloth tacked up in gathers over the windows and hemmed with pins,—all this, revealed at once, had the surprise of a conjurer's trick, or, if one were predisposed that way, the entrancement of a miracle.

She was a little entranced, herself, partly with fatigue for she had put in, one after the other, two unusually laborious days, but partly no doubt with her own magic, with this almost convincing simulation of a home which she and her assistants had produced. It didn't matter that she had gone slack and silent, because Sylvia, who just before supper had shown a disposition to dreamy elegiac melancholy, rebounded, as soon as she was filled with food, to the other end of the scale altogether and swept Rush after her into a boisterous romp, which none of Aunt Lucile's remonstrant asides to her nephew was effectual to quell.

She was an amazing creature, this product of the latest generation to begin arriving at the fringes of maturity, a reedy young thing, as tall as Graham, inches taller than Rush. She had the profile of a young Greek goddess and the grin of a gamin. She was equally at home in a ballgown—though she was not yet out—or in a pair of khaki riding breeches and an olive drab shirt. She was capable of assuming a manner that was a genuine gratification to her great aunt or one that startled her father's stable men. She read French novels more or less at random, (unknown to her mother. She had a rather mischievous uncle who was responsible for this development) and she was still deadly accurate with a snowball. A bewildering compound of sophistications and innocence, a modern young sphinx with a riddle of her own.

Mary watched her tussling and tumbling about with Rush, pondering the riddle but making no great effort to find an answer to it. Was she child or woman? To herself what was she? And what did Rush think about her? They were evidently well established on some sort of terms. Rush, no doubt, would tell you—disgustedly if you sought explanation—that Sylvia was just a kid. That he was fond of her as one would be of any nice kid and that her rough young embraces, her challenges and her pursuits, meant precisely what those of an uproarious young—well, nephew, say,—would mean. Only his eagerness to go on playing the game cast a doubt upon that explanation.

They went out abruptly after a while, just as it was getting dark, to settle a bet as to which of them could walk the farthest along the top rail of a certain old fence. Miss Wollaston saw them go with unconcealed dismay, but it was hard to see how even a conscientious chaperon could have prevented it so long as the child's elder brother would do nothing to back her up. To Mary, half-way in her trance, it didn't seem much to matter what the relation was or what came of it. It was a fine spring night and they were a pair of beautifully untroubled young animals. Let them play as they would.

Their departure, did, however, arouse Graham to the assumption of his duties as host and he launched himself into a conversation with Miss Wollaston; a fine example, Mary thought, of what really good breeding means. Her aunt's questions about life in the navy were not the sort that were easy to answer pleasantly and at large. They drew from him things he must have been made to say a hundred times since his return and sometimes they were so wide of the mark that it must have been hard not to stare or laugh. He must have been wishing, too, with all his might down in the disregarded depths of his heart, that the old lady would yield to the boredom and fatigue that were slowly creeping over her. Soon! Before that pair of Indians came back. But by nothing, not even the faintest irrepressible inflection of voice was that wish made manifest.

It broke over Mary suddenly that this would never happen. Aunt Lucile might die at her post, but she'd never, in Graham's presence, retire through a door which was known to lead to her bedroom. She rose and going around to her aunt's chair, laid a light hand on her shoulder. But she spoke to Graham.

"Let's go out and bring in the wanderers," she said. "Aunt Lucile has had a pretty long day and I know she won't be able to go to sleep until Sylvia is tucked in for the night."

When the door had closed behind them and they stood where the path, already faintly indicated, led down to the road, he stopped with a jerk and mutely looked at her.

"Do you know where that fence of theirs is?" she asked.

"Yes, I guess so," he said. Then—it was almost a cry—"Must we go there? Right away?"

"I don't know that we need." (Why should he be tortured like that! What did it matter if the rigidity of some of her nightmare-born resolutions got relaxed a little?) "Where do you want to go with me?"

He didn't answer for a minute, but when he did speak his voice was steady enough. "There's a place up on the top of this hill where the trees open out to the east, a lovely place. I went up there last night after Rush had turned in. There'll be a moon along in a few minutes and you can see it come up, from there. Could we wait for it?—I suppose Miss Wollaston..."

"No, she'll be all right," Mary said. "Now that she thinks we're looking for them."

As she moved up the slope she added, "I've a sort of interest in the moon, myself, to-night."

"Perhaps if you'll take my hand—" he said stiffly. "It is dark here under the trees."

Her single-minded intention had been to make him a little happier. She liked him better to-night than ever, and that was saying a lot. But this elaborate covering up of what he really wanted under the pretended need of guiding her, tried her patience. The pretense was for himself, too, as much as for her. He was holding her off at arm's length behind him as if they were scaling an Alp!

In the spirit of mischief, half irritated, half amused, she crowded up to his side and turned her hand so that their palms lay together. And she said in a voice evenly matter-of-fact, "That's nicer, isn't it?"

He didn't succeed in producing anything audible in answer to that, but he began presently, and rather at random, to talk. As if—she reflected, mutinously,—some fact that must on no account be looked at would emerge, un-escapable, the moment he stopped.

But the bewitching loveliness of the place he led her to made amends, sponged away her irritation, brought back the Arcadian mood of the day. A recently fallen apple tree just on the crest of the hill, offered in its crotched arms a seat for both of them. With an ease which thrilled her he lifted her in his hands to her place and vaulted up beside her. His arm (excusably, again, for the hand was seeking a hold to steady him), crept around behind her.

Once more he began to talk,—of nature, of the farm, of how it was the real way to live, as we were meant to. One couldn't, of course, cut off the city altogether. There were concerts and things. And the companionship of old friends. Even at that it would be lonely. They had felt it already. That was why it was such a marvelous thing to have her here. She made a different world of it. Just as she had made what seemed like a home out of that old apple house. No one could do that but a woman, of course …

She was no longer irritated by this. She barely listened, beyond noting his circuitous but certain approach to the point of asking her, once more, to marry him.

Her body seemed drugged with the loveliness of the night, with fatigue, with him, with the immediacy of him,—but her mind was racing as it does in dreams.

Nature was not, of course, the gentle sentimentalist Graham was talking about, but one did get something out of close communion with her. A sense of fundamentals. She was a—simplifier of ideas. Plain and straightforward even in her enchantments. That moon they were waiting for…. Already she was looking down upon a pair of lovers, somewhere,—a thousand pairs!— with her bland unseeing face. And later to-night, long after she had risen on them, upon a thousand more.

Of lovers? Well perhaps not. Not if one insisted upon the poets' descriptions. But good enough for nature's simple purposes. Answering to a desire, faint or imperious, that would lead them to put on her harness. Take on her work.

Anthony March had never put on a harness. A rebel. And for the price of his rebellion never had heard his music, except in his head. Clear torment they could be, he had told her, those unheard melodies. Somehow she could understand that. There was an unheard music in her. An unfulfilled destiny, at all events, which was growing clamorous as the echo of the boy's passion-if it were but an echo-pulsed in her throat, drew her body down by insensible relaxations closer upon his.

The moon came up and they watched it, silent. The air grew heavy. The call of a screech-owl made all the sound there was. She shivered and he drew her, unresisting, tighter still. Then he bent down and kissed her.

He said, presently, in a strained voice, "You know what I have been asking. Does that mean yes?"

She did not speak. The moon was up above the trees, yellow now. She remembered a great broad voice, singing:

"Low hangs the moon. It rose late.
It is lagging-O I think it is heavy with love, with love"

With a passion that had broken away at last, the boy's hands took possession of her. He kissed her mouth, hotly, and then again; drew back gasping and stared into her small pale face with burning eyes. Her head turned a little away from him.

"… Whichever way I turn, O I think you could give me
My mate back again if you only would,
For I am almost sure I see her dimly whichever way I look.
O rising stars!…"

The languor was gone. She shivered and sat erect, he watching her in an agony of apprehension. She looked slowly round at him.

"You haven't answered!" His voice broke over that into a sob. "Will you marry me, Mary?"

"I don't know," she said dully, like one struggling out of a dream. "I will if I can. I meant to for a while, I think. But ..."

He leaped to the ground and stood facing her with clenched hands. "I ought to be shot," he said. "I'm not fit to touch you—a white thing like you. I didn't mean to. Not like that. I meant ..."

She stared for an instant, totally at a loss for the meaning—the mere direction of what he was trying to say. Then, slipping down from the branch, she took him by the arms. "Don't!" she cried rather wildly. "Don't talk like that! That's the last impossibility. Listen. I'm going to tell you why."

But he was not listening for what it might be. He was still morosely preoccupied with his own crime. He had been a beast! He had bruised, once more, the white petals of a flower!

It was not that her courage failed. She saw he wouldn't believe. That he couldn't be made to believe. It was no use. If he looked at her any longer like that, she would laugh.

She buried her face in her arms and sobbed.

He rose to this crisis handsomely, waited without a word until she was quiet and then suggested that they go and find Rush and Sylvia. And until they were upon the point of joining the other pair nothing more was said that had any bearing on what had happened in the apple tree. But in that last moment he made a mute appeal for a chance to say another word.

He reminded her that she had said she would marry him if she could. This was enough for him. More than he deserved. He was going back to the beginning to try to build anew what his loss of self-control had wrecked. She need say nothing now. If she'd wait, she'd see.

# CHAPTER XIV
## A CLAIRVOYANT INTERVAL

It was still May and the North Carolina mountain-side that John Wollaston looked out upon was at the height of its annual debauch of azalea blooms, a symphonic romance in the key of rose-color with modulations down to strawberry and up to a clear singing white. For him though, the invalid, cushioned and pillowed in an easy chair, a rug over his knees, these splendors and the perfume of the soft bright air that bathed them had an ironic significance.

He had arrived with Paula at this paradise early in the week, pretty well exhausted with the ordinary fatigues of less than a day's journey in the train. They were feeding him bouillon, egg-nogs and cream. On Paula's arm he had managed this afternoon, his first walk, a matter of two or three hundred yards about the hotel gardens, and at the end of it had been glad to subside, half reclining into this easy chair, placed so that through the open door and the veranda it gave upon, he could enjoy the view of the color-drenched mountain-side.

He had dismissed Paula peremptorily for a real walk of her own. He had told her, in simple truth, that he would enjoy being left to himself for a while. She had taken this assurance for an altruistic mendacity, but she had yielded at last to his insistence and gone, under an exacted promise not to come back for at least an hour.

It offered some curious compensations though, this state of helplessness—a limpidity of vision, clairvoyant almost. For a fortnight he had been like a spectator sitting in the stalls of a darkened theatre watching the performances upon a brilliantly lighted stage, himself—himselves among the characters, for there was a past and a future self for him to look at and ponder upon. The present self hardly counted. All the old ambitions, desires, urgencies, which had been his impulsive forces were gone—quiescent anyhow. He was as sexless, as cool, as an image carved in jade.

And he was here in this lover's paradise—this was what drew the tribute of a smile to the humor of the high gods—with Paula. And Paula was more ardently in love with him than she had ever been before.

The quality of that smile must have carried over to the one he gave her when she came back, well within her promised hour, from her walk. One couldn't imagine anything lovelier or more inviting than the picture she made framed in that doorway, coolly shaded against the bright blaze that came in around her. She looked at him from there, for a moment, thoughtfully.

"I don't believe you have missed me such a lot after all," she said. "What have you been doing all the while?"

"Crystal-gazing," he told her.

She came over to him and took his hands, a caress patently enough through the nurse's pretext that she was satisfying herself that he had not got cold sitting there. She relinquished them suddenly, readjusted his rug and pillows, then kissed him and told him she was going to the office to see if there were any letters and went out again. She was gone but a moment or two; returning, she dropped the little handful which were addressed to him into his lap and carried one of her own to a chair near the window.

He dealt idly with the congratulatory and well-wishing messages which made up his mail. There was but one of them that drew even a gleam of clearly focused intelligence from him. He gave most of his attention to Paula. She was a wonderful person to watch,—the expressiveness of her, that every nerve and muscle of her body seemed to have a part in. She had opened that letter of hers with nothing but clear curiosity. The envelope evidently had told her nothing. She had frowned, puzzled, over the signature and then somehow, darkened, sprung to arms as she made it out. She didn't read it in an orderly way even then; seemed to be trying to worry the meaning out of it, like one stripping off husks to get down to some sort of kernel inside. Satisfied that she had got it at last, she dropped the letter carelessly on the floor, subsided a little deeper into her chair and turned a brooding face toward the outdoor light and away from him.

"Are you crystal-gazing, too?" he asked. Unusually, she didn't turn at his voice and her own was monotonous with strongly repressed emotion.

"I don't need to. I spent more than a week staring into mine."

That lead was plain enough, but he avoided, deliberately though rather idly, following it up. The rustle of paper told her that he had turned back to his letters.

"Anything in your mail?" she asked.

"I think not. You can look them over and see if I've missed anything. To a man in my disarticulate situation people don't write except to express the kindness of their hearts. Here's a letter from Mary designed to prevent me from worrying about her. Full of pleasant little anecdotes about farm life. It's thoroughly Arcadian, she says. A spot designed by Heaven for me to rusticate in this summer when—when we go back to town. Somehow, I never did inhabit Arcady. There's a letter from Martin Whitney, too, that's almost alarmingly encouraging in its insistence that I mustn't worry. If only they knew how little I did—these days!"

"Well, that's all right then," she said. "Because those were Doctor Darby's orders. You weren't to be excited or worried about anything. But, John, is it really true that you don't? Not about anything?"

The fact that her face was still turned away as she asked that question gave it a significance which could not be overlooked.

"It's perfectly true," he asserted. "I don't believe I could if I tried. But there's something evidently troubling you. Let's have it. Oh, don't be afraid. You've no idea what an—Olympian position one finds himself in when he has got half-way across the Styx and come back. Tell me about it."

"You know all about it already. I told you the first day you could talk—that I was going to give up singing altogether except just for you,—when you wanted me to. I knew I'd been torturing you about it. I thought perhaps you'd get well quicker,—want to get well more—if you knew that the torture wasn't to go on. It was true and it is true. Perhaps you thought it was just one of those lies that people tell invalids—one of those don't-worry things. Well, is wasn't.

"But you made me promise I wouldn't do anything—wouldn't break my Ravinia contract—until we could talk it all out together. Your temperature went up a little that afternoon and when Doctor Darby asked me why, I told him. He said I mustn't, on any account, speak again to you about it until you brought the subject up yourself. I don't know whether he'd call this bringing it up or not, but anyway that's it. I've kept my promise to you though," she concluded. "I haven't written. They still think I am going to sing this summer."

"I am very glad of that," he said quietly. "I thought the thing was settled by our first talk. I didn't realize that you had taken it merely as an—adjournment."

She was still turned rigidly away from him, but the grip of one of her hands upon the arm of a chair betrayed the excitement she was laboring under, while it showed the effort she was making to hold it down.

"I didn't think, though," he went on, "that that resolution of yours to give up your whole career,—make ducks and drakes of it, in obedience to my whim—was nothing more than one of those pious lies that invalids are fed upon. I knew you meant it, my dear. I knew you'd have done it—then—without a falter or a regret."

"Then or now," she said. "It's all the same. No, it isn't! Now more than then. With less regret. Without a shadow of a regret, John,—if it would bring you back to me."

The last words were muffled, for she had buried her face in her hands.

He had heard the ring of undisguised passion in her voice without an answering pulse-beat, sat looking at her thoughtfully, tenderly. The reflection that occupied his mind was with what extravagant joy he would have received such an assurance only a few weeks ago. On any one of those last days before his illness fastened upon him;—the Sunday he had gone to Hickory Hill alone because Paula had found she must work with March that day; the evening when he had made his last struggle against the approaching delirium of fever in order to telephone for an ambulance to get him out of that hated house. What a curious compound of nerve ends and gland activities a man's dreams—that he lived by, or died for—were!

She pulled him out of his reverie by a deliberate movement of resolution, taking her hands away from her face, half rising and turning her chair so that she faced him squarely.

"I want to know in so many words," she said, "why you're glad that I'm still bound to that Ravinia thing. You seem to want me to sing there this summer, as much as you hated the idea of my doing it before. Well, why? Or is it something you can't tell me? And if I sing and make a success, shall you want me to go on with it, following up whatever opening it offers; just as if—just as if you didn't count any more in my life at all?"

Before he could answer she added rather dryly, "Doctor Darby would kill me for talking to you like this. You needn't answer if it's going to hurt you."

"No," he said, "it isn't hurting me a bit. But I'll answer one question at a time, I think. The first thing that occurred to me when you spoke of the Ravinia matter was that I didn't want you to break your word. You had told them that they could count on you and I didn't want you, on my account, to be put in a position where any one could accuse you of having failed him. My own word was involved, for that matter. I told LaChaise I wouldn't put any obstacles, in your way. Of course, I didn't contract lobar pneumonia on purpose," he added with a smile.

The intensity of her gaze did not relax at this, however. She was waiting breathlessly.

"The other question isn't quite so easy to answer," he went on, "but I think I would wish you to—follow the path of your career wherever it leads. I shall always count for as much as I can in your life, but not—if I can help it—as an obstacle."

"Why?" she asked. "What has made the perfectly enormous difference?"

It was not at all an unanswerable question; nor one, indeed, that he shrank from. But it wanted a little preliminary reflection. She interrupted before he was ready to speak.

"Of course, I really know. Have known all along. You haven't forgiven me."

He echoed that word with a note of helplessness.

"No," she conceded. "That isn't it, exactly. I can't talk the way you and Mary can. I suppose you have forgiven me, as far as that goes. That's the worst of it. If you hadn't there'd be more to hope for. Or beg for. I'd do that if it were any good. But this is something you can't help. You're kind and sweet to me, but you've just stopped caring. For me. What used to be there has just—gone snap. It's not your fault. I did it myself."

"No," he said quickly. "That's where you're altogether wrong. You didn't do it. You had nothing to do with the doing of it."

She winced, visibly, at the implication that, whoever was responsible, the thing was done.

"Paula, dearest!" he cried, in acute concern. "Wait! There are things that can't be dealt with in a breath. That's why I was trying to think a little before I answered."

Even now he had to marshal his thoughts for a moment before he could go on. It was too ridiculous, that look of tragic desperation she wore while she waited! He averted his eyes and began rather deliberately.

"You are dearer to me now—at this moment, as we sit here—than ever you've been before. I think that's the simple literal truth. This matter of forgiveness—of your having done something to forfeit or to destroy my—love for you… Oh, it's too wildly off the facts to be dealt with rationally! I owe you my life. That's not a sentimental exaggeration. Even Steinmetz says so. And you saved it for me at the end of a period of weeks—months I guess—when I had been devoting most of my spare energies to torturing you. Myself, incidentally, but there was nothing meritorious about that. In an attempt to assert a—proprietary right in you that you had never even pretended to give me. That I'd once promised you I never would assert. The weight of obligation I'm under to you would be absolutely crushing—if it weren't for one thing that relieves me of it altogether. The knowledge that you love me. That you did it all for the love of me."

She moved no nearer him. These were words. There was no reassurance for her in them. One irrepressible movement of his hands toward her, the mere speaking of her name in a voice warmed by the old passion, would have brought her, rapturous, to his knees.

"There's no such thing as a successful pretense between us, I know," he said. "So I'll talk plainly. I'm glad to. I know what it is you miss in me. It's gone. Temporarily I suppose, but gone as if it had never been. That's a—physiological fact, Paula."

She flushed hotly at that and looked away from him.

"I don't know exactly what a soul is," he went on. "But I do know that a body—the whole of the body—is the temple of it. It impenetrates everything; is made up of everything. Well, this illness of mine has, for these weeks, made an old man of me. And I'm grateful to it for giving me a chance to look ahead, before it's too late. I want to make the most of it. Because you see, my dear, in ten years—or thereabouts—the course of nature will have made of me what this pneumonia has given me a foretaste of. Ten years. You will be—forty, then."

She was gazing at him now, fascinated, in unwilling comprehension. "I hate you to talk like that," she said. "I wish you wouldn't."

"It's important," he told her crisply. "You'll see that in a minute, if you will wait. Before very long—in a month or so, perhaps—I shall be, I suppose, pretty much the same man I was—three months ago. Busy at my profession again. In love with you again. All my old self-assurance back; the more arrogant if it isn't quite the real thing. So now's the time, when the fogs one moves about in have lifted and the horizon is sharp, to take some new bearings. And set a new course by them. For both of us.

"There is one fact sitting up like a lighthouse on a rock. I'm twenty-four years older than you. Every five years that we live together from now on will make that difference more important. When you're forty-five—and you'll be just at the top of your powers by then—I shall be one year short of seventy. At the end, you see, even of my professional career. And that's only fifteen years away. Even with good average luck, that's all I can count on. It's strange how one can live along, oblivious to a simple sum in arithmetic like that."

She had been on her feet moving distractedly about the room. Now she came around behind his chair and gripped his body in her strong arms.

"You shan't talk like that!" she said. "You shan't think like that! I won't endure it. It's morbid. It's horrible."

"Oh, no, it's not," he said easily. "The morbidity is in being afraid to look at it. It was morbid to struggle frantically, the way I did all the spring, trying to resist the irresistible thing that was drawing you along your true path. It was a cancerous egotism of mine that was trying to eat you up, live you up into myself. That, thank God, has been cut out of me! I think it has. Don't misunderstand me, though. I'm not going to relinquish anything of you that I can keep;—that I ever had a chance to keep."

He took her hands and gently—coolly—kissed them.

"Then don't relinquish anything," she said. "It's all yours. Can't you believe that, John?"

He released her hands and sank back slackly in his chair. "Victory!" he said, a note of inextinguishable irony in his voice. "A victory I'd have given five years of my life for last March. Yet I could go on winning them—a whole succession of them—and they could lead me to nothing but disaster."

She left him abruptly and the next moment he heard her fling herself down upon his bed. When he rose and disengaged himself from his rug, she said, over an irrepressible sob or two, that he wasn't to mind nor come to her. She wasn't going to cry-not more than a minute.

He came, nevertheless, settled himself on the edge of the bed and took possession of her hands again.

"I wouldn't have told you all this," he said—"for you don't need any lessons in arithmetic, child—if I dared trust myself to remember, after the other thing had come back. Now I'm committed—don't you see?—not to play the fool, tragically or ludicrously, as the case might be, trying to dispute the inevitable. And I shall contrive to keep a lot, my dear. More than you think."

Later, the evening of that same day, he asked her what was in the letter that had provoked their talk. Did they want her back in Chicago for rehearsals or consultations? Because if they did there was no reason in the world why she should not go. At the rate at which he was gaining strength there would not be the slightest reason—he gave her his professional word of honor—why she should not go back in a day or two.

"I should have to go back," she said, "if I were going to sing March's opera. There is such a lot of work about a new production that there would be no time to spare."

"But," he asked, "isn't March's opera precisely what you are going to sing?"

"No," she said rebelliously. "It's not. There wasn't anything in the contract about that. I'll carry out the contract this summer. I'll keep my word and yours, since that is what you want me to do. But I won't sing 'Dolores' for anybody."

He did not press her for the reason.

After a little silence, she said, "Lucile thought I'd fallen in love with him. So did Rush, I guess,—and poor old Nat. Did you, John?"

"I tried to, hard enough," he confessed.

She stared. "Tried to!"

"That would have been the easier thing to fight," he said. "There's nothing inevitable about a man,—any man. I'd have stood a chance at least, of beating him, even though he had a twenty-year handicap or so. But the other thing,—well, that was like the first bar of the Fifth Symphony, you know; Fate knocking at the door. Clear terror that is until one can get the courage to open the door and invite Fate in."

# CHAPTER XV
# THE END OF IT

About a week later—just at the beginning of June, this was—Paula did go back to Chicago, leaving her husband to go on gaining the benefit, for another ten days or so, of that wine-like mountain air. It was an unwelcome conviction that he really wanted her to go, rather than any crying need for her at Ravinia that decided her to leave him. The need would not be urgent for at least another fortnight since it had been decided between her and LaChaise that she should make her debut in *Tosca*, an opera she had sung uncounted times.

Since their momentous conversation in which John had attempted to revise the fundamentals of their life together, they had not reverted to the main theme of it; had clarified, merely, one or two of its more immediate conclusions. Paula was to carry out in spirit as well as in letter the terms of her Ravinia contract exactly as if it were still to be regarded as the first step of her reopened career. What she should do about the second step in case it offered itself to her was a bridge not to be crossed until they came to it.

John had professed himself content to let it remain at that, but she divined that there was something hollow in his profession. It was possible, of course, that his restlessness represented nothing more than a new stage in his convalescence. It didn't seem possible that after the candors of that talk he could still be keeping something back from her. Yet that was an impression she very clearly got. Anyhow, her presence was doing him no good, and on that unwelcome assurance, she bade him a forlorn farewell and went home.

It was a true intuition. John heaved a sigh of relief when she was gone. In his present enfeebled state she was too much for him. The electrical vitality of her overpowered him. Even before his illness he had had moments—I think I have recorded one of them—when her ardent strength paralyzed him with a sort of terror and these moments were more frequent now.

There was, too, a real effort involved in presenting ideas to her (intellectual ideas, if they may be so distinguished from emotional ones). He didn't know, now, whether she had fully understood what he had been driving at that day; whether anything had really got through to her beyond a melancholy realization that his love had cooled. He had always been aware of this effort, but in the days of his strength he hadn't minded making it.

Now he was conscious of wishing for some one like Mary,—indeed, for Mary herself. They talked the same language, absolutely. Their minds had the same index of refraction, so that thoughts flashed back and forth between them effortlessly and without distortion. He thought of her so often and wished for her so much during the first two days of his solitude that it seemed almost a case for the psychical research people when he got a telegram from her.

It read: "Aunt Lucile worried you left alone especially traveling. Shall you mind or will Paula if I come down and bring you back, Mary."

There was a situation made clear, at all events. He grinned over it as he despatched his wire to her. "Perfectly unnecessary but come straight along so that we can play together for a week or two before starting home."

Play together is just what they did. Enough of his strength soon came back to make real walks possible and during the second week, with a two-horse team and a side-bar buggy, they managed, without any ill effect upon him, an excursion across the valley and up the opposite mountainside to a log cabin road-house where they had lunch.

Mary, a born horsewoman, did the driving herself, thus relieving them of the impediment to real companionship which a hired driver would have been. In an inconsecutive, light-hearted way difficult to report intelligibly, they managed to tell each other a lot. She let him see, with none of the rhetorical solemnities which a direct statement would have involved, her new awareness of his professional eminence. A dozen innuendoes, as light as dandelion feathers, conveyed it to him; swift brush-strokes of gesture and inflection sketched the picture in; an affectionate burlesque of awe completed it, so that he could laugh at her for it as she had meant he should.

She told him during their drive what the source of her illumination was; described Anthony March's visit on that most desperate day of all, the vividness of his concern over the outcome of the fight and his utter unconcern about the effect of it upon his own fortunes. She had been reading Kipling aloud, out at the farm, to the boys and Aunt Lucile and a memory of it led her to make a comparison—heedless of its absurdity—between the composer and Kirn's lama. "He isn't, anyhow, tied to the 'wheel of things' any more than that old man was."

"I'd like to have come down that day and heard him talk," John said. "Because it's the real thing, with him. Not words. He wouldn't be a bad person to go to," he added musingly, "if one had got himself into a real *impasse*—or what looked like one. Paula has chucked his opera, you know."

She nodded, evidently not in the least surprised and, no more, perturbed by this intelligence. "He won't mind that," she explained. "The only thing he really needs, in the world, is to hear his music, but this, you see, wasn't his any more. He had been trying to make it Paula's. He had been working over it rather hopelessly, because he had promised, but it was like letting him out of school when he found that she had forgotten all about him;—didn't care if she never saw him again."

She caught, without an explanatory word, the meaning of the glance her father turned upon her, and went straight on. "Oh, it seems a lot, I know, to have found out about him in one short talk, but there's nothing—personal in that. He doesn't, I mean—save himself up for special people. He's there for anybody. Like a public drinking fountain, you know. That's why he would be such a wonderful person—to go to, as you said. No one could possibly monopolize him."

She added, after a silence, "It seems a shame, when he wants so little that he can't have that. Can't hear, for example, that opera of his the way he really wrote it."

"We owe him something," her father said thoughtfully. "He got rather rough justice from Paula, anyhow. I suppose a thing like that could, perhaps, be managed—if one put his back into it."

She understood instantly, as before, and quite without exegesis, the twinge of pain that went across his face. "You *will* have a back to put into things again, one of these days. It wants only courage to wait for it, quite patiently until it comes. You've plenty of that. That's one of he things Mr. March told me about you," she added with the playful purpose of surprising him again. "Only I happened to know that for myself."

"It's more than I can be sure of," he said. "I've been full of bravado with Paula, telling her how soon I was going to be back in harness again; cock-sure and domineering as ever, so that she'd better make hay while the sun shone. But it was I, nevertheless, who made her go home so that she could start to work—when the whistle blew. Some one was going to have to support the family, I told her, and it didn't look as if it were going to be me."

This speech, though it ended in jest, had begun, she knew, in earnest. He meant her to understand that, and left her to judge for herself where the dividing line fell. She answered in a tone as light as his, "Paula could do it easily enough." But she was not satisfied with the way he took it. The mere quality of the silence must have told her something. She turned upon him with sudden intensity and said, "Don't tell me you're worrying—about three great healthy people like us. You have been, though. Whatever put it into your mind to spend half a thought on that?"

"Why, it was a letter from Martin Whitney," he said. "Oh, the best meant thing in the world. Nothing but encouragement in it from beginning to end, only it was so infernally encouraging, it set me off. No, let me talk. You're quite the easiest person in the world to tell things to. I've been remiss, there's no getting away from that. I've never taken money-making very seriously, it came so easily. I've spent my earnings the way my friends have spent their incomes. Well, if I'd died the other day, there wouldn't have been much left. There would have been my life insurance for Paula, and enough to pay my debts, including my engagements for Rush, but beyond that, oh, a pittance merely. Of course with ten years' health, back at my practise, even with five, I could improve the situation a lot."

She urged as emphatically as she dared—she wanted to avoid the mistake of sounding encouraging—that the situation needed no improvement. The income of fifty thousand dollars would take care of Paula, and beyond that,—well, if there were ever two healthy young animals in the world concerning whom cares and worries were superfluous, they were herself and Rush.

He told her thoughtfully that this was where she was; wrong. "Rush, to begin with, isn't a healthy young animal. That's what I couldn't make Martin Whitney understand. He's one of the war's sacrifices precisely as much as if he had had his leg shot off. He needs support; will go on needing it for two or three years, financial as well as moral. He mustn't be allowed to fail. That's the essence of it. He's—spent, you see; depleted. One speaks of it in figurative terms, but it's a physiological thing—if we could get at it—that's behind the lassitude of these boys. It all comes back to that. That they're restless, irresolute. That they need the stimulus of excitement and can't endure the drag of routine. They need a generous allowance, my dear,—even for an occasional failure in self-command, those two boys out at Hickory Hill."

She had nothing to say to that, though his pause gave her opportunity. A sudden surmise as to the drift of that last sentence, silenced her. And it was a surmise that leaped, in the next instant, to full conviction. He was pleading Graham's cause with her! Why? Was it something that had been as near his heart as that, all along? Or had some one—Rush—or even Graham himself—engaged his advocacy?

She said at last, rather breathlessly (it was necessary to say something or he would perceive that his stratagem had betrayed itself): "Well, at the gloomy worst, Rush is taken care of. And as for me, I'm not a war sacrifice, anyhow. That's not a possible conception—even for a worried convalescent. Did you ever *see* anything as gorgeous as that tree, even in an Urban stage setting?"

"No," he said, "the war wasn't what you were sacrificed to."

She held her breath until she saw he wasn't going on with that. But he seemed willing to follow her lead to lighter matters, and for the rest of their excursion they carried out the pretense that there was nothing like a cloud in their sky.

That evening, though, after she had bidden him good night, she changed her mind and came back into his room. There had been something wistful about his kiss that, determined her.

"Which of them wrote to you about me?" she asked.

"Both," he told her. "Of course I should have known you'd guess. Forgive me for having tried to—manage you. I'll show you both their letters if you like. It's a breach of confidence, of course, but I don't know that I could do better."

"I'll read Rush's," she said. "Not the other."

She carried it over to the lamp, and for a while after she had taken in its easily grasped intent she went on turning its pages back and forth while she sought for an end of the tangled skein of her thoughts to hold on by.

Finally, "Do you want me to marry him, dad?" she asked. Then, before he could answer she hurried on. "I mean, would it relieve you from some nightmare worry about me if I did?—This has to be plain talk, doesn't it, if it is to get us anywhere?"

"That's a fair question of yours," he said. But he wasn't ready at once with an answer. "It *would* be such a relief, provided you really wanted to marry him. That goes to the bottom of it, I think. My responsibility is to make it possible for you to—follow your heart. To marry or not as you wish. To marry a poor man if you wish. But if Graham is your choice and all that holds you back from him is some remediable misunderstanding—or failure to understand ..."

"I don't know whether it's remediable or not," she said; and added, "I told him I would marry him if I could. Did he tell you that?"

It was a mistake to have quoted that expression to her father. He took it just as Graham had. Of course! What else could he think? She sat with clenched hands and a dry throat, listening while he tried to enlighten what he took to be her innocent misunderstanding.

They had never spoken, she realized, about matters of sex. For anything he really knew to the contrary she might have been as ignorant as a child. He was actually talking as one talks to a child;—kindly, tolerantly, tenderly, but with an unconscious touch of patronage, like one trying to explain away—misgivings about Santa Claus! There were elements, inevitably, in a man's love for a woman, that a young girl could not understand. Nothing but experience could bring that understanding home to her. This was what in one way after another, he was trying to convey.

But the intuition which, in good times or bad, always betrayed their emotions to each other, showed him that he was, somehow missing the mark. Her silence through his tentative little pauses disconcerted him heavily. He ran down at last like an unwound clock.

It was only after a long intolerably oppressive silence that she found her voice. "The misunderstanding isn't what you think," she said. "Nor what Graham thinks. It's his misunderstanding, not mine. He thinks that I am—a sort of innocent angel that he's not good enough for. And the fact is that I'm not—not innocent enough for him. Not an angel at all. Not even quite—good."

But she got no further. The plea for comprehension, for an ear that would not turn away from her plain story, never was made. In a smother of words he halted her. Affectionately, with a gentleness that achieved absolute finality. She was overwrought. She carried paradox too far. In her innocence she used a form of speech that she didn't know the meaning of, and should be careful to avoid. Her troubles, with patience, would work themselves out in the end. Meanwhile let her as far as possible stop thinking about them.

But she had got, during the intaken breath before he began to speak, a sensation,—as sharp and momentary as the landscape revealed in a lightning flash,—of a sudden terror on his part; as of one finding himself on the edge of an abyss of understanding. For that one glaring instant before he had had time to turn his face away he had known what she meant. But he never would look again. Never would know.

# CHAPTER XVI
# FULL MEASURE

Ravinia is one of Chicago's idiosyncrasies, a ten-weeks' summer season of grand opera with a full symphony orchestra given practically out-of-doors. Its open pavilion seats from fifteen hundred to two thousand people and on a warm Saturday night, you will find twice as many more on the, "bleachers" that surround it or strolling about under the trees in the park. The railroad runs special trains to it all through the season from town, and crammed and groaning interurbans collect their toll for miles from up and down the shore.

It had begun as an amusement park with merry-go-rounds, Ferris-wheels and such—to the scandalized indignation of numerous super-urban persons whose summer places occupied most of the district roundabout. They took the enterprise into their own hands, abolished the calliope, put a symphony orchestra into the bandstand and, eventually, transformed the shell into a stage and went in for opera; opera popularized with a blue pencil so that no performance was ever more than two hours long, and at the modest price of fifty cents.

Its forces, recruited chiefly from among the younger stars at the Metropolitan, give performances that want no apologetic allowance from anybody. It has become an institution of which the town and especially the North Shore is boastful.

Paula foresaw no easy conquest here. Her social prestige, part of which she enjoyed as John Wollaston's wife and part of which she had earned during the last four years for herself, counted as much against her as it did in her favor. It was evident from the way the announcements of her prospective appearance at Ravinia had been elaborated in the society columns of the newspapers that it would arouse a lot of curiosity. It would be one of the topics that everybody, in the social-register sense of the word, would be talking about and in order to talk authoritatively everybody—four or five hundred people this is to say—would have to attend at least one of her performances.

Nothing less than a downright unmistakable triumph would convince them. She was a professional in the grain and yet in this adventure she would be under the curse of an amateur's status, a thing she hated as all professionals do.

It was evidently from an instinct to cut herself off as completely as possible from these social connections of hers that she rented for the summer, a furnished house in the village of Ravinia, within a mile or so of the park. John was rather disconcerted over this when she told him about it. She greeted him with it as an accomplished fact upon his return to Chicago with Mary. She made a genuine effort to explain the necessity, but explanations were not in Paula's line and she didn't altogether succeed.

She made it clear enough, though, that she didn't want to be fussed by the attentions of friends or family, of her husband least of all. She didn't want to be congratulated nor encouraged. She didn't want to be asked to little suppers or luncheons nor to be made the objective of personally conducted tourist parties back stage. She didn't want to be called to the telephone, ever, except on matters of professional business by her Ravinia colleagues.

All of this, John pointed out, could be accomplished at home. He, himself, could deal with the telephoners and the tourists. This was about all apparently that he was going to be good for this summer; but a watchdog's duties he could perform in a highly efficient manner.

"But a home and a husband are the very first things I've got to forget about," cried Paula. "Oh, can't you see!"

Darkly and imperfectly, he did. The atmosphere of the home in which one has been guarded and pampered as a priceless possession was—must be—enervating, and to one who was screwing up her powers to their highest pitch for a great effort like this, it would be poisonous—malarial! He would have been clearer about it, though, but for the misgiving that, consciously or not, Paula was punishing him for having insisted that she carry her contract through. Or—if that were too harsh a way of putting it,—that she was coquetting with him. Having told her down there in the South that he didn't care for her in a loverlike way, he might now have an opportunity of proving that he did—over obstacles!

It gave him a twinge, for a fact, but he managed to ask good-humoredly if this meant that he was to be barred from the whole show, from performances as well as from rehearsals and the Ravinia house.

"I won't care," she said with a laugh of desperation, "after I've once got my teeth in. But until then... Oh, I know it sounds horrible but I don't want even to—feel you; not even in the fringe of it.

"I'll tell you who I would like, though," she went on over a palpable hesitation and with a flush of color rising to her cheeks. "I can't live all alone up there of course. I could get along with just a maid, but it would be easier and nicer if I could have some one for a—companion. And the person I'd choose, if she'd do it, is Mary."

He said, not quite knowing whether to be pleased or not, that they could ask her about it at all events. They were rather counting on her out at Hickory Hill but he didn't know that that need matter. Only wasn't Mary—family, herself, a reminder of home?

"Not a bit," said Paula, with a laugh. "Not but what she likes me well enough," she went on, trying to account for her preference (these Wollastons were always concerned about the whys of things) "but she stands off a little and looks on; without holding her breath, either. And then, well, she'd be a sort of reminder of you, after all."

Put that way, he couldn't quarrel with it, though there was a challenge about it that chilled him a little. Watched over by his own daughter (this was what it came to) Paula would be beyond suspicion—even of Lucile.

Mary, when the scheme was put up to her was no less surprised than John had been, but she was pleased clear through, and with a clean-cutting executive skill he had hardly credited her with, she thought out the details of the plan and revised the rest of their summer arrangements to fit.

The Dearborn Avenue house should be closed and her father should move out to the farm. The apple house was now remodeled to a point where it would accommodate him as well as Aunt Lucile very comfortably. The boys and the servants could live around in tents and things. She'd want only one maid for the cottage at Ravina and the small car which she'd drive herself.

The sum of all the activities that Mary proposed for herself added up to a really exacting job; housekeeper, personal maid, chauffeur, chaperon and secretary. It was with a rather mixed lot of emotions that John thought of delivering her over to be tied to Paula's chariot wheels like that. One of the two women who loved him serving the other in a capacity so nearly menial! The thought of it gave him an odd sort of thrill even while he shrank from it. Certainly, he would not have assented to it, had it not been so unmistakably what Mary herself wanted. Her reasons for wanting it he couldn't feel that he had quite fathomed.

There was, as a matter of fact, nothing fine-spun about them. It was a job in the first place and gave her, therefore, she mordantly told herself, an excuse for continuing to exist. It was an escape from Hickory Hill. (Clear cowardice this was, she confessed. That situation would have to be met and settled one way or the other before long; but her dread of both the possible alternatives had mounted since her frustrated attempt to confide in her father.) The third reason which she avowed to everybody, was simple excited curiosity for a look into a new world. The mystery and the glamour of it attracted her. Paula's proposal gave her the opportunity to see what these strange persons were like when they were not strutting their little while upon the stage.

Paula, of course, was, fundamentally, one of them. It was remarkable how that simple discovery interpreted her. When you saw her surrounded by them, working and quarreling with them, talking that horrible polyglot of French, Italian and English, which she slipped into so easily, you realized how exotic the environment of the Dearborn Avenue house must have been to her and how strong a thing her passion for John Wollaston, to enable her to endure five years of it,—of finikin social observances,—of Aunt Lucile's standards of propriety!

Mary took real comfort in her companionship; found an immense release from emotional pressure in it. One might quarrel furiously with Paula (and it happened Mary very nearly did, as shall be related presently, before they had been in the cottage three days), but one couldn't possibly worry one's self about her, couldn't torture one's self feeling things with Paula's nerves. That was the Wollaston trick. What frightful tangles the thing that goes by the name of unselfishness, the attempt to feel for others, could lead a small group like a family into!

Another thing that helped was that during the fortnight of rehearsal before the season opened, there wasn't time to think. They were pelted by perfectly external events, a necessity for doing this, an appointment to do that, an engagement somewhere else. It was like being caught out in a driving rain. You scuttled along-snatched a momentary shelter where you could.

Even getting the clothes Paula needed would have filled the time of a woman of leisure to the brim. A bridal trousseau would have been nothing to it. But with Paula these activities had to be sandwiched in with daily rehearsals,—long ones, too,—hours with Novelli while she memorized half-forgotten parts, interviews with reporters, struggles with photographers, everything that the diabolic ingenuity of the publicity man could contrive. He, by the way, regarded Paula as his best bet and lavished his efforts upon her in a way that stirred her colleagues (rivals, of course), to a frenzied exasperation, over his sinister partiality to this "society amateur."

(They all but enjoyed a terrible revenge, for as poetic justice narrowly missed having it, the extent of her advance publicity and the beauty of her clothes proved to be the rocks she went aground on. Only a lucky wave came along and floated her off again.)

Mary's quarrel with Paula, though it never came off,—never for that matter got through to Paula's consciousness, even as an approach to one,— had, all the same, a chain of consequences and so deserves to be recorded. The opera management was supposed to supply Paula with a piano and they found one already installed in the Ravinia house when they moved in, a small grand of a widely advertised make. Paula dug half a dozen vicious arpeggios out of it and condemned it out of hand. Then in the midst of a petulant outburst which had, nevertheless, a humorous savor (the management would promise and pretend till kingdom come. They'd even take real trouble to get out of complying with her simple request for a new piano), she pulled herself up short and stared at Mary.

"What idiots we are! I am, anyhow. I'd forgotten all about March. He can make a piano out of anything. When he's tuned this, I won't want another. I've got his telephone number somewhere. You don't happen to remember it, do you?—Why? What makes you look like that?"

For Mary was staring at her—speechless. Paula's affairs had driven her own pretty well out of her mind. She had stopped thinking about Graham. She'd given over worrying about Rush. But she had not forgotten Anthony March. The alternative possibility that Paula might have gone on with his opera, that he might have been, but for what her father spoke of as rough justice, attending rehearsals of it, hearing that big orchestra making a reality of its unheard melodies, had been much in her mind. She had wondered whether it was not really in Paula's. Along with a regret for his downcast hopes. He was, in a way, the ladder she had climbed by. Hearing her sing those wonderful songs of his was what had led LaChaise to offer her this opportunity. And Paula didn't know, Mary was sure, of anything that mitigated his disappointment. To her, he was merely one who had tried and, pitiably, failed. She must, it seemed, have felt sorry about it and Mary had considerately avoided all reference to him.

Now it appeared that Paula had blankly forgotten all about him. Remembered him only when she wanted him to tune the piano. She callously proposed to exact this service of him, and if possible, over the telephone!

"I suppose," Mary said, when she had found her voice, "that I look the way I feel. Paula, you *wouldn't* do that!"

"Why not?" Paula demanded. And then with a laugh, "I wouldn't forget to pay him this time. And it would be nice to see him again, too. Because I really liked him a lot."

"Well, if you do like him, you wouldn't, would you, want to do anything—cruel to him? Anything that he might take as—a willful insult? Because it could be taken like that, I should think."

She spoke with a good deal of effort. Paula's surprise, the incredulous way she had echoed the word cruel, the fact that there was still an unshaken good humor in the look of curiosity that she directed upon her stepdaughter, all but overwhelmed Mary with a sudden wave of helpless anger.

What could one do with a selfishness as insolent as that? What was there to say?

Paula got up, still looking at her in that puzzled sort of way, came over to her chair, sat down on the arm of it and took her by the shoulders.

"You're trembling!" she said. "I suspect I am working you too hard. You mustn't let me do that, you know. John will never forgive me if I do. Why, about March, did you mean because I wouldn't sing his opera? He knew all the time I wouldn't unless he could get it right. And he knew he wasn't getting it right. He wanted to give it up long before he did, only I wouldn't let him. But as for being insulted, bless you, he isn't like that. And perhaps if he came I could get him all the pianos out here to keep in tune. There must be dozens!"

At that Mary laughed in a recoil of genuine amusement. She could imagine that Anthony March would laugh himself. In one particular Paula was unquestionably right. He wouldn't feel insulted. He was just the last person in the world to be accessible to such a petty emotion.

She returned Paula's hug and extricated herself from the chair.

"You needn't worry about me, at all events," she said. "I'm not tired a bit. But could we worry a little about Mr. March? About his opera, I mean? Don't you suppose we could get Mr. LaChaise to put it on? The way he originally wrote it.—I mean for somebody else to sing."

"Fournier could sing it in a rather interesting way," Paula remarked speculatively. "Only I don't believe he'd sing in English. Certainly there's nobody else."

"Perhaps if he saw the score ..." Mary began.

"Gracious!" Paula broke in, a little startled, not much. "I haven't an idea where that score is. I may have sent it back to him, but I don't believe I did."

"No," Mary told her. "It's here. When I closed up the house, I brought it along. He might be interested enough in it I should think," she persisted, "if you and Mr. LaChaise told him how good it was,—to learn it in English. Or it might, I suppose,—the whole thing I mean,—be translated into French. There might, anyhow, prove to be something we could do."

"Good heavens, child!" Paula said, "we're up to the eyes now, all three of us. Will be for weeks as far as that goes. We simply couldn't think of it." Through a yawn she added, "Not that it wouldn't be a nice thing to do if we had time."

Paula's notion of getting March to come up and tune her piano was not damped at all by the wet blanket of Mary's objection to it. From town that day, Mary having driven her in for more fittings and photographers, Paula telephoned to the Fullerton Avenue house and later told Mary in an acutely dissatisfied manner that she had got simply nowhere with the person with whom she had talked. "She pretends,—oh, it was his sister or his mother, I suppose,—that they don't know anything whatever about him. Haven't seen him for ever so long. Haven't an idea how to get word to him. If only I had time to drive out there … But I haven't a minute of course."

Mary observed that she didn't see what good it would do to be told in person what Paula had just learned over the telephone. She could drive out there herself if there was any point in it, during the hour when Paula was engaged with her dressmaker.

Paula jumped at this suggestion. She was one of those persons whom telephones never quite convince. So Mary, rather glad of the errand, though convinced of its futility so far as Paula's designs were concerned, drove out to the Fullerton Avenue house and presently found herself in a small neat parlor talking to a neat old lady who was not, perhaps, as old as she looked, about Anthony March.

For anything that bore upon the obtainability of his service for the Ravinia piano the telephone conversation would have done as well. His mother had seen him for only a short time, a little more than a week ago and judged from what he then said that he was upon the point of going away, though not for a long absence—a month, perhaps. She had not asked where he meant to go and he had volunteered nothing. It was possible that he did not know himself.

Mary remained in doubt, for the first five minutes or so of her call, whether the stiff guarded precision of this was a mark of hostility to the whole Wollaston clan or whether it was nothing but undiluted New England reserve. She ventured a tentative, "I suppose he didn't say especially why he was going," and on getting a bare negative in reply, went on, a little breathlessly:—"I didn't mean that impertinently;—only all of us were very much interested in him and we liked him too well, especially father and I, to be content to lose track of him. I hope he wasn't ill;—didn't go away because of that."

"He told me that he was not," Mrs. March answered. "Though if I might have had my way with him, I would have put him to bed for a week. However," she added, with a fine smile, "I never did have my way with him and neither has his father had his. And I judge it to be as well that we have not."

No, there was no hostility about it. She perceived the genuineness in her visitor's concern and was perhaps really touched by it. But even so she was sparing of details. Anthony had never lived a life regulated by rule and habit. He worked at his music much too hard when the call, as she termed it, was upon him, and obviously quite forgot to take proper care of himself. And then he went away, as on this occasion, to recuperate in his own manner.

Mary adventured again just as she was getting up to take her leave. "It must want a good courage," she said, "to let him go like that; not to keep trying, at least, to hold him back in sheltered ways."

She got a nod of acknowledgment of the truth of this, but no words at all. But she found herself, afterward, in possession of an impression so clear that one would think it must have needed a long exchange of unreserved confidences to have produced it. The man's mother loved him, of course; one might take that for granted. And was proud of him; of course—perhaps—again. But beyond all that, she rejoiced in him; in his emancipation from the line and precept which had so tightly confined her; in his very vagabondage.

She was not much in his confidence, though. Mary had made that out from the way she had received her own resume of the status of his opera. His mother had known nothing of his hopes, neither when Paula raised them up nor later when she cast them down. It was odd about that—and rather pitiable. She would have welcomed her son's confidences, Mary was sure, with so real a sympathy, if he could only have believed it. But the crust of family tradition was too thick, she supposed, to make even the attempt possible.

This failure of his fully to understand the person traditionally the nearest and dearest to him in all the world had, upon Mary's mind, the effect of, somehow, solidifying him; making him more completely human to her— where it might have been expected to work the other way. It proved the last touch she needed to quicken the concern she had from the beginning felt for him into an entirely real thing, a motivating principle. If it was possible to get that opera of his produced, she was going to do it.

She stopped at the Dearborn Avenue house on her way down-town to get her little portable typewriter and carry it out to Ravinia with her. In the odd hours of the next few days she copied March's libretto in English, triple spaced, out of his score and this, with a lead pencil, she took to carrying around with her to Paula's rehearsals, to her dressing-room, everywhere. A phrase at a time, syllable by syllable, she began putting it into French.

On the last Saturday night in June the Ravinia season opened with *Tosca* sung in Italian; Paula singing the title part and Fournier as "Scarpia." A veteran American tenor, Wilbur Hastings, an old Ravinia favorite, sang "Cavaradossi." Taken as a whole, the performance was quite as good as any one has a right to expect any opening night to be. The big audience which went away good-naturedly satisfied, had had its moments of really stirring enthusiasm. Fournier scored a well deserved triumph with a "Scarpia" that was characterized by a touch of really sinister distinction. Hastings, incapable as he was of subtleties or refinements, did as usual all the obvious things pretty well and got the welcome he had so rightly counted upon. But Paula fell unmistakably short of winning the smashing success she had so ardently hoped for.

She did not, of course, fail. Wallace Hood, to take him for a sample of her admiring friends, went home assuring himself that her success had been all he or any of the rest of them could have wished. And he wrote that same night a letter to John Wollaston out at Hickory Hill saying as much. Her beauty, he told John, had been a revelation even to him and there could be no doubt that the audience had been deeply moved by it. Her acting also had taken him by surprise. It was a talent he had not looked for in her and he was correspondingly delighted by this manifestation of it. In the great scene with Fournier when he stated the terms of his abominable bargain to her, Wallace had hardly been able to realize it was Paula that he saw on the stage.

When it came to her singing (he knew John would want his most impartial honest judgment)—here where he had been surest of her, she came nearest to disappointing him. It was a shame, of course, to subject a lovely voice like hers to singing in the great vacancy of all outdoors, to say nothing of forcing it into competition with a shouter and bellower like Hastings. But he felt sure when she was a little better accustomed to her surroundings, she would rise superior even to these drawbacks.

This was somewhere near the facts, though stated with a strong friendly bias. Paula was nervous, never really got into the stride of her acting at all. The strong discrepancy between Fournier's methods and Hastings' served perhaps to prevent her getting into step with either. And she sang all but badly. There had been only one rehearsal in the pavilion and at that she had been content merely to sketch her work in, singing off the top of her voice. When she really opened up at the performance, the unfamiliar acoustics of the place frightened her into forcing, with the result that she was constantly singing sharp.

Paula herself, though disappointed, didn't feel too badly about it, knowing that all her difficulties were merely matters of adjustment, until she read what the critics said about her in the papers the next morning. What they said was not on the face of it, severe;—came, indeed, to much the same thing as Wallace Hood's verdict. But the picture between the lines which they unanimously presented, was of a spoiled beauty, restless for the publicity that private life deprived her of, offering in a winning manner to a gullible public, a gold brick.

Paula was furiously angry over this, justifiably, too. Her work had been professional even in its defects and deserved professional judgment. The case was serious, too, for if that notion of her once got fairly planted in the minds of her public, it would be almost impossible to eradicate it.

But Anthony March had not been mistaken when he spoke of her as a potential tamer of wild beasts. Her anger was no mere gush of emotions, to spend itself and leave her exhausted. It was a sort that hardened in an adamantine resolution. The next chance she got, she'd show them! Unluckily, she wasn't billed to sing again until toward the end of the week. It happened, however, that the Sunday papers, taking away with one hand, gave in a roundabout but effective fashion with the other.

The opera billed for that night was *Pagliacci*. A young American baritone with a phenomenal high A, was to sing "Tonio" and a new Spanish soprano was cast for "Nedda." When this young woman saw the Sunday papers she, too, went into a violent rage. Her knowledge of English was not sufficient to enable her to draw any comfort from the subtle cruelties which the critics had inflicted on Paula in the news section. But the music and drama supplements which had been printed days before, devoted as they were to the opening of the season, simply made Paula the whole thing. The Spanish young lady's rage was of a different quality from Paula's. She wept and stormed. She demanded like Herodias, the head of that press agent on a charger. Simply that and nothing more. And when she failed to get it, she went to bed.

The management, disconcerted but by no means at the end of its resources, decreed a change of the bill to *Lucia*. They were ready to go on with *Lucia* which had been billed for Tuesday night. All they needed was to bring the scenery out from town in a truck. This they ordered done; but at five o'clock, about two miles south of the park, the truck went through a bridge culvert and rolled all the way to the bottom of a ravine. The driver escaped with his life but the production of *Lucia* was smashed to splinters.

Mary chanced upon this piece of information and brought it straight to Paula. "Tell them to go ahead with *Pagliacci*, then," Paula said. "I'll sing 'Nedda' myself. Get LaChaise on the phone and let me talk to him."

She did sing it without any rehearsal at all. And she gave a performance which for most of the persons who saw it, made her the, and the only, "Nedda"; though—or perhaps, because—she didn't give the part quite its traditional characterization; adapted it with the unscrupulousness of the artist to her own purpose.

Paula's "Nedda" was a sulky slattern, indifferent, lazy, smoldering with passion,—dangerous. The sensuous quality of her beauty had never been more apparent than it was in the soiled cheap mountebank fineries which she had worn for so many performances of the part in Europe. And this beauty, of course, did a lot of the work for her. Explained the tragedy all by itself. And, indeed, tragedy hung visibly over her from the moment of her first entrance upon the stage in the donkey cart. She was the sort of woman men kill and are killed for.

She played the part with an extreme economy of movement, with a kind of feline stillness which made her occasional explosions into action, as when she attacked Tonio with the whip, literally terrifying. She sang it carelessly and therefore in a manner absolutely gorgeous. She swept them all, critics as well as the immense audience, clean off their feet.

Also, by way of a foot-note, the managerial announcement that Madame Carresford had volunteered for the part at six o'clock, to rescue them from the necessity of closing the park and was to sing it absolutely without rehearsal, exploded for all time the notion that there was anything of the amateur about her.

"You can do anything," LaChaise told her as she came out into the wings. And he kissed her on both cheeks rather solemnly, in the manner of one conferring a decoration. In full measure pressed down and running over, that was how Paula's success came to her.

# CHAPTER XVII
# THE WAYFARER

By the time Paula had got back to her dressing-room after the long series of tumultuous curtain calls was over, the rush of her friends to express their congratulations in person had begun. After the *Tosca*, performance she had been adamant about seeing anybody but to-night with a laugh she said, "I don't care. For a few minutes. If they're people I really know."

So Mary took her station beside the Rhadamanthus at the stockade gate—in a proper opera-house, he would have been the stage door-keeper—to pick out the sheep from the goat-like herd of the merely curious who, but for firm measures, would have stormed the place. Those who came down again, pushed out by the weight of new arrivals, lingered about the gate talking things over with Mary. It amused her to see how radically their attitude had changed. Such people as the Averys, the Cravens and the Byrnes, who in a social way had known Paula well, seemed to regard her now as a personage utterly remote, translated into another world altogether. And when they asked about John Wollaston, as most of them did, there was an undertone almost of commiseration about their inquiries, though on the surface this didn't go beyond an expressed regret that he hadn't been here to witness the triumph.

Mary drove them all away at last, even the lingerers in Paula's dressing-room, left her safely in the hands of her dresser and went out into the automobile park to get her car. Coming up softly across the grass and reaching in to turn on the lights, she was startled to discover that there was a man in it. But before she had time more than to gasp, she recognized him as her father.

"I didn't want to push my way in with the mob," he explained, after apologizing for having frightened her. "The car, when I spotted it, seemed a safe place to wait. And the privacy of it," he added, "will be grateful, too, since I'm not perfectly sure that Paula won't refuse outright to see me."

Mary smiled at this and said she hoped he hadn't missed the performance.

"No," he told her somberly, "I didn't miss—any of it." Then on a different note, "Now we'll see whether those dogs of critics won't change their tune."

"Paula herself changed the tune," Mary observed. Then, "She's longing to see you, of course. And there's no reason why you should wait. No one's with her now except her dresser."

She led the way, without giving him a chance to demur, to the gate to the stockade and turned him over to the gatekeeper.

"Please take Doctor Wollaston up to his wife's dressing-room," she said. And with a momentary pleasure in having evaded introducing him as Madame Carresford's husband, she turned away and went back to the car.

For the moment the spectacle of her father in the rôle of a young lover touched her no more acutely than with a mild half-humorous melancholy. She even paid the tribute of a passing smile to the queer reversal of their rôles, her own and his. She was more like a mother brooding over the first love-affair of an adolescent son. It was so young of him, younger, she believed, than any act she herself could be capable of, to have come to Paula's performance without letting her know and waited shyly alone in the dark while the herd of her acquaintances crowded in and monopolized her. Pathetically young, almost intolerably pathetic in a man in his middle fifties. She wondered if he had come up for *Tosca* the night before and gone away without a word.

She had spoken quite without authority in assuring him of Paula's welcome. Paula had not, she thought, spoken of him once either in connection with her disappointment the night before or with her triumph to-night. Yet that he would get a lover's welcome she had very little doubt. It was his moment certainly. Paula left alone up there at last, sated with an overwhelming success, tired, relaxed…

With an effort of will Mary settled herself a little more deeply in the seat behind the wheel and lighted a cigarette. She hated having to wait, having to be found waiting when they came down together. She wished she could just—disappear. It wasn't possible, of course.

It was not very long before they came down. "She says I may stay two days," John told Mary as they squeezed into their seats in the little roadster. "Then, relentlessly, she's going to turn me out." But his voice was beyond disguise that of a lover who has prospered.

Mary drove them in almost unbroken silence all the way, down the ravine road and up through the woods to the house in the village. Then she went on with the car to their garage which stood in a yard of a neighbor, two or three doors away. She rejected with curt good-humor her father's offer to help her with this job. It was what she always did by herself, she said, and took a momentary perverse pleasure, which she despised herself for, in the obvious fact that this troubled him.

Back in the cottage living-room, ten minutes later perhaps, she found him alone and heard then, the explanation of his having come. They had got the Sunday papers out at Hickory Hill as usual in the middle of the morning but had found no reference to the performance of *Tosca* the night before. John had spent a good part of the day fretting over the absence of any news as to how Paula's venture had succeeded and puzzling over the lack of it in the papers. Then the obvious explanation had struck one of the boys, that the papers that came out to Hickory Hill on Sunday were an early edition.

He had had old Pete drive him straight into town, at that, and there he had found the news-stand edition containing the criticisms. The unfairness of them had disturbed him greatly. Orders or no orders, he hadn't been able to endure the thought of leaving Paula to suffer under the sting of a sneer like that without making at least an effort to comfort her. He had driven out to Ravinia without any idea that she was to sing again that night; had been told of it at the park where he had stopped for the purpose of picking up some one who could conduct him to her house. Learning that she was about to sing again, he had exerted all his will power and waited until this second ordeal should be over.

"It was as much one for me as it could have been for her," he concluded. "I don't know what stage fright is, but vicarious stage fright is the devil. I never was so terrified in my life. I hope nobody I knew saw me. I took pains they shouldn't, for I must have looked like a ghost."

"There's nothing the matter with your looks now," she told him. "Hickory Hill must be just the place for you."

"It would be," he assented, "if it were possible for me to be whole-heartedly there. By the way, we've got a visitor. Anthony March."

She felt herself flush at that with clear pleased surprise. "Oh, that's as nice as possible," she said. "But how in the world did it happen? How did you find him? Paula was trying to and couldn't."

"Was she?" Her father's voice, she thought, flattened a little on the question. "Why, he found us. He turned up on foot—Friday morning, it must have been—with a knapsack on his shoulders; came to the farm-house door and asked if he should tune the piano. Luckily, I happened to be about and caught him before he could get away. He was combining a walking trip, he said, with his own way of earning a living and I persuaded him to stay for a few days and make us a visit."

The last part of that sentence, Paula, coming down into the room from up-stairs, heard.

"Who?" she asked. "Who's the visitor you've been persuading?"

It was just a good-natured way of showing her interest in anything that her husband might happen to be talking about. But when he answered, "Anthony March," she came into focus directly.

"Thank goodness, you've found him!" she said. "I had about given him up. — And I really need him."

"I thought," said John, "that you had given him up. Are you going to do his opera, after all?"

"Opera!" said Paula blankly, as if she had never heard of such a thing. "No, I want him to see if he can fix this beastly piano they've given me so that it's fit to work with."

And John, after a moment-laughed.

It was a shattering sort of laugh to Mary. She stared at the man who uttered it as if he were — what he had for the moment become — a stranger. He was not, certainly, the man who, down in North Carolina had talked about March with her, regretted the "rough justice" he had had from Paula and considered the possibility of repairing it. That momentary blank look of his had shown that he perceived the insensitive egotism of his wife's attitude. Not even now that her success was an established thing had she a regretful thought for the man who had hoped to share it with her. She had forgotten those hopes. All she remembered now about Anthony March was that he could tune pianos better than any one else.

This Mary's father saw and yet he laughed. A cruel laugh. He had felt for the moment a recurrence of the old jealousy. In his relief from it, he, a reassured lover, triumphed in the humiliation of one he had supposed his rival.

Mary managed to hide her face from him — superfluously because he wasn't looking at her — and thought up, desperately, a few more questions about how they were getting on at Hickory Hill.

But she went on feeling from moment to moment more horribly in the way, and at last with a simulated yawn she said she was going to bed. "This — vicarious success is rather tiring," she told her father; "almost as bad as vicarious stage fright." And then to Paula, "Is there any reason, if you're going to keep father here for two days, why I shouldn't steal a holiday?"

"Go away, do you mean?" Paula asked with a faint flush. "Why,—where would you go?"

"I could drive over to Hickory Hill," Mary said, "either by myself in the little car or with Pete in the big one. Whichever you wouldn't rather have here."

"I think that's a capital idea," John said. "Oh, you'd better take the big car with Pete. It would be rather a long drive for you all by yourself in the little one."

This was not the real reason, of course. He wouldn't want a chauffeur under foot while he was honeymooning about with Paula.

Owing to a late start and an errand which at the last moment Paula wanted done in Chicago, it was getting on toward four o'clock when Pete drove Mary up to the loading platform of the old apple house at Hickory Hill. The farm Ford was standing there idling in a syncopated manner and apparently on the point of departure somewhere. Where, was explained a moment later by the emergence of Sylvia Stannard in her conventional farm costume of shirt and breeches with a two-gallon jug in each hand.

"Oh," she said, "then the big car can take Miss Wollaston over to Durham, can't it?—so she won't have to ride in the Ford which she hates. How do you do? I'm awfully glad you've come. We weren't expecting you, were we? Was anybody, I mean?"

Mary allowed herself a laugh at this young thing with her refreshing way of saying first whatever first came into her head and letting this serve as a greeting, said she was sure the big car and Pete were equal to taking her aunt to the four-miles-distant village.

"That's all right then. I won't have to wait for her," said Sylvia, letting down her jugs into the tonneau of the Ford. "I'll run straight along with this. They must be simply perishing for it. Isn't it hot, though!"

Mary wanted to know who they were and what they were perishing for.

"Lemonade," said Sylvia, "for the boys out in the hay field. It's perfectly gorgeous out there but hot enough to frizz your hair."

"Where is the hay field?" Mary asked. "Is it very far?"

"It's just over in the northeast eighty," said Sylvia, with a rather conscious parade of her mastery of bucolic vernacular. "But you don't want to walk. It would be awfully jolly if you would come along with me."

"Wait two minutes until I've said hello to Aunt Lucile and I will," said Mary, and turned to go into the house.

"Don't step on any of the piano," Sylvia called after her. "It's spread all over the place."

They had made a good many changes in the apple house since Mary had gone to Ravinia, but the thing that drew a little cry of surprise from her was this old square piano. The case of it stood snugly in the corner of the west wall. But the works were spread about the room in a manner which made Sylvia's warning less far-fetched than it seemed.

The feeling that caught Mary at sight of it was more than just surprise. Its dismantled condition brought to her a half-scared but wholly happy reassurance that Anthony March was really here.

Her journey to Hickory Hill had been, so she had told herself at intervals during the day, merely a flight from her father and Paula. There was no real reason for thinking that she would find March at the end of it. Week-end visits usually ended Monday morning, and it was probable that he would have gone hours before she arrived. She was conscious now of having commanded herself not to be silly when she was fretting over the late start from Ravinia and Paula's errand in town. It *would* be nice to see him again! He was probably out in the hay field with the others.

She gave her aunt a rather absent-minded greeting and a highly condensed summary of her news. Her father was well and was stopping on with Paula for a day or two.

"He's taken over my job," she concluded mischievously, "maid, chauffeur and chaperon. Paula doesn't mind now that she's made such an enormous hit and she doesn't sing again until Thursday. Pete will take you in the big car to Durham."

"Well, that's Heaven's mercy," exclaimed Miss Wollaston. "I don't like to drive with Sylvia in any car and I don't like riding in a Ford no matter who drives. But Sylvia driving a Ford—her own car's broken down somehow—is simply frightful."

"She's waiting for me now," said Mary, "to take me out to the hay field. I must run before she grows any more impatient."

And run was precisely what she did, down the slope to where Sylvia awaited her, a lighter-hearted creature altogether than she had supposed this morning that it was possible for her to be.

She got an explanation of the piano from Sylvia. She had gone with Rush and Mr. March to an auction sale late Saturday afternoon at a farm three or four miles away. Just for a lark. They hadn't meant seriously to buy anything. But this old piano, Mr. March having sworn that he would make it play despite the fact that half the keys wouldn't go down at all and the rest when they did made only the most awful noises, they had bought for eleven dollars, and had fetched home in the truck on Sunday.

"I think he's terribly nice," Sylvia confided. "You know him, don't you? He's quite old, of course. — Well, over thirty he says; but he's awfully — don't you know — well preserved. There are a whole lot of things he can do."

Mary laughed. "That is remarkable. How old are you, you nice young thing? Going on six? Lookout! You'll smash the lemonade!"

"We're going to surprise them," Sylvia announced when they had arrived, miraculously without disaster, at the northeast eighty. They had careened through the wagon gate and halted under an oak tree at the edge of the field. "I'll go and tell them I've brought the lemonade, but I won't say anything about you. You keep out of sight behind the tree. Then Graham won't want to go and brush his hair."

It startled Mary to realize that she had forgotten all about Graham. Not even the sight of his sister had recalled the — highly special nature of the state of things between them nor suggested the need for preparing an attitude to greet him with. At all events she wouldn't follow Sylvia's suggestion and pop out at him from behind a tree.

He was, it happened, the first person the child encountered in her flight across the field; the others, indistinguishable at that distance, were in a group a little farther away. Mary walked out to meet him when she saw him coming toward her and competently gave the encounter its tone by beginning to talk to him — about how hot it was and how nice the hay smelled and how good it seemed to be back here at Hickory Hill — while they were still a good twenty paces apart. You couldn't strike any sort of sentimental note very well when you had to begin at a shout. Then she led him back to the lemonade, gave him a cigarette and answered at length and with a good deal of spontaneous vivacity his obligatory questions about Paula and the opening of the Ravinia season.

She was in the full tide of this — and was, since she had sat down upon a small boulder Graham had insisted she take possession of, screened by the trunk of the tree — when Sylvia hailed her brother from, not very far away with the statement that Rush wouldn't stop for anything or anybody until once more around the field. It was March, then, who was audibly coming along with her. Mary rose, broke off about Paula, and moved the single step it needed to give her sight of him.

She saw nothing else but him. She saw his head go back as from the actual impact of the sight of her. She saw the look, unmistakable as a blast from a trumpet, that flamed into his face. And then her world swam. Paula wasn't singing now, "Hither, my love! Here I am! Here!" Nor could Paula come upon him now, from anywhere, and take him by the shoulders and kiss his cheek and lead him away with her. This moment was not Paula's— whatever the other had been.

And the rest, standing there looking on, hadn't seen the bolt fall! They were talking as idly and easily as if this were nothing but a hot summer afternoon in the hay field.

"I told him," she heard Sylvia saying, "that there was another nice old person he knew here with the lemonade, who thought I was only about six.—Were you surprised when you saw who she was?—I'm going to take him back to the apple house with us, now that Mary's come, so that he can have the piano ready to dance by to-night." This last, apparently, to Graham.

She even heard herself join in,—the voice was hers anyhow—when Graham, commenting upon the view across the field, remarked that it was so intensely farm-like that it had almost the look of a stage setting.

"It is like something," she said then. "It's like the first act of *Le Chemineau*. We ought to have a keg of cider instead of two jugs of lemonade and we should have brought it in a wheelbarrow instead of in the Ford."

"Well, we couldn't take Mr. March back in a wheelbarrow," Sylvia said, "so I'm glad it isn't the first act of whatever-you-call-it. Because he's simply got to fix the piano well enough for jazz."

Mary couldn't remember that he spoke a word, but he got into the back seat of the Ford with her when Sylvia slid under the wheel.

"If you'll promise," Sylvia said to March at the end of the breathless mile back to the apple house, "if you'll promise to go straight to work at it and never stop until it'll play the *Livery Stable Blues*, then I'll go back to the hay field and see that Rush gets some of the lemonade before those laborers drink it all up. You'll see to him, won't you, Mary? Stand right over him and be severe, so that we can dance to-night. You aren't as excited about it as you ought to be. I think I'll come in and start him."

And this she did while the Ford executed a little jazz rhythm of its own outside. She didn't stay more than a minute or two though. When she saw him fairly occupied, tools in hand, over his task, she darted away again with a last injunction to severity upon Mary.

She had seen nothing. The two were left alone.

Mary sat where she could watch his fine skilled hands at work. The negligent precision with which they accomplished their varied tasks occupied her, made it possible to continue for a while the silence she needed until her world should have stopped swimming; until the blindness of that revelation should have passed.

She had been wrong about him again. He was not an Olympian. (But, of course, Olympians themselves weren't, if it came to that; not always.) He could never, she had been telling herself since that day when they had had their one talk together, belong to any one. He did not—save himself up for special people. He was just there, the same for everybody, like, she had half humorously observed to her father, a public drinking fountain.

If that was the rule, she, Mary Wollaston, was the exception to it. Not Paula with her opulent armory, but she who had listened with him, clinging to him, while Paula sang; she, who had talked to him while Paula fought for her husband's life; she, whom he had come upon in the shade of the oak tree at the edge of the hay field; she who sat near him, silent now. This was the meager total that outweighed those uncounted hours of Paula's. Somehow she had acquired a special significance for him.

Was she trying to evade saying that he had fallen in love with her. What was the good—except that it sounded sweet—of using a phrase which could be packed like a hand-bag with anything you chose to put into it? Graham was in love with her. That boy in New York, whom she had found in a panic of lonely terror lest he should prove a coward in the great ordeal he was facing overseas had been for a few hours in love with her. What would be the content of the phrase for a man like this?

Was she in love with him? Her thoughts up to now had been deep, submerged, almost formless, but this question came to the surface and touched her lips with a smile. Well, and what did the phrase mean to her?

All she could think of as she sat so still watching him, was those fine hands of his, working as skillfully and swiftly as her father's ever worked but at this humble task. She kept her eyes away for just a little longer from his face. She wanted those hands. She wanted them with an intensity that made it impossible at last to let the silence endure any longer.

"Paula..." she said, and stopped in sheer surprise that her voice had come at all; then began again, "Paula wanted you to tune her piano. At Ravinia. I was angry, at that, until she reminded me that you wouldn't be."

His hand laid down the small, odd shaped tool it held, but the next moment picked it up again.

"I shouldn't have minded tuning her piano," he told her.

"I know," she said. "I knew as soon as I had had a minute in which to—gather you up. And when I had done that, I helped her try to find you. I had a special reason, a different one from Paula's, for hoping that we could. And for my reason," she went on, trembling a little and finding it harder to make her words come steadily, "it isn't—yet, too late.

"You see if you were there with her where she could see you every day—there'd be a lot of pianos there she said; enough to keep you going—she'd remember you again. She is like that. Lots of people are, I suppose. When she doesn't see you, she forgets. But if she remembered how much she liked you and how good your opera was,—the real one, the one you wrote for yourself—she might do something about it.—To get it played—so that you could hear it. Now that she's had a great success, she could do almost anything quite easily, I think. Infinitely more than I. I've been trying, but I haven't got very far."

He laid down the tool once more and locked his hands together. "You have been trying?" he repeated. The tension, like the grip of his hands, was drawing up almost unbearably.

"There's a French baritone there, Fournier, who could play your officer's part. As you meant it to be played, I think. But he doesn't sing in English. I thought it might be possible, if you didn't mind its being sung in French, to translate it. That's one of the things I've been—trying to do."

And then with a gasp and a sob, "Oh, don't,—don't hurt them like that!" she reached out and took the hands she wanted.

He responded to the caress, as before, so quickly that one could hardly have known where it began; only Mary did know. She looked up then into his face, steadily, open-eyed, though she could not see much for the blur.

"This time," he said, laboriously,—"this time it isn't the song."

She shook her head.

"I couldn't have waited, like that," he told her, three breaths later, "except for being afraid that if I tried to touch you, you wouldn't be there at all. Like a fairy story;—or a dream. I have never been sure that the other time wasn't."

"It's real enough," she said. "You're sure now, aren't you?"

His answer, the one she meant him to make, was to draw her up into a deep embrace, his lips upon hers.

"What does it mean?" he asked, when they had drawn back from it.

She smiled at that. "You don't need ask. That's the Wollaston trick, to ask for meanings and reasons." She added, a moment later, "It means whatever it says to your heart."

It was at her half-humorous suggestion that he went back, presently, to work at the piano. She settled contentedly near him where with an outstretched hand she could occasionally respond to his touch. They hadn't, either of them, very much to say.

Once the work was interrupted, when he asked, rather tensely, "Do you want me to come to Ravinia?"

She found herself at a loss for a categorical reply. She'd have thought that a whole-hearted yes would have been the only thing she could say.

"I don't want you—tortured any more with unheard melodies," she answered after a moment's reflection.

His nod, decisive as it was, struck her as equivocal. But she was too happy to probe into anything this afternoon. There would be plenty of time; unstinted hours. It was with no more than a mild regret that she heard, under the windows, the return of the big car with Aunt Lucile. This inextinguishable happiness expressed itself in the touch of impudent mischief with which she slipped up close behind Anthony March and, in the last possible instant before her aunt's entrance into the room, bent down and kissed him; then flashed back to her decorously distant chair.

It was funny how calm she was. This day that was closing down over the hill behind the apple house couldn't be, it seemed, the same that had dawned over the lake at Ravinia. The whole Ravinia episode, even as she told Lucile and March about it, seemed remote, like something out of a book; but became for that very reason, rather pleasant to dwell upon. Sylvia came in pretty soon for a critical survey of what March had accomplished with the piano, volunteered to help and attempted to. But having pled some of Anthony's arrangements of loose parts, she was sacked off the job and sent back to the hay field to bring the boys in for supper.

After supper the excitement over the piano increased. They all gathered round March like people watching a conjurer's trick when he slid the action into place and proved, chromatically, that every hammer would strike and every key return.

"But it isn't tuned at all," Sylvia wailed. "It will be hours before you can play on it."

"Minutes," March corrected with a grin. And they watched, amazed,—but less so really than an ordinary piano tuner would have been,—at the way he caught octaves, fifths and fourths, sixths and thirds up and down that keyboard like a juggler keeping seven tennis balls in the air.

"There you are," he said suddenly, before it seemed that he could be half-way through and began playing a dance.

"But you can play tunes!" cried Sylvia. "I thought you only did terribly high-brow things. That's what Rush said."

"I was pianist in the best jazz orchestra in Bordeaux," March told her.

He stayed there at the piano quite contentedly for more than an hour. Some of the musical jokes he indulged in (his sense of humor expressed itself more easily and impudently in musical terms than in any other) were rather over his auditors' heads. Parodies whose originals they failed to recognize, experiments in the whole-tone scale that would have interested disciples of Debussy, but his rhythms they understood and recognized as faultless.

And Mary danced. With Graham when she must, with Rush when she could. The latter happened oftener than you would have supposed.

"Those Wollastons can certainly dance," Sylvia remarked to her brother. "I wonder they'll have anything to do with us. Let's just watch them for a minute.—Here, we'll turn the piano around so Mr. March can see, too."

It was queer, Mary reflected, how easy it was for her and also, she was sure, for her lover, to acquiesce in a spending of the hours like that; how little impatient she was of the presence of these others that kept them apart. She gave no thought to any maneuver, practicable or fantastic, for stealing away with him, not even when, as the party broke up for the night it became evident that chance was not going so to favor them.

She realized afterward that there had been something factitious about her tranquillity. What he had said in the moment before their first embrace had been on that same note. He had been afraid to touch her for fear that— as in a fairy story, or a dream,—she wouldn't be there. All that afternoon and evening, despite an ineffable security in their miracle, she had walked softly and so far as the future was concerned, avoided trying to look.

Something in his gaze when he said good night to her, gave her a momentary foreboding, though she told herself on the way up to the tent she was to share with Sylvia that this was nothing but the scare that always comes along with a too complete happiness.

But in the morning when her aunt told her that March had gone, she realized that it had been more than that.

It was in the presence of the others who had gathered in the apple house for breakfast that she heard the news, and this was perhaps a mercy; for the effort she had to make to keep from betraying herself rallied her forces and prevented a rout.

To the others his having gone like that seemed natural enough, — likably characteristic of him, at any rate. In his note to Miss Wollaston he had merely said that he realized that he must be off and wished to make the most of the cool of the morning. He hoped she would understand and pardon his not having spoken of his intention last night.

"It's the crush Sylvia had on him that accounts for that," Graham observed. "He was afraid of the row she'd make if he let on."

Sylvia's riposte to this was the speculation that Mary had scared him away, but one could see that her brother's explanation pleased her.

"Anyhow," she concluded, "he was good while he lasted."

What held Mary together was the obvious fact that none of them saw — no more than they had seen — anything. Not one curious or questioning glance was turned her way. A sense she was not until later able to find words for, that she was guarding something, his quite as much as her own, from profaning eyes, gave her the resolution it needed to carry on like that until she could be alone. Naturally, — or at all events plausibly — alone. She wouldn't run away from anybody.

Toward eleven o'clock chance befriended her. She hid herself in the old orchard, lay prone upon the warm grass, her cheek upon her folded forearms, and let herself go. She did not cry even now. Grief was not what she felt, still less resentment.

She was lonely as she had never been before, and frightened by her loneliness. All the familiar things of her life seemed far away, unreal. She wanted a hand to hold; — his — oh, one of his! — until she could find her way into a path again.

She had known, she reflected, — somewhere in the depths of her she had known — from the first moment of their meeting, that he would go away. This was why she had been so careful not to look beyond the moments as they came; not to tempt Nemesis by asking nor trying for too much.

There happened to be, rather uncannily, a genuine proof that this was true. While she had been still dazed with that first look of his, there in the oak shade at the edge of the field, she had said that it was like the first act of *Le Chemineau*. That had been speaking all but with the tongue of prophecy. Deeply as the story had impressed her when she heard it, she had spoken with no conscious sense of the likeness between that wayfarer — whom neither love nor interest nor security could tempt away from the open road which called him,—and Anthony March. It was an inner self that knew and found a chance to speak. It was that same self who had answered for her when he asked whether she wanted him to come to Ravinia.

He had come to his decision then, with just that nod of the head. And she, forlorn, was glad he had cast this temptation aside. That he was plodding now sturdily along his highway. She flushed with shame at the thought of him, ubiquitous among those egotists at Ravinia, enlisting their interest, reminding Paula how much she liked him.

Why had he not hated her for suggesting such a thing? He had loved her for it, she knew, because he understood the longing to comfort and protect him which lay behind it. But that sort of comfort was not for him. The torture of the unheard melodies, instead.

He did love her. This, utterly, she knew. His going away, even with no farewell at all, cast no flaw upon the miraculous certainty of that. Their one unreserved embrace remained the symbol of it.

She pressed her hands to her face and with a long indrawn breath surrendered to the memory of it. It was hers—for always.

The family were sitting at dinner when she came down to the apple house, and after a rather startled look at her, demanded to know where she had been.

"Asleep in the orchard," she said. "And not altogether awake yet."

But she knew she must get away from them. The look she saw in Graham's face would have decided that.

# CHAPTER XVIII
# A CASE OF NECESSITY

She told Rush when they left the table, that she had some shopping to do in town for Paula and meant to go on the afternoon train. She was expected back at Ravinia to-morrow anyhow. Beyond trying to persuade her to let Pete drive her in he made no protest, but she could see that he was troubled about it and she wasn't much surprised to find Wallace Hood waiting on the station platform when her train got in.

She didn't, very much, mind Wallace. There was no appearance of his being there in the rôle of guardian because she wasn't considered safe to leave to herself. You could always trust Wallace to do a thing like that perfectly.

It was a great piece of luck for him he told her. He had called up Hickory Hill to congratulate John upon Paula's enormous success; had learned from Rush of Mary's visit and that she was even then on the way to Chicago. He had just dropped round at the station in the hope of being able to pick her up for dinner. She had some shopping to do he understood and he wouldn't detain her now.

"Oh, nothing that matters a bit," said Mary. "It was an excuse merely, for running away from Hickory Hill."

There was something to be said for a man like Wallace as a confidant. He was perfectly safe not to guess anything on his own account. He seemed touched by her candor and hugged her arm against his side as they walked along, a gesture of endearment such as he hadn't indulged in for half a dozen years.

"So if you have nothing better to do," she went on, "we can begin our evening now. Though I suppose I had better find, first, a place to sleep."

"Frederica Whitney's in town for a day or two, just for a flying visit to Martin. She'd be glad to take you in, I'm sure."

"Oh, I think not," said Mary. "Not if I can get anything with four walls at the Blackstone."

She thought from his glance at her that he attached some special significance to her unwillingness to go to the Whitney house and hastened to assure him this was not the case.

"Frederica's a dear. Only I just happen to feel like not being anybody's guest to-night. Oh, and I didn't mean you by that either."

"It's nice to be nobody in that sense," he said.

His next suggestion was that he get his car, start north up the shore with her, have dinner at one of the taverns along the road and deliver her in good season for a night's sleep in the cottage at Ravinia.

But this suggestion was declined rather more curtly.

"To-morrow is as soon as I want to go there," she said. "Pete's going over then to get father so I shall go on duty. But meanwhile I'll let him enjoy his holiday in peace."

He made no further demur to telephoning over to the Blackstone.

On his coming back presently with the news that he had a room for her, she said, "Then we've nothing on our minds, have we? Except finding a place for dinner that's quiet and—not too romantic. I *am* glad you came to meet me."

She was quite sincere about this. It would have been ghastly she reflected, to have spent the evening alone in a hotel bedroom with her own thoughts, if those she had entertained on the train coming in were a fair sample.

He was being just as nice to her as possible. By his old-fashioned standards, no hotel was a proper place for a young girl to spend a night in alone. Yet beyond offering two alternative suggestions, he forbore trying to dissuade her. So when he chose the Saddle and Cycle as their anchorage for the evening, she endorsed his choice with the best appearance of enthusiasm she could muster, though she'd rather have gone to a place where three out of four of the other diners wouldn't in all probability be known to her.

Arriving, however, in the unclassified hour between tea and dinner, they found they had the place pretty much to themselves and settled down in a secluded angle of the veranda for a leisurely visit. They began on Paula, of course, her retrieved failure and her sensational success. How sorry Wallace was not to have been there for her "Nedda." (He didn't go in much for Sunday entertainments of any sort, Mary remembered.) Well, it had been just as splendid as everybody said it was. That was one thing, at any rate, that had been put beyond discussion. Even the pundits were, for the moment anyhow, silenced.

He was curious as to how the intimate details of this strange life she had a chance to observe, struck her. How she liked Paula's colleagues; to what extent the glamour evaporated when one was behind the scenes.

She satisfied him as well as she could, though her opportunities, she said, were a good deal narrower than he took them to be. She had, herself, so much to do as Paula's factotum that there wasn't much leisure for loafing about. And this launched her into a humorously exaggerated account of what was involved in being secretary, chauffeur and chaperon to a successful opera star. But she pulled up when she saw he was taking it seriously.

"It's shocking she should work you like that," he said in a burst of undisguised indignation. "Of course, it's precisely what Paula would do. She has very little common consideration, I'm afraid, for anybody."

Mary could not remember having heard him speak like that, in all the years she'd known him, of anybody; she was sure he never had so spoken of any one who bore the name of Wollaston. Taken aback as she was she changed her tune altogether and tried to reassure him.

"But that's what I'm there for, Wallace dear! To be worked. And you've no idea how I like having something to do which amounts, in a small way, to a job."

"It's too hard for you, though," he persisted. "It isn't what you were trained for. And it's rather, as I said,—shocking. If it was all understood from the first, then so much the worse for the understanding. I hope your father, when he went up there, didn't discover what your duties were supposed to be."

"No," Mary said rather dryly, "I don't believe he did."

"Well," he said thoughtfully, at the end of a short silence, "I am profoundly thankful that she's made so—solid a success."

Up to this moment none of their talk had been quite real to Mary. She had betrayed no inattention to him and when it had come her turn to carry on the conversational stream she had done so adequately and even with a certain vivacity. But it had meant no more than an occupation; something that passed the time and held her potential thoughts at bay.

This last observation of his, though, struck a different note. He had done full justice to his pleasure in Paula's success at the very beginning of their talk. Now he meant something by it. Leaning forward a little for a keener look at him, she asked what it was that he meant.

He was a little surprised to be brought to book like that, but he made hardly an effort to fence with her. "I was glad, I meant, for purely non-sentimental reasons. Her success may prove, I suppose, a practical solution of some difficulties."

"Practical?" she echoed. "You don't mean,—yes, I suppose you do mean,—money difficulties. Do you mean that Paula's going to be invited to support the family now?" She finished with a little laugh and he winced at it. "Father said something like that to me one day while I was down south with him," she explained. "Only he said it as a joke,—a sort of joke. That's why I laughed."

"He talked to you then about his affairs?" Wallace asked. "May I ... Do you mind telling me what he said?"

"Of course not, if I can remember. He'd been remiss, he said, about making money. He said that if he had died, then when he was so ill, there wouldn't have been, beyond his life insurance which was for Paula, much more than enough to pay his debts. Practically nothing for Rush and me is what that came to. I pointed out to him that we could take care of ourselves, and he said that anyway as soon as he could get back into practise, he'd begin to make a lot of money and save. It must be a good deal worse,—the whole situation I mean—than I took it to be, for you to mean that seriously about Paula."

She had managed an appearance of composure but in truth she was badly shaken. Money matters was just about the one real taboo that she respected and to break over this habitual reticence even with an old friend like Wallace troubled her delicacy. The notion she got from the look in his face that there was something dubious about her father's solvency, was terrifying. She hid her hands under the table so that he shouldn't see they were trembling. She wanted the truth from him now, rather than vaguely comforting generalties, and if she betrayed her real feelings, these latter were what she would drive him back upon.

"Can you tell me," she asked after a pause, "exactly how bad it is?"

He couldn't furnish details. He told her though that there couldn't be any doubt her father's affairs were more involved than his summary of them had made them appear. "He isn't a very good bookkeeper, of course,—never was; and he has never taken remonstrances very seriously. Why, about all I know is that Martin Whitney is worried. He tried to dissuade John from going in anywhere near so heavily on the Hickory Hill project.—And that, of course, was before we had any reason to suppose that his ability to earn money was going to be ..."

It was apparent that he discarded the word that came to his tongue here and cast about for another; "interfered with," was what he finally hit upon.

"Then he's your aunt's trustee and I believe that complicates the situation, though just how much I don't know. Rush didn't get a letter from Martin this morning, did he?"

"I don't know," Mary said numbly.

"I thought perhaps," he explained, "that might be the reason why you didn't want to go to their house tonight. Rush doesn't quite understand Martin's position nor do justice to it. Martin wants to have a really thorough talk with him I know, as soon as possible."

"Wallace ..." Mary asked, after another silence, "what was the word you didn't say when you spoke of father's earning power being—interfered with? Was it—cut off? Do you mean that father isn't—ever going to be well?"

Startled as he was, he did not attempt a total denial; answered her, though with an effort, candidly.

"It's not hopeless, at all," he assured her. "It really is not. If he'll rest, live an outdoor life for the next year or two, he has a good chance to become a well man again. It's probable that he will,—practically so. But if he attempts to take up his practise in the autumn it will simply be, so Darby declares, suicide."

"That means tuberculosis, I suppose," she said.

He nodded; then involuntarily he reached his hands out toward her, a gesture rare with him and eloquent equally of sympathy and consternation. He hadn't in the least meant to tell her all that—nor indeed any of it. Her hands met his with a warm momentary pressure and then withdrew. He had, for a fact, pretty well forgotten where they were.

"If you knew," she said, "how kind you've been not to try to—spare me. No, don't bother. I'm not going to cry. Just give me a minute..."

It was less than that before she asked, in a tone reassuringly steady, "Does father know, himself?"

"He's been warned, but he's skeptical. Steinmetz says there's nothing surprising about that. It's his all but universal experience with men of his own profession. Of course this summer out at Hickory Hill is so much to the good. And if he can get sufficiently interested to stay there the year round, why, there's no knowing. The investment in that farm may prove the wisest one he ever made."

"If it were only possible,"—she was quoting what her father had said to her the other night at Ravinia,—"for him to be whole-heartedly there! And he could be—for it's a place one can't help loving and he and Rush are wonderful companions—he could be whole-heartedly there if it weren't for Paula."

It was precisely at this point, he indicated to her, that Paula could come in by relieving him of the necessity of getting back into practise. Martin would look out for the fixed indebtedness on the farm. He would probably be willing, in case John made it his home and put his own mature judgment at the disposal of the two young partners, to finance still further increases in the investment. But for the ordinary expenses of living during the next year or two, Paula should cease being a burden and become a support. "Do you think," he finished by asking, "that she has any idea what the situation really is?"

Mary replied to this question a little absently. "Father insisted that she carry out the Ravinia contract. She told me so herself and seemed, I don't know why, just a little resentful about it. But I'm sure she can't have any idea that there was a need for money at the back of it. It has irritated her rather whenever she has caught me economizing up there. And father will never tell her any more pointedly than he has, you can be sure. Some one of us will have to do it."

"You're on very good terms with her, aren't you?" Wallace asked. He added instantly, though with an effort, "I'm willing to tell her if you wish me to."

She smiled very faintly at that for she knew how terrifying such a prospect would be to him. "Whoever told Paula," she said, "she'd eventually attribute it, I think, back to me. So I may as well, and rather better, do it directly."

The tension slackened between them for a while after that. The talk became casual. Wallace, it was easy to see, was enormously relieved. Mary had been put in unreserved possession of the facts and had endured them better than he could possibly have hoped. He began chatting about the farm again, not now as an incubus but as a hopeful possibility. Both the boys had real mettle in them and might be expected to buckle down and show it. Rush would forget the disillusionment of his holiday hopes when the necessities of the case were really brought home to him. And as for Graham …

Wallace broke off short there, flushed, and made a rather panicky effort to retrieve the slip. He was in the family enough to be a part of the Graham conspiracy. Poor Graham, distracted by her innocent inability to make up her mind to marry him! He would be all right as soon as her maidenly hesitations should have come to an end, and she'd made him the happiest man in the world with the almost inevitable yes.

She had gone rather white by the end of a long silence. Finally:

"Wallace," she began in a tone so tense that he waited breathlessly for her to go on, "do you remember I asked you once, the day I came home from New York, if you couldn't find me a job? I know you didn't think I meant it and I did not altogether—then. But I mean it now. I need it—desperately.— Wallace, I can't ever marry Graham. I know I can't. And I can't go on being dependent on father while he's dependent on Paula."

He caught at a straw. "Paula is really very fond of you," he said.

"Yes, in a way," Mary agreed; "though she sometimes has regarded me a little dubiously. But if she ever saw me—coming between her and father, or father turning ever so little away from her—toward me, whether it was any of my doing or not, she'd—hate me with her whole heart. It may not be very logical but it's true."

Then she brought him back from the digression. "Anyhow, it's on my own account, not Paula's—nor even father's—that I want a job. Father will feel about it, of course, as you do and so will Rush and—and the rest. And I don't want it to hurt anybody more than necessary. I'd rather stay here but I suppose on their account I'd better go away. And you know so many people—in so many places. There's your sister in Omaha. I remember how much trouble you said she had finding a nursery governess. I'd be pretty good at that I think. I could teach French and—I'd be nice to children."

For a moment she wildly thought she had won him. She saw the tears come into his eyes.

"Anything I have in the world, my dear, or anything I can command is yours. On any terms you like."

But there he disposed of the tears and got himself together, as if he'd remembered some warning. She could imagine Rush over the telephone, "Of course, she's terribly run down with that damned war work of hers; not quite her real self, you know."

She saw him summon a resolute smile and heard the familiar note of encouragement in his voice. "We'll think about it," he told her. "After all, things aren't, probably, as black as they look. And sometimes when they look darkest it's only the sign that they're about to change their faces altogether. Anyhow, we've stared at them long enough to-night, haven't we? And all I meant was to take you out for a jolly evening! Don't you think we might save it, even yet? Is there anything at the theatres you'd like to see?"

"Some musical show?" she asked. "Yes, I'd like that very much. Thank you."

# CHAPTER XIX
# THE DRAMATIST

Mary returned to Ravinia—went on duty, as she put it to Wallace—the following afternoon rather taut-drawn in her determination to have things out with Paula at once. But the mere attitude and atmosphere of the place, as before, let her down a little.

It was restful to have her days filled up with trivial necessary duties; an hour's errand running in the small car; a pair of soiled satin slippers to clean with naptha; a stack of notes to answer from such unknown and infatuate admirers as managed to escape the classification feebleminded and were entitled therefore to have the fact recognized (this at a little desk in the corner while Novelli at the piano and Paula ranging about the room, ran over her part in half-voice in the opera she had rehearsed yesterday with the orchestra and was to sing to-night), a run to the park for a visit to Paula's dressing-room in the pavilion in order to make sure, in conference with her dresser, that all was in order for to-night; a return to the cottage in time to heat Paula's milk (their maid of all work couldn't be trusted not to boil it); then at seven, driving Paula to the park for the performance, spending the evening in her dressing-room or in the wings chatting sometimes with other members of the force whom she found it possible to get acquainted with; occasional incursions into the front of the house to note how something went or, more simply, just to hear something she liked; driving Paula home again at last, undressing her; having supper with her—the most substantial meal of the day—talking it over with her; and so, like Mr. Pepys—to bed.

It might shock Wallace Hood, a schedule like that, but there were days when to Mary it was a clear God-send.

She decided within the first twenty-four hours to wait for some sort of lead from Paula before plunging into a discussion of her father's affairs. It would take the edge off if the thing weren't too glaringly premeditated. Paula just now was doing all she could. Mary opened all her mail and would know if any offer came in that involved future plans. She accepted the respite gratefully.

She had a use to put it to. For the first two or three days after her return, she had not been able to turn to anything that associated itself with

Anthony March without such an emotional disturbance as prevented her from thinking at all. The mere physical effect of those sheets of score paper was, until she could manage to control it, such as to make any continuance of the labor of translating his opera, impossible.

By a persistent effort of will she presently got herself in hand however and went on not only with her translation but with the other moves in her campaign to get *The Outcry* produced. Her first thought was that something might be accomplished directly through LaChaise. Her simple plan had been to make friends with him so that when she urged the arguments for producing this work, they'd be—well—lubricated by his liking for her.

She began saying things to him on a rather more personal note, things with a touch of challenge in them. There was no gradual response to this but suddenly—a week or ten days after her return from Hickory Hill this was— he seemed to perceive her drift. He turned a look upon her, the oddest sort of look, startled, inquiring, lighted up with a happy though rather incredible surmise. It was an exclamatory look which one might interpret as saying, "What's this! Do you really mean it!"

Mary got no further than that. She didn't mean it, of course, a serious love-affair with LaChaise, and she tried for a while to feel rather indignant against an attitude toward women which had only two categories; did she offer amorous possibilities or not. An attitude that had no half lights in it, no delicate tints of chivalry nor romance. LaChaise would do nothing for the sake of her blue eyes. He had no interest whatever in that indeterminate, unstable emotional compound that goes, between men and women, by the name of friendship.

She tried to call this beastly and feel indignant about it, but somehow that emotion didn't respond. She had more real sympathy for and understanding of an attitude like that than she had for one like Graham's. It was simpler and more natural. It involved you in no such labyrinths of farfetched absurdities and exasperating cross-purposes as Graham's did.

It was characteristically,—wasn't it?—a Latin attitude; or would it be fairer to say that its antithesis as exemplified by Graham was a northern specialty? She extracted quite a bit of amusement from observing some of the results of individual failures to understand this fundamental difference, all the more after she had Jimmy Wallace to share observations with. He was a dramatic critic, but he consented to take a fatherly, or better avuncular, interest in the Ravinia season during the month of his musical colleague's vacation.

The special episode they focused upon was Violet Williamson's flirtation with Fournier. She was a pretty woman, still comfortably on the east side of forty, socially one of the inner ring, spoiled, rather, by an enthusiastic husband but not, thanks to her own good sense, very seriously. James Wallace was an old and very special friend of hers and she commandeered his services as soon as he appeared at Ravinia, in her campaign for possession of the French baritone.

Mary had reflected over this and talked it out pretty thoroughly with Jimmy before it occurred to her that she might be able to turn it to her own account—or rather to her lover's. For that matter, why not, while she had him under her hand, recruit Jimmy as an aid in the campaign?

"Do you mind being used for ulterior purposes?" she asked him.

He intimated that he did not if they were amusing, as any of Mary's were pretty sure to be.

"I'm interested in an opera," she told him, "or rather, I'm very much interested in a man who has written one. Father and I have agreed that he's a great person and everybody seems willing to admit that he's a musical genius. Paula considered the opera, but gave it up after she had kept him working over it for weeks because the soprano part wasn't big enough. It would be just the thing for Fournier."

Jimmy raised the language difficulty. "The book's in English, I suppose," he said.

"It's been translated into French," Mary said, and then admitted authorship by adding, "after a fashion; as well as an amateur like me could do it." She didn't mind a bit how much Jimmy knew. Not that he wasn't capable of very acute surmises but that whatever he brought up he wouldn't have the flutters over.

"Does Fournier like it himself?" he wanted to know. "Does he see the personal possibilities in it, I mean?"

"I haven't shown it to him yet," Mary said. "I want him to hear about it in just the right way first. If Paula would only say just the right thing! She means to but she forgets. LaChaise would back her up, I think, if she took the lead. Otherwise ... well, he isn't looking for trouble, I suppose, and of course, it would mean a lot."

"Somebody has to put his back into an enterprise of that sort," Jimmy observed.

"I can't, directly," she said, "not with LaChaise nor with Mr. Eckstein. But you see," she went on, "if Violet happened to hear, from somebody who was in the way of getting inside information, about a small opera that had a sensational part for a baritone, she'd work it and make her husband too, and since he's one of the real backers and a friend of Mr. Eckstein's, they'd be likely to accomplish something."

"Lead me to it," said Jimmy. "Give me your inside information and leave Violet to me."

He got a little overflow from the fulness of her heart at that that would have rewarded him amply for a more arduous and less amusing prospect than he was committed to. It was always touch and go whether this summer plunge into musical criticism wouldn't bore him frightfully. Pretentious solemnities of any kind were hard for him to tolerate and an opera season is, of course, stuffed with these, even a democratized blue-penciled out-of-doors affair like this. It was a great relief to find him a mind as free from sentimental resonances as Mary Wollaston's swimming about in it. They saw eye to eye over a lot of things.

They were in whole-hearted agreement for example about a certain impresario, Maxfield Ware, who created a sensation among the company and staff by turning up ostentatiously unaccounted for from New York and looking intensely enigmatical whenever any one asked him any questions. He was a sufficiently well-known figure in that world for surmises to spring up like round-eyed dandelions wherever he trod.

It wasn't long before everybody knew, despite the concealments which his ponderous diplomacy never cast aside, that his objective was Paula. She divined this before he had made a single overt move in her direction and pointed it out to Mary with a genuine pleasure sounding through the tone of careless amusement she chose to adopt.

"You wouldn't have anything to do with a person like that, would you?" Mary was startled into exclaiming. "Of course, if he were genuinely what he pretends to be and the things he boasts were true...."

"Oh, he's genuine enough," said Paula. "A quarter to a half as good as he pretends and that's as well as the whole of that lot will average. Though he isn't the sort you and John would take to, for a fact."

It was not the first time Mary had found herself bracketed with her father in just this way. It wasn't a sneering way, hardly hostile. But Mary by the second or third repetition began reading an important significance into it. Paula in her instinctive fashion was beginning to weigh alternatives, one life against the other, a thing it wasn't likely she had ever attempted before.

There was a tension between John and Paula which Mary saw mounting daily over the question of his next visit to Ravinia. Paula wanted him, was getting restless, moody, as nearly as it was possible for her to be ill-natured over his abstention. Yet it was evident enough that she had not invited him to come; furthermore, that she meant not to invite him. Once Mary would have put this down to mere coquetry but this explanation failed now to satisfy altogether. There was something that lay deeper than that. Some sort of strain between them dating back, she surmised, to the talk her father had referred to down in North Carolina in the jocular assertion that he had told Paula she would have to begin now supporting the family. Had the same topic come up again during his visit to Ravinia?

The perception of this strain in their relation increased Mary's reluctance to bring the topic up herself, in default of a lead from Paula, out of nowhere. It almost seemed as if Paula consciously avoided giving her such a lead, sheered away whenever she found they were "getting warm" in that direction.

There were hours when the undertaking she had committed herself to with Wallace Hood seemed fantastic. Between two persons like her father and Paula a meddler could make such an incalculable amount of mischief. All the current maxims of conduct would support her in a refusal to interfere. It was exclusively their affair, wasn't it? Why not let them settle it in their own way?

Yet there were other hours when she put her procrastinations down to sheer cowardice. This occurred whenever she got a letter from her aunt at Hickory Hill.

Miss Wollaston was a dutiful but exceedingly cautious correspondent, but beneath the surface of her brisk little bulletins were many significant implications. Rush had made two or three trips to town for consultations with Martin Whitney ... Doctor Steinmetz, presence unaccounted for, had been a guest one day at lunch... Graham's father had come out one Saturday and after he had been exhaustively shown over the place the men had talked until all hours.... The building program was to be curtailed for the present; to be resumed, perhaps when prices weren't so high nor labor so hard to get.... The new Holstein calves had come. Mary had been told, hadn't she, of the decision to constitute the herd in this manner instead of buying all milking cows.... Sylvia, declaring that Rush and Graham had got too solemn to live with, had finally obeyed her mother and gone home to the Stannards' summer place at Lake Geneva.

Mary read these letters to Paula as they came in the hope of provoking some question that would make it possible to tell John Wollaston's wife the tale of his necessities, but nothing of the sort happened. Paula did observe (a little uneasily?) apropos of Steinmetz' visit:

"John says he's taken quite a fancy to him. He told me he was going to get him to come out if he could."

The other casts brought up nothing whatever.

As it happened Mary paid dear for her procrastination. Paula sent her into town one day with a long list of errands, a transparently factitious list, which, taken in connection with an unusual interest she displayed in the item of lunch, made it more than sufficiently plain to Mary that for the day she wasn't wanted at Ravinia.

She concealed, successfully she thought, the shock she felt at these new tactics of Paula's, studied the list and said she thought she should be able to return on the three o'clock train. She made a point however of not coming back until the four-fifteen. It was nearly six before she got back to the cottage, but the contented lazy tone in which Paula from up-stairs answered her hail, made it plain that her tardiness had not been remarked. However Paula had spent her day, the upshot of it was satisfactory.

"Shall I come up?" Mary asked.

"Come along," Paula answered. "I'm not asleep or anything and besides I want to talk to you."

"I think I got everything you want," Mary said from Paula's doorway, "or if not exactly, what will do just about as well."

Paula, stretched out on the bed rather more than half undressed, with the contented languor of a well fed lioness yet with some passion or other smoldering in her eyes, made no pretense at being interested in Mary's success in executing her commissions.

"I had Max to lunch to-day," she said. "I knew you hated him and then. it was complicated enough anyway. I suppose it might have been better if I'd told you so right out instead of making up all those things for you to do in town, but I couldn't quite find the words to put it in somehow and I had to have it out with him. He's been nagging at me for a week and he's going away to-morrow. He's given me until then to think it over."

There was no use trying to hurry Paula. Mary took off her hat, lighted a cigarette and settled herself in the room's only comfortable chair before she asked, "Think what over?"

"Oh, the whole thing," said Paula. "What he's been harping on for the last week.—He *is* a loathsome sort of beast," she conceded after a little pause. "But he's right about this. Absolutely."

Was her father ever fretted, Mary wondered, by this sort of thing? Did his nerves draw tight, and his muscles, too, waiting for the idea behind these perambulations to emerge?

"I can imagine a lot of things that Mr. Maxfield Ware would be right about," she observed. "Which one is this?"

"About me," said Paula. "About what I'd have to do if I wanted to get anywhere. He thinks I've a good chance to get into the very first class, along with Garden and Farrar and so on. And unless I can do that, there's no good going on. I'd never be happy as a second rater. Well, that's true. And my only chance of getting to the top, he says, is in being managed just right. I guess that's true, too. He says that if I take this Metropolitan contract that LaChaise has been talking about, go down to New York as one of their 'promising young American sopranos' to sing on off-nights and fill in and make myself generally useful, I simply won't have a chance. They wouldn't get excited about me whatever happened. They'd go on patronizing me and yawning in my face no matter how good I was. I'd do just as well, he says, so far as my career is concerned, to stay right here in Chicago and get Campanini to give me two or three appearances a season;—make a sort of amateur night of it for the gold coast to buzz about. I'd have a lot easier time that way and it would come to the same thing in the end. And he says that unless I want to go in for his scheme, that's what I'd better do. Well, and he's right. I can see that, plainly enough."

Mary refrained from asking what Max's scheme was. She'd learn, no doubt, in her stepmother's own good time. She nodded a tentative assent to Max's general premises and waited.

"He certainly was frank enough," Paula went on after a while. "He wants to make a real killing he says. Something he's never quite brought off before. He says the reason he's always failed before is that he's had to go and mix a love-affair up with it somehow. He's either fallen in love with the woman or she with him or if it was a man he was managing, they both went mad over the same woman. Something always happened anyhow to make a mess of it. But he says he isn't interested in me in the least in that way and that he can see plainly enough that I'm not in him. But imagine five years with him!"

She broke off with a shudder, not a real shudder though. The sort one makes over a purely imaginary prospect. Some expression of her feeling must have betrayed itself in Mary's face, for Paula, happening to look at her just then, sat up abruptly.

"Oh, I know," she said. "It's all very well, but that's the sort of person you have to go in with and that's the sort of scheme you have to go into if you're going to get anywhere. Something of the sort anyhow,—I never heard of one exactly like this. But this is what he proposes: we're each to put up twenty thousand dollars. That's easy enough as far as I'm concerned because what I put up isn't to be spent at all. It's just to be turned over to somebody—some banker like Martin Whitney—as a guarantee that I won't break my contract. He says he wouldn't take on anybody in my position without a guarantee like that. He's to spend the money he puts up for publicity and other things but he's to get paid back out of what I earn. He's to be my manager absolutely. I'm to go wherever he says; carry out any contracts he makes for me. He's to pay my expenses and guarantee me ten thousand a year beyond that. If he doesn't pay me that much, then it's he that breaks the contract. And of course, he can't make me do anything that would ruin my voice or my health. He says he's going to work me like a dog. That's what he thinks I need. He says he can get me in with the Chicago company for their road tour before their regular season opens here. He won't let me sing either in Chicago or New York until I've landed, but he wants me to go to New York this winter and coach with Scotti, if we can get him. Then go to Mexico City in the spring and then down to Buenos Aires for their winter season there. That's July and August, of course, when it's summer up here. By that time he thinks we'll be ready for Europe; London or Paris. He's rather in favor of London. He knows all the ropes and he'll buy the people that have to be bought and square the people that have to be squared and work the publicity. He says he's the best publicity man in the world and I guess he knows. Then after a year or two over there, he thinks we'll be ready to come back to the Metropolitan and clean up."

"And what," asked Mary, "is his share of the clean-up to be?"

"Oh, a half," said Paula; "we'd be equal partners. That's fair enough, I suppose. I sat there all through lunch while he was talking, hating him; hating his big blue chin, and his necktie and his great shiny finger-nails and the way he ate, and feeling, of course, perfectly frightfully unhappy. I told him I'd let him know what I would do sometime before to-morrow noon, and as soon as I could I got rid of him. And then I came up here and cried and cried. And that's something I haven't done for a long while. I felt as if he was a big spider that had been running about all over me tying me up in his web. And as if I was a fly and couldn't get out. There is something spidery about him, you know. The way he goes back and forth and the way he's so patient and indirect about it all. It seemed like the end of the world to me before he finished, as if I never was going to see John again. Oh, I cried my eyes out. Well, and then about an hour ago I came to. I realized that I hadn't signed his horrible contract and that I needn't. And that when this beastly season was over,—and it isn't going to last much longer, thank goodness,—I could go home to John and lock up the piano and never look at a score again. It was like coming out of a nightmare."

Mary dared not stop to think. She took the plunge.

"There's something about father you've got to be told. I promised Wallace Hood weeks ago that I'd tell you. I guess he and Martin Whitney think you know about it by now."

"Something I've got to be told about John?" Paula echoed incredulously. "Why, I was talking with him over the telephone not ten minutes before you came in."

"Oh, I know. It's nothing like that," Mary said. "But they say he has tuberculosis. Not desperately, not so that he can't get well if he takes care of it. If he lives out-of-doors and doesn't worry or try to work. But if he takes up his practise again this fall, they say,—Doctor Steinmetz says,—that it will be—committing suicide. That's one thing. And the other is that he's practically bankrupt. Anyhow, that for a year or two, until he can get back into practise, he'll need help. That's why Wallace and Mr. Whitney wanted you told about it."

There hadn't been a movement nor a sound from Paula. Mary, at the end of that speech was breathless and rather frightened.

Finally Paula asked, "Does he know about it?—his health I mean."

"He's been told," Mary answered, "but he doesn't believe it. They nearly always are skeptical, Doctor Steinmetz says."

"He's probably right to be. He's a better doctor than six of Steinmetz will ever be."

Another pause; then, once more from Paula, "Did he tell you about the other thing,—about his money troubles,—when you were down in North Carolina with him?"

Mary flushed at the hostile ring there was to that. "He told me a little," she said, "but not much more, I thought, than he had already told you."

"Told me?" Paula swung herself off the bed and on to her feet in one movement. "He told me nothing."

"He urged you to carry out your Ravinia contract, didn't he?" Mary asked, as steadily as she could.

Paula stood over her staring. "Oh," she exclaimed, and, a moment later she repeated the ejaculation in a drier tone and with a downward inflection. She added presently, "I'm not clever the way you are at taking hints. That's the thing it will be just as well for you both to remember." She began bruskly putting on her dressing-gown. "I'm going down-stairs to telephone to Max," she explained. "He's got the paper all drawn up, not the final contract but an agreement to sign one of the sort I told you about. I'm going to tell him that if he will bring it back with him now, I'll sign it."

Mary stood between her and the door. "Don't you think it would be—fairer to wait?" she asked; "before you signed a thing like that. Until at least, you were no longer angry with me for having told you too much or with father because he had told you too little."

Paula pulled up at that and stood looking at her stepdaughter with a thoughtful expression that was almost a smile. "I am angry," she admitted, "or I was, and just exactly about that. It's queer the way you Wollastons, you and your father, anyhow, are always—getting through to things like that. What you say is fair enough. I guess you're always fair. Can't help being, somehow. But I can't put off telephoning to Max. You see I called up John at Hickory Hill an hour ago. I told him I had made up my mind to stop singing. I told him I didn't want any career. That I just wanted to—belong to him. And I asked him to come to me as fast as he could. He's on the way now. So it's important, you see, that Max should get here first."

# CHAPTER XX
# TWO WOMEN AND JOHN

Paula seemed calm enough after that one explosion but she moved along toward the accomplishment of her purpose, to get herself thoroughly committed to Max before John's arrival, with the momentum of a liner leaving its pier. Mary made two or three more attempts at dissuasion but their manifest futility kept her from getting any real power into them. She was, to tell the truth, in a panic over the prospect of that evening;—her father arriving triumphant in Paula's supposed surrender to find Maxfield Ware with his five years' contract in his pocket. And the responsibility for the disaster would be attributed to herself; was indeed so attributable with a kind of theatrical completeness seldom, to be found in life. It didn't often happen that any one was as entirely to blame for a calamity to some one else as Mary was for this *volte-face* of Paula's.

She did not run away altogether. Paula, indeed, didn't know that she had fled at all, for Maxfield Ware's tardiness about coming back the second time supplied her with a pretext.

It was nearly eight o'clock before he came and Paula, who was momentarily expecting John's arrival by then, was in an agony of impatience to sign his papers and get him out of the house again. Ware may have divined her wish and loitered out of mischievous curiosity as to the cause of it. Or he may, merely, have been prolonging an experience which he found agreeable. Anyhow, he wouldn't be hurried and he wouldn't go. But Paula finally turned a look of despairing appeal upon Mary who thereupon announced her intention of going to to-night's performance in the park. She would drive, of course, and would be glad to take Mr. Ware along. Or, for that matter, she would set him down first wherever he might want to go. He smiled upon her with the fatuous smile of one who finds he has made an unexpected conquest and said he would be delighted to accompany Miss Wollaston anywhere.

She took him, driving pretty fast, to the Moraine Hotel and was glad the distance was not greater, for after various heavy-handed and unquenchable preliminaries he kissed her as nearly on the mouth as possible, clinging to a half-lit cigar the while, just before she whipped around into the hotel drive. She avoided a collision with one of the stone posts narrowly enough to startle him into releasing her,—he hadn't realized the turn was so close— and stopped at the lighted carriage door with a jerk that left him no option but to get out at once.

She nodded a curt good night and drove back to the park; went to one of the dressing-rooms and washed her face. Then she came around in front to hear Edith Mason sing *Romeo and Juliet*. She didn't get just the effect she anticipated from this lovely performance because Polacco, who is Miss Mason's husband, came and sat down beside her—there was nothing spidery about him, thank goodness—and in a running and vivacious commentary expressed his lively contempt for this opera of Gounod's. At its best it was bad *Faust*. Its least intolerable melodies were quotations from *Faust*,—an assertion which he proved from time to time by singing, and not very softly either, the original themes to the wrath of all who sat within a twenty-five foot radius of them.

Mary felt grateful to him for giving her something that was not maddening to think about and after the performance went with him and his wife to supper so that it was well after midnight before she returned to the cottage.

It was an ineffable relief to find it dark. Her habit on warm nights was to sleep on the gloucester swing in the screened veranda and she made it her bed to-night, though beyond a short uneasy doze of two, she didn't sleep at all.

At half past eight or so, just after she had sat down to breakfast, she heard her father coming down the stairs. She tried to call to him but could command no voice and so waited, frozen, until he appeared in the doorway.

"I thought I heard you stirring down here and that it perhaps meant breakfast. Paula won't be down, I suppose, for hours. She fell asleep about four o'clock and has been sleeping quietly ever since."

This was exactly like Paula, of course. She was the vortex of the whole tempest, but when she had thoroughly exhausted the emotional possibilities of it she sank into peaceful slumber like a baby after a hard cry.

No wonder she was too much for these two Wollastons who sat now with dry throats and tremulous hands over the mockery of breakfast! Mary, although she knew, asked her father whether he wanted his coffee clear or with cream in it and having thus broken the spell, went on with a gasp:

"I'm glad Paula isn't coming down. It gives you a better chance to tell me just how you feel about my having interfered. I did run away last night.

You guessed that, I suppose. But it wasn't to evade it altogether. My— whipping, you know."

It had an odd effect on both of them, this reference to her childhood; her hand moved round the table rim and covered his which rested on the edge of it.

"Did your mother ever punish you?" he asked. "Corporeally? It's my recollection that she did not. I was always the executioner. I doubt now if that was quite fair."

"Perhaps not," she asserted dubiously. "In general it isn't fair of course. It probably wasn't in the case of Rush. But with me,—I don't think I could have borne it to have mother beat me. It would have seemed an insufferable affront. I'd have hated her for it. But there was a sort of satisfaction in having you do it."

After another moment of silence she smiled and added, "I suppose a Freudian would carry off an admission like that to his cave and gnaw over it for hours."

He stared at her, shocked, incredulous. "What do you know about Freud?" he demanded.

"One couldn't live for two years within a hundred yards of Washington Square without knowing at least as much about it as that," she told him,— and was glad of the entrance of the maid with another installment of the breakfast. There was no more talk between them during the meal. But at the end of it she faced him resolutely.

"We must have this out, dad. And isn't now as good a time as any?"

He followed her out into the veranda but the sounds from the dining-room, where the maid had come in to clear away the breakfast, disturbed him so Mary suggested a walk.

"Get your hat and we'll go over to the lake. I know a nice place not far, an open field right at the edge of the bluff with one big tree to make it shady. At this hour of the morning we are sure to have it all to ourselves."

He said as they walked along, "I've no reproaches for you. Not this morning. I've thought over a lot of ground since four o'clock."

He said nothing more to the point until they reached the spot which Mary had selected as their destination—it lived up handsomely to all her promises—and settled themselves under the shade of the big tree.

"I suppose," he added then, "that I ought to forgive Whitney and Hood. Their intentions were the best and kindest, of course. But I find that harder to do."

He sat back against the trunk of the tree, facing out over the lake; she disposed herself cross-legged on the grass near by just within reaching distance. She offered him her cigarette case but he declined. Of late years, since his marriage to Paula, he had smoked very little. As a substitute, now, he picked up a forked bit of branch, and began whittling it.

"I'm as much to blame as they are," she said, presently. "More, really. Because, if I hadn't procrastinated-o-ut of cowardice, mostly,—until yesterday, when she was half-way over the edge, it might never have come to Maxfield Ware at all. After the situation had dramatized itself like that, there was only one thing she could do. Of course, they didn't foresee that five years' contract, any more than I did."

He nodded assent, though rather absently to this. "I'm not much interested in the abstract ethics of it," he said. "It's disputable, of course, how far any one can be justified in making a major interference in another's life; one that deprives him of the power of choice. That's what you have done to me—the three of you. If the premises are right, and the outcome prosperous, there's something to be said for it. But in this case ..."

"They aren't mistaken, are they, dad? Wallace and Mr. Whitney?—Or Doctor Steinmetz?"

"Why, it's reasonable to suppose that Whitney understands my financial condition better than I do. I mean that. It's not a sneer. But what he and Hood don't allow for is that I've never tried to make money. They've no idea what my earning power would be if I were to turn to and make that a prime consideration. A year of it would take me out of the woods, I think."

She waited, breathless, for him to deal with the third name. She was pretty well at one with Paula in the relative valuation she put upon her father's opinion and that of the throat and lung specialist.

"Oh, as for Steinmetz," John Wollaston said, after a pause, querulously, "he's a good observer. There's nothing to be said against him as a laboratory man. But he has the vice of all German scientists; he doesn't understand imponderables. Never a flash of intuition about him. He managed to intimidate Darby into agreeing with him. Neither of them takes my recuperative powers into account."

He seemed to feel that this wasn't a very strong line to take and the next moment he conceded as much.

"But suppose they were right," he flashed round at her. "Am I not still entitled to my choice? I've lived the greater part of my life. I've pulled my weight in the boat. It should be for me to choose whether I spend the life I have left in two years or in twenty. If they want to call that suicide, let them. I've no religion that's real enough to make a valid argument against my right to extinguish myself if I choose."

She wasn't shocked. It was characteristic of their talks together, this free range among ethical abstractions, especially on his part.

"You act on the other theory though," she pointed out to him. "Think of the people you've patched together just so that they can live at most another wretched year or two."

"That's a different thing," he said. "Or rather it comes to the same thing. The question of shortening one's life is one that nobody has a right to decide except for himself."

Then he asked abruptly. "What sort of person is Maxfield Ware?"

She attempted no palliations here.

"He kissed me last night," she said, "taking his cigar out of his mouth for the purpose. He's not a sort of person I can endure or manage. Paula hates him as much as I do, but she can manage him. He'd never try to kiss her like that."

"Oh, God!" cried John. "It's intolerable." He flung away his stick, got to his feet and walked to the edge of the bluff. "Think of her working, traveling,—living almost,—with a man like that! You say she can manage him; that she can prevent him from trying to make love to her. Well, what does that mean, if you're right, but that she—understands him; his talk; his ideas; his point of view. You can't make yourself intelligible to a man like that; she can. It's defilement to meet his mind anywhere—any angle of it. She's given him carte blanche, she says, to manage the publicity for her. Do you realize what that means? He's licensed to try to make the public believe anything that he thinks would heighten their interest in her. That she dresses indecently; that she's a frivolous extravagant fool; that she has lovers. You know how that game is played."

Mary did know. She ran over a list of the great names and opposite every one of them there sprang into her mind the particular bit of vulgar réclame that had been in its day some press agent's masterpiece. She was able further to see that Paula would regard the moves of this game with a large-minded tolerance which would be incomprehensible to John. After all, that was the way to take it. If you were a real luminary, not just a blank white surface, all the mud that Mr. Maxfield Ware could splash wouldn't matter. You burnt it off. None of those great names was soiled.

She tried to say something like this to her father, but didn't feel sure that she quite had his attention. He did quiet down again however and resumed his seat at the foot of the tree. Presently he said:

"She's doing it for me. Because my incompetence has forced it upon her. She'd have taken the other thing; had really chosen it." Then without a pause, but with a new intensity he shot in a question. "That's true, isn't it? She meant what she said over the telephone?" As Mary hesitated over her answer he added rather grimly, "You can be quite candid about it. I don't know which answer I want."

"She meant every word she said over the telephone," Mary assured him. "You couldn't doubt that if you had seen her as I did afterward."

She didn't pretend though that this was the complete answer. The reflective tone in which she spoke made it clear that there was more to it than that.

"Go on," John said, "tell me the rest of it. I think, perhaps, you understand her better than I do."

Mary took her time about going on and she began a little doubtfully. "I always begin by being unjust to Paula," she said. "That's my instinct, I suppose, reproaching her for not doing what she would do if she were like me. But afterward when I think her out, I believe I understand her pretty well."

"Paula exaggerates," she went on after another reflective pause. "She must see things large in order to move among them in a large way. Her gestures, those of her mind I mean, are—sweeping. If she weren't so good-natured, our—hair-splitting ways would annoy her. Then it's necessary for her to feel that she's—conquering something."

That last word was barely audible and the quality of the silence which followed it drew John Wollaston's gaze which had been straying over the lake, around to the speaker. She had been occupying her hands while she talked, collecting tiny twigs and acorn cups that happened to be within reach but now she was tensely still and paler than her wont, he thought.

"You needn't be afraid to say what's in your mind," he assured her.

"It wasn't that," she told him. "I realized that I had been quoting somebody else. Anthony March said once of Paula that if she had not been an artist she might have been a *dompteuse*."

John settled himself more comfortably against his tree trunk. A contact like this with his daughter's mind must have been inexpressibly comforting to him after a night like the one he had just spent. Its rectitude;

its sensitiveness; the mere feel and texture of it, put his jangling nerves in tune.

"Is Ware the wild beast she has an inclination to tame in this instance?" he asked.

"He's nothing but a symbol of it," Mary said. Then she managed to get the thing a little clearer. "What she'd have done if she'd been like us and what we'd have had her do—Mr. Whitney and Wallace and I,—would have been to make a sort of compromise between her position as your wife and a career as Paula Carresford. We'd have had her sign a contract to sing a few times this winter with the Metropolitan or the Chicago company, go on a concert tour perhaps for a few weeks, even give singing lessons or sing in a church choir. That would probably have been Mr. Whitney's idea. Rather more than enough to pay her way and at the same time leave as much of her to you as possible.

"But that's the last thing in the world it would be possible for Paula to do. She must see a great career on one side,—see herself as Geraldine Farrar's successor,—and on the other side she must see a perfect unflawed life with you. So that whichever she chooses she will have a sense of making the greatest possible sacrifice. She couldn't have said to you what she did over the telephone if Mr. Ware hadn't convinced her that a great career was open to her and she couldn't have signed his contract if it had not involved sacrificing you."

She propped herself back against her hands with a sigh of fatigue. "There's some of the hair-splitting Paula talks about," she observed.

"It may be fine spun," her father said thoughtfully, "but it seems to me to hold together. Isn't there any more of it?"

"Well, it was balanced like that, you see," Mary went on; "set for the climax, like the springs in a French play, when I came along at just the moment and with just the word, to topple it over. Being Paula, she couldn't help doing exactly what she did. So, however it comes out, I shall be the one person she won't be able to forgive."

She knew from the startled look he turned upon her that this last shot had come uncannily close. She fancied she must almost literally have echoed Paula's words. If she needed any further confirmation she would have found it in the rather panicky way in which he set about trying to convince her that she was mistaken, if not in the fact at least in the permanence of it.

She insisted no further, made indeed no further attempt at all to carry the theme along and though she listened and made appropriate replies when they were called for, she let her wordless thought drift away to a dream that it was Anthony March who shared this shade and sunshine with her and that veiled blue horizon yonder. It was easier to do since her father had drifted into a reverie of his own. They need not have lingered for they had sufficiently talked away all possible grounds of misunderstanding, even if they had not reconciled their disagreement.

It occurred to her to suggest that they go back, but she dismissed the impulse with no more than a glancing thought. It was his burden, not hers, that remained to be shouldered at the cottage and it might be left to him to choose his own time for taking it up. Paula seldom came down much before noon anyhow.

As for John Wollaston, he was very tired. Paula's volcanic moments always exhausted him. He never could derationalize his emotions, cut himself free; and while he felt just as intensely as she did, he had to carry the whole superstructure of himself along on those tempestuous voyages. In the mood Paula had left him in this morning, there was nothing in the world that could have satisfied and restored him as did his daughter's companionship. The peace of this wordless prolongation of their talk together was something he lacked, for a long while, the will to break.

It was not far short of noon when they came back into the veranda together. He had walked the last hundred yards, after a look at his watch, pretty fast and after a glance into both the down-stairs rooms, he called up-stairs to his wife in a voice that had an edge of sudden anxiety in it. Then getting no response, he went up, two at a time.

Mary dropped down, limp with a sudden premonition, upon the gloucester swing in the veranda. The maid of all work, who had heard his call, came from the kitchen just as he was returning down the stairs. Mrs. Wollaston had gone away, she said. Pete had reported with the big car at eleven o'clock and Paula, who apparently had been waiting for him, had driven off at once having left word that she would not be back for lunch.

"All right," John said curtly. "You may go."

He was so white when he rejoined Mary in the veranda that she sprang up with an involuntary cry and would have had him lie down, where she had been sitting. But the fine steely ring in his voice stopped her short.

"Have you any idea," he asked, "where she has gone or what she has gone to do? She came down," he went on without waiting for her answer,— "and looked for me. Waited for me. And thanks to that—walk we took, I wasn't here. Well, can you guess what she's done?"

"It's only a guess," Mary said, "but she may have gone to see Martin Whitney."

"Martin Whitney?" he echoed blankly. "What for? What does she want of him?"

"She spoke of him," Mary said, "in connection with the money, the twenty thousand dollars..."

He broke in upon her again with a mere blank frantic echo of her words and once more Mary steadied herself to explain.

"Her agreement with Mr. Ware required her to put up twenty thousand dollars in some banker's hands as a guarantee that she would not break the contract. She mentioned Martin Whitney as the natural person to hold it. So I guessed that she might have gone to consult him about it;—or even to ask him to lend it to her. As she said, it wouldn't have to be spent."

"That's the essence of the contract then. It's nothing without that. Until she gets the money and puts it up. Yet you told me nothing of it until this moment. If you had done so—instead of inviting me to go for a walk—and giving her a chance to get away..."

He couldn't be allowed to go on. "Do you mean that you think I did that—for the purpose?" she asked steadily.

He flushed and turned away. "No, of course I don't. I'm half mad over this."

He walked abruptly into the house and a moment later she heard him at the telephone. She stayed where she was, unable to think; stunned rather than hurt over the way he had sprung upon her.

He seemed a little quieter when he came out a few minutes later. "Whitney left half an hour ago for Lake Geneva," he said. "So she's missed him if that's where she went. There's nothing to do but wait."

He was very nervous however. Whenever the telephone rang, as it did of course pretty often, he answered it himself, and each time his disappointment that it was not Paula asking for him, broke down more or less the calm he tried to impose upon himself. He essayed what amends good manners enabled him to make to Mary for his outrageous attack upon her. It went no deeper than that. The discovery that Paula was gone and simultaneously that he need not have lost her obliterated—or rather reversed—the morning's mood completely.

It was after lunch that he said, dryly, "I upset your life for you, half a dozen years ago. Unfairly. Inexcusably. I've always been ashamed of it. But it lends a sort of poetic justice to this."

She made no immediate reply, but not long afterward she asked if she might not go away without waiting for Paula's return. "It would be too difficult, don't you think?—for the three of us, in a small house like this."

He agreed with manifest relief. He asked if it was not too late to drive that afternoon to Hickory Hill, but she said she'd prefer to go by train anyhow. That was possible she thought.

He did not ask, in so many words, if this was where she meant to go. There was no other place for her that he could think of.

# CHAPTER XXI
# THE SUBSTITUTE

It was a good guess of Mary's that Paula had gone to borrow the twenty thousand dollars but it was to Wallace Hood, not to Martin Whitney, that she went for it; and thereby illustrated once more how much more effective instinct is than intelligence.

Martin, rich and generous as he was, originator as he was of the edict that Paula must go to work, would never have been stampeded as Wallace was in a talk that lasted less than half an hour, into producing securities to the amount that Paula needed and offering them up in escrow for the life of Maxfield Ware's contract.

Wallace was only moderately well off and he was by nature, cautious. His investments were always of the most conservative sort. This from habit as well as nature because his job — the only one he had ever had — was that of estate agent. But Paula's instinct told her that he wouldn't find it possible to refuse. I think it told her too, though this was a voice that did not make itself fairly heard to her conscious ear, that he would be made very fluttered and unhappy by it whether he granted her request or not.

What he would hate, she perceived, was the suddenness of the demand and the irrevocable committal to those five years; the blow it was to those domesticities and proprieties he loved so much. The fact that he would be made sponsor for those unchartered excursions to Mexico, to South America, and so on, under the direction of a libidinous looking cosmopolite like Maxfield Ware.

Why she wanted to put Wallace into the flutters she couldn't have told. She was, as I say, not quite aware that she did. But he had been running up a score in very minute items that was all of five years old. The fact that all these items went by the name of services, helpful little acts of kindness, made the irritation they caused her all the more acute.

I don't agree with Lucile Wollaston's diagnosis, that Paula could not abide Wallace merely because he refused to lose his head over her, but there was a grain of truth in it. What she unconsciously resented was the fundamental unreality of his attitude to her. Actually, he did not like her, but the relation he had selected as appropriate to the first Mrs. Wollaston's successor was one of innocent devotion and he stuck, indefatigably, to the pose. So the chance to put his serviceability to the proof in consternating circumstances like these, afforded her a subtle satisfaction. He'd brought it upon himself, hadn't he? At least it was he and no other who had put Mary up to the part she had played.

None of this, of course, came to the surface at all in the scene between them. She was gentler than was her wont with him, very appealing, subdued nearer to his own scale of manners than he had ever seen her before. But she did not, for a fact, allow him much time to think.

He asked her, with a touch of embarrassment, whether John was fully in her confidence concerning this startling project, and if she had won his assent to it.

"He knows all about it," she said—and with no consciousness of a *suppressio veri* here. "We hardly talked of anything else all last night. I didn't get to sleep till four. He doesn't like it, but then you couldn't expect he would. For that matter neither do I. Oh, you don't know how I hate it! But I think he sees it has to be. Anyhow, he didn't try very hard to keep me from going on with it—And Mary, of course, is perfectly satisfied."

Even his not very alert ear caught something equivocal in those last sentences, and he looked at her sharply.

"Oh, I'm worn to ribbons over it!" she exclaimed, and this touch of apology served for the tearing edge there had been in her voice. "I couldn't let him see how I feel about it. It would be a sort of relief to have it settled. That's why I came straight to you to-day."

He tried, but rather feebly, to temporize. We mustn't let haste drive us farther than we really wanted to go. The matter of drawing the formal contract, for instance, must be attended with all possible legal safe-guards, especially when we were dealing with a person whose honor was perhaps dubitable.

"I thought we might go round to see Rodney Aldrich about it, now," she said. "He's about the best there is in that line, isn't he? Why don't you telephone to his office and find out if he's there."

This seemed as good a straw as any to clutch at. The chance of catching as busy a man as Aldrich with a leisure half hour was very slim. The recording angel who guarded his wicket gate would probably give them an appointment for some day next week, and this would leave time for a confirmatory talk with John. But, unluckily, Rodney was there and would be glad to see Mrs. Wollaston as soon as she could be brought round.

"Then, that's all right," Paula said with a sigh of relief. "So if you really believe I'll keep my word and don't mind putting up the money for me, it's as good as settled."

There was one more question on his tongue. "Does John know that you have come to me for it?" But this, somehow, he could not force himself to ask. Implicitly she had already answered it—hadn't she?

"Of course I believe, in you, in everything, my dear Paula. And I'm very much—touched, that you should have come to me. And my only hope is that it may turn out to have been altogether for the best."

And there was that.

It was not until late that night that his misgivings as to the part Mary might have played in this drama really awoke, but when they did he marveled that they had not occurred to him earlier. He recalled that Mary had prophesied during their talk at the Saddle and Cycle that Paula would attribute to her the suggestion—whoever might make it—that an operatic career for John's wife was desirable and necessary for financial reasons. She had said too, in that serious measured way of hers, "If Paula ever saw me coming between her and father, whether it was my doing or not, she would hate me with her whole heart."

Had that prediction been justified? There were half a dozen phrases that Paula had allowed herself to use this afternoon, which added up to a reasonable certainty that it was altogether justified. It was not easy for him to admit to himself that he didn't like Paula; that he knew her and had long known her for a person incapable of following any lead save that of her own primitive straightforward desires.

His self-communings reached down deeper into him than they had done for many a long year. He convicted himself, before his vigil was over, of flagrant cowardice in having allowed Mary to undertake the burden of that revelation. What harm would it have done any one, even himself, beyond an hour's discomfort, to have drawn down Paula's lightnings on his own head? Her enmity, even though it were permanent, could not seriously have changed the tenor of his ways.

But to Mary, such a thing could easily be a first-class disaster. Could John be relied upon to come whole-heartedly to her defense. No, he could not. Indeed—this was the thought that made Wallace gasp as from a dash of cold water in the face—John's anger at this interference with his affairs and at the innocent agent of it was likely to be as hot as his wife's. Momentarily anyhow. What a perfectly horrible situation to have forced the girl into;—that fragile sensitive young thing!

And now above all other times, when, for some reason not fully known to him, she was finding her own life an almost impossibly difficult thing to manage. He remembered the day she had come back from New York; how she had flushed and gone pale and asked him in a moment of suddenly tense emotion if he couldn't find her a job. It had been that very night, hadn't it?—when Paula had given that recital of Anthony March's songs—that she had disappeared out of the midst of things and never come back during the whole evening. When one considered her courage a flight like that told a good deal.

Then there had been that something a little short of an engagement with Graham Stannard, which must have distressed her horribly;—any one with a spirit as candid as hers and with as honest a hatred of all that was equivocal. The family had seemed to think that it would all come out right in the end somehow, yet the last time she had talked with him she had said, cutting straight through the disguise his thought had hidden itself behind, "I know I can't ever marry Graham."

And it was a young girl harassed with perplexities like these, whom he had permitted in his stead to beard the lioness. Well, if there was anything in the world, any conceivable thing, that he could do to repair the consequences of his fault, he would do it. If that lovers' misunderstanding with Graham could, after all, be cleared away it would be the happy, the completely desirable solution of the problem. But if it could not ... A day-dream that it was he who stood in Graham Stannard's shoes, offering her harbor and rest and a life-long loyalty, formed the bridge over which he finally fell asleep.

She called him to the telephone the next morning while he was at breakfast; just to tell him she was in town, she said, and to ask him if he had heard anything from his sister in Omaha as to whether she wanted a nursery governess. He had to admit, of course, that he had not even written to her, and felt guiltier and more miserable than ever.

"Do write to-day, though, won't you?" she urged. "And give me the best character you can. Because I am going to get some sort of job just as soon as possible."

In reply to the inarticulate noise of protest he made at this she went on, "Our family has simply exploded. I fled for my life last night. So you see I'm really in earnest about going to work now."

"I want to come and see you at once," he said. "Where are you?"

"At home," she answered, "but I'm going out this minute for the day. If you'd like a picnic tea here at half past five, though, come and I'll tell you what I've been doing."

He asked if this meant that she was staying all by herself in the Dearborn Avenue house without even a servant, and at his lively horror over this she laughed with an amusement which sounded genuine enough to reassure him somewhat. She ended the conversation by telling him that she had left her father with the impression that she was going straight to Hickory Hill. She was writing Aunt Lucile a note saying she meant to stay in town for a few days. "But if you get any frantic telephone calls in the meantime, tell them I'm all right."

He wondered a good deal, as his hours marched past in their accustomed uneventful manner, what she could be doing with hers. It was an odd locution for her to have employed that she was "going out for the day." He couldn't square it with any sort of social activity. The thing that kept plaguing his mind despite his impatient attempts to dismiss it as nonsense, was the possibility that she was actually looking for that job she'd talked about. Answering advertisements!

Toward four, when he had stopped trying to do anything but wait for his appointment with her, Rush and Graham came in, precipitately, and asked for a private talk with him. He took them into his inner office, relieved a little at the arrival of reenforcements but disappointed too.

"If you're anxious about Mary," he began by saying, "I can assure you that she is all right. She's at the Dearborn Avenue house, or was last night and will be again later this afternoon. I talked to her on the phone this morning."

"Thank God!" said Rush.

Graham dropped into a chair with a gesture of relief even more expressive.

Rush explained the cause of their alarm. Old Pete had driven in to Hickory Hill around two o'clock with a letter, addressed to Mary, from Paula, and on being asked to explain offered the disquieting information that she had left Ravinia for the farm, the afternoon before. They had driven straight to town and to Wallace as the likeliest source of information.

In the emotional back-lash from his profound disquiet about his sister, suddenly reassured that there was nothing—well, tragic to be apprehended, Rush allowed himself an outburst of brotherly indignation. He'd like to know what the devil Mary meant by giving them a fright like that. Why hadn't she telephoned last night? Nothing was easier than that. Or more to the point still, why hadn't she come straight out to the farm as she had told her father she meant to do, instead of spending the night in town?

Wallace would have let him go on, since it gave him a little time he wanted for deciding what line to take. But Graham, it seemed, couldn't stand it.

"Shut up, Rush!" he commanded. (You are to remember that he was three years his partner's senior.) "Mary never did an—inconsiderate thing in her life. If she seems to have forgotten about us, you can be dead sure there's a reason."

"I agree with Stannard," Wallace put in, "that she wants to be dealt with—gently. She must have been having a rather rotten time."

He hadn't yet made up his mind how far to take them into his confidence as to what he knew and guessed, but Rush made an end of his hesitation.

"Tell us, for heaven's sake, what it's all about.—Oh, you needn't mind Graham. He's as much in it as any of us. I suppose you know how he stands."

Wallace was conscious of an acute wish that they had not turned up until he'd had a chance to see Mary, but somehow he felt he couldn't go behind an assurance like that. So he told them what he had pieced together.

Rush grunted and blushed and said he'd be damned, but it was not a theme—this contention between his father and his stepmother—that he could dwell upon. He got hold at last of something that he could be articulate about, and demanded to know why, in these circumstances, Mary hadn't come straight to them at Hickory Hill instead of camping out, for the night, all by herself in the Dearborn Avenue house.

"She has an idea she must find a job for herself," Wallace said, feeling awkwardly guilty as if he had betrayed her; but the way Rush leaped upon him, demanding in one breath what the deuce he meant and what sort of job he was talking about, made it impossible to pull up.

He recounted the request Mary had made of him, concerning his sister in Omaha, and, last of all, stated his own misgiving—nothing but the merest guess of course—that she had been putting in this day answering advertisements. "She said she'd give me a picnic tea at five-thirty and tell me what she'd been doing."

"Well, it'll be no picnic for her," Rush exploded angrily. "I'll see her at five-thirty myself. She must be plumb out of her head if she thinks she'll be allowed to do a thing like that."

Once more, before Wallace could speak, it was Graham who intervened. "I want you to leave this to me," he said gravely. "I don't know whether I can settle it or not, but I'd like to try." He turned to Wallace. "Would you mind, sir, letting me go to tea with her at half past five in your place?"

It is possible that, but for Wallace's day-dream of himself offering Mary the shelter and the care she so obviously needed, he might have persisted in seeing her first and assuring her that he was to be regarded as an ally whatever she decided to do. Her voice as she had said, "I know I can never marry Graham" echoed forlornly in his mind's ear. But a doubt faint and vague as it was, of his own disinterestedness held him back. Graham was young; he was in love with her. That gave him right of way, didn't it?

So he assented. It was agreed that Rush should dine with Wallace at his apartment. Graham, if he had any news for them should communicate it by telephone. Instantly!

# CHAPTER XXII
# THE FUNDAMENTAL DIFFERENCE

The instinct to conceal certain moods of depression and distress together with the histrionic power to make the concealment possible may be a serious peril to a woman of Mary Wollaston's temperament. She had managed at the telephone that morning to deceive Wallace pretty completely. Even her laugh had failed to give her away.

She was altogether too near for safety to the point of exhaustion. She had endured her second night without sleep. She had not really eaten an adequate meal since her lunch in town the day Paula had engineered her out of the way for that talk with Maxfield Ware.

There was nothing morbid in her resolution to find, at the earliest possible moment, some way of making herself independent of her father's support. Having pointed out Paula's duty as a bread winner she could not neglect her own, however dreary the method might be, or humble the results. In any mood, of course, the setting out in search of employment would have been painful and little short of terrifying to one brought up the way Mary had been.

A night's sleep though and a proper breakfast would have kept the thing from being a nightmare. As it was, she felt, setting out with her clipping from the help-wanted columns of a morning paper, a good deal like the sole survivor of some shipwreck, washed up upon an unknown coast, venturing inland to discover whether the inhabitants were cannibals. Even the constellations in her sky were strange.

Where, then, was Anthony March? Nowhere above her horizon, to-day at all events. The memory of him had been with her much of the two last sleepless nights. She had told over the tale of her moments with him again and again. (Did any one, she might have wondered, ever love as deeply with so small a treasury of golden hours for memory to draw upon?) But she could not, somehow, relate him at all to her present or her future. Her love for him was an out-going rather than an in-coming thing. At least, her thoughts had put the emphasis upon that side of it; upon the longing to comfort and protect him, to be the satisfaction to all his wants. Not—passionately not—to cling heavily about his neck, drag at his feet, steal his wayfarer's liberty,—no, not the smallest moment of it! This present helplessness of hers then, which heightened her need for him, served also to bolt the doors of her thoughts against him.

Her recollection of the next few hours, though it contained some vignettes so sharp and deeply bitten in as to be, she fancied, ineffaceable, was in the main confused. She must have called upon ten or a dozen advertisers in various suburban districts of the city (she avoided addresses that were too near home and names where she suspected hers might be known). Her composite impression was of flat thin voices which she could imagine in excitement becoming shrill; of curious appraising stares; of a vast amount of garrulous irrelevancy; of a note of injury that one who could profess so little equipment beyond good will should so disappoint the expectation her first appearance had aroused. The background was a room—it seemed to have been in every case the same—expensively overfurnished, inexpressive, ill-fitting its uses, like a badly chosen ready-made coat. The day was not without its humors, or what would have been humors if her spirit could have rebounded to them. Chiefly, the violent antagonism she found aroused in two or three cases by the color of her hair.

The residuum of her pilgrimages was three addresses where she might call about the middle of next week, in person or by telephone, to learn the advertiser's decision. Well it would convince Wallace Hood that she was in earnest. That was something.

Wallace's coming to tea became, as the day wore on, more and more something to look forward to. All the things about him which in more resilient hours she had found irritating or absurd, his neutrality, his appropriateness, his steady unimaginative way of going always one step at a time, seemed now precisely his greatest merits. The thought of tea in his company even aroused a faint appetite for food in her and lent zest to her preparations for it. When she stopped at the neighborhood caterer's shop for supplies she bought some tea cakes in addition to the sandwiches she had ordered in the morning. She had managed to get home in good enough season to restore the drawing-room somewhat to its inhabited appearance, to set out her tea table, put on her kettle, and then go up-stairs and change her dress for something that was not wilted by the day's unusual heat. She was ready then to present before Wallace an *ensemble* which should match pretty well her tone at the telephone this morning.

But when she answered the ring she supposed was his and flinging open the door saw Graham Stannard there instead, she got a jarring shock which her overstrung nerves were in no condition to endure.

"I persuaded Mr. Hood to let me come to tea in his place," he said. "It was rather cheeky of me to ask him, I'm afraid. I hope you will forgive me."

The arrest of all her processes of thought at sight of him lasted only the barest instant. Then her mind flashed backward through a surmise which embraced the whole series of events. An alarm at Hickory Hill over her failure to arrive (which somehow they had been led to expect), a dash by Graham (Rush not available, perhaps), into town for news. To Wallace Hood, of course. And Wallace had betrayed her. In the interest of romantic sentiment. The happy ending given its chance. A rich young adoring husband instead of a job as nursery governess in Omaha!

It took no longer for all that to go through her mind than Graham needed for his little explanatory speech on the door-step. There he stood waiting for her answer. The only choice she had was between shutting the door in his face without a word, or graciously inviting him to come in and propose to her—for the last time, at all events. It was not, of course, a choice at all.

"I'm afraid it's a terribly hot day for tea," she said, moving back from the doorway to make room for him to come in. "Wallace likes it, though. I might make you something cold if only I had ice, but of course there isn't any in the house. It's nice and cool, though, isn't it; from having been shut up so long?"

Anything,—any frantic thing that could be spun into words to cover the fact that she had no welcome for him at all, not even the most wan little beam of friendly tenderness. She had seen the hurt look come into his eyes, incipient panic at the flash of anger which had not been meant for him. She must float him inside, somehow, and anchor him to the tea table. There she could get herself together and deal with him—decently.

He came along, tractably enough, sat in the chair that was to have been Wallace's, and talked for a while of the tea, and how hot it was this afternoon, and how beautifully cool in here. It was hot, too, out at Hickory Hill but one thought little of it. The air was drier for one thing. He and Rush had commented on the difference as they drove in to-day.

"Oh, Rush came in with you, did he?" she observed.

He flushed and stammered over the admission and it was easy to guess why. The fact that her brother, as well as Wallace, was lurking in the background somewhere waiting for results gave an official cast to his call that was rather—asinine. She came to the rescue.

"I suppose he and Wallace had something they wanted to talk about," she commented easily, and he made haste to assent.

She steadied herself with a breath. "Did Wallace tell you," she asked, "about our explosion at Ravinia over Paula's new contract? And how furious both father and Paula are with me about it? And how I'm out looking for a job? He didn't say anything about his sister, did he; whether he'd written to her to-day or not?"

"Not whether he'd written. But he told us the rest. How you wanted to go to work. As a nursery governess."

He paused there but she did not break in upon it. She had given him all the lead he needed. With the deliberate care that a suddenly tremulous hand made necessary he put down his teacup and spoke as if addressing it.

"I think you're the bravest—most wonderful person in the world. Of course, I've known that always. Not just since I came back last spring. But this, that Mr. Hood told us this afternoon, somehow—caps the climax. I can't tell you how it—got me, to think of your being ready to do—a thing like that."

The last thing she would have done voluntarily was to put any obstacles in his way. Her program, on the contrary was to help him along all she could to his declaration, make a refusal that should be as gentle as was consistent with complete finality, and then get rid of him before anything regrettably—messy ensued. But to have her courage rhapsodized over like this was a thing she could not endure.

"It's nothing," she said rather dryly, "beyond what most girls do nowadays as a matter of course. I'm being rather cowardly about it, I think—on account of some silly ideas I've been more or less brought up with perhaps, but..."

"What if they do?" he broke in; "thousands of them at the stores and in the offices. It's bad enough for them—for any sort of woman. But it's different with you. It's horrible. You aren't like them."

She tried to check herself but couldn't. "What's the difference? I'm healthy and half-educated and fairly young. I have the same sort, pretty much, of thoughts and feelings. I don't believe I like being clean and warm and well-fed and amused and admired any better than the average girl does. I ought to have found a job months ago, instead of letting Rush bring me home from New York. Or else gone to work when I came home. But every one was so horrified..."

"They were right to be," he interrupted. "It is a horrible idea. Because you aren't like the others. You *haven't* the same sort of thoughts and feelings. A person doesn't have to be in love with you to see that. Your father and Rush and Mr. Hood all see it. And as for me—well, I couldn't endure it, that's all. Oh, I know, you can act like anybody else; laugh and dance and talk nonsense and make a person forget sometimes. But the other thing is there all the while—shining through—oh, it can't be talked about!—like a light. Of—of something a decent man *wants* to be guided by, whatever he does. And for you to go out into the world with that, where there can't be any protection at all ... I can't stand it, Mary. That's why I came to-day instead of Mr. Hood."

She went very white during that speech and tears came up into her eyes. Tears of helpless exasperation. It was such a cruelly inhuman thing to impose an ideal like that upon a woman. It was so smug, so utterly satisfactory to all romantic sentimentalists. Wallace would approve every word of it. Wallace had sent him to say just this;—was waiting now to be told the good news of his success.

The fact is worth recalling, perhaps, that away back in her childhood Wallace had sometimes reduced her to much this sort of frantic exasperation by his impregnable assumption that she was the white-souled little angel she looked. Sitting here in this very room he had goaded her into committing freakish misdemeanors.

She was resisting now an impulse of much the same sort, though the parallel did not, of course, occur to her. It was just a sort of inexplicable panic which she was reining in with all her might by telling herself how fond she really was of Graham and how terrible a thing it would be if she hurt him unnecessarily. She dared not attempt to speak so she merely waited. She was sitting relaxed, her head lowered, her chin supported by one hand. This stillness and relaxation she always resorted to in making any supreme demand upon her self-control.

He looked at her rather helplessly once or twice during the silence. Then arose and moved about restlessly.

"I know you don't love me. I've gone on hoping you could after I suppose I might have seen it wasn't possible. You've tried to and you can't. I don't know if one as white as you could love any man—that way. Well, I'm not going to ask any more for that. I want to ask, instead, that we be friends. I haven't spoiled the possibility of that, have I?"

She was taken utterly by surprise. It didn't seem possible that she had even heard aright and the face he turned to, as he asked that last question, was of one pitiably bewildered, yet lighted too by a gleam of gratitude.

"You really mean that, Graham?" she asked in a very ragged voice. "Is that what you came to-day to tell me?"

Mary Wollaston | 209

"I mean it altogether," he said earnestly. "I mean it without any—reservations at all. You must believe that because it's the—basis for everything else."

She repeated "everything else?" in clear interrogation; then dropped back rather suddenly into her former attitude. Everything else! What else was there to friendship but itself?

He turned back to the window. "I've come to ask you to, marry me, Mary, just the same. I couldn't be any good as a friend, couldn't take care of you and try to make you happy, unless in the eyes of the world I was your husband. But I wouldn't ask,—I promise you I wouldn't ask anything,—anything at all. You do understand, don't you? You'd be just as—sacred to me …"

Then he cried out in consternation at the sight of her, "Mary! What is it?"

The tension had become too great, that was all. Her self-control, slackened by the momentarily held belief that it was not needed, had snapped.

"I understand well enough," she said. "You would say good night at my bedroom door and good morning at the breakfast table. I've read of arrangements like that in rather nasty-minded novels, but I didn't suppose they existed anywhere else. I can't think of an existence more degradingly sensual than that;—to go on for days and months and years being 'sacred' to a man; never satisfying the desires your nearness tortured him with—to say nothing of what you did with your own!

"But that such a thing should be offered to me because I'm too good to love a man honestly…. You see, I'm none of the things you think I am, Graham. Nor that you want me to be. Not white, not innocent. Not a 'good' woman even, let alone an angel. That's what makes it so—preposterous."

He had been staring at her, speechless, horrified. But at this it was as if he understood. "I ought not to have worried you to-day," he said, suddenly gentle. "I know how terribly overwrought you are. I meant—I only meant to make things easier. I'm going away now. I'll send Rush to you. He'll come at once. Do you mind being alone till then?"

She answered slowly and with an appearance of patient reasonableness, "It's not that. It's not what Rush calls shell-shock. There is many a shabby little experimental flirt who has managed to keep intact an-innocence which I don't possess. That is the simple-physiological truth."

Then, after a silence, with a gasp, "I'm not mad. But I think I shall be if you go on looking at me like that. Won't you please go?"

# CHAPTER XXIII
# THE TERROR

Graham Stannard made his well-meant but disastrous proposal to Mary at half past five or so on a Friday afternoon. It was a little more than twenty-four hours later, just after dark on Saturday evening, that she came in, unheralded, more incredibly like a vision than ever, upon Anthony March in his secret lair above the grocery.

He was sitting at his work-table scoring a passage in the third act of *The Dumb Princess* for the wood-wind choir when her knock, faint as it was, breaking in upon the rhythm of his theme, caused his pen to leap away from the paper and his heart to skip a beat. But had it actually been a knock upon his door? Such an event was unlikely enough.

He uttered a tentative and rather incredulous "Come in" as one just awakened speaks, humoring the illusion of a dream.

But the door opened and the Dumb Princess stood there, pallid, wistful, just as she had looked before her true lover climbed the precarious ivy to her tower and tore away the spell that veiled her.

March sat debating with himself,—or so it seemed to him afterward; it was a matter of mere seconds, of course,—why, since she was a vision, did she not look as she had on one of the occasions when he had seen her. The night of the Whitman songs; the blazing afternoon in the hay field.

She was different to-night, and very clearly defined, in a plain little frock of dark blue—yet not quite what one ordinarily meant by dark blue—cut out in an unsoftened square around the neck, and a small hat of straw, the color of the warmer sort of bronze. These austerities of garb, dissociated utterly with all his memories, gave her a poignancy that was almost unbearable. Why had the vision of her come to him like that?

She smiled then and spoke. "It is really I. I've come with a message for you."

Until she spoke he could do nothing but stare as one would at an hallucinatory vision; but her voice, the first articulate syllable of it, brought him to his feet and drew him across the room to where she stood. He was almost suffocated by a sudden convulsion of the heart, half exultation, half terror. The exultation was accountable enough. The high Gods had given him another chance. Why he should be terrified he did not at the time know, but he was—from that very first moment.

He came to her slowly, not knowing what he was to do or say. All his mental powers were for the moment quite in abeyance. But when he got within hand's reach of her it was given to him to take both of hers and stoop and kiss them. He'd have knelt to her had his knees ever been habituated to prayer. Then he led her to his big hollow-backed easy chair which stood in the dormer where the breeze came in, changed its position a little and waited until, with a faintly audible sigh, she had let herself sink into it.

How tired she was! He had become aware of that the moment he touched her hands. Whatever her experience during the last days or weeks had been, it had brought her to the end of her powers.

He felt another pang of that unaccountable terror as he turned away, and he put up an unaddressed prayer for spiritual guidance. It was a new humility for him. He moved his own chair a little nearer, but not close, and seated himself.

"I can conceive of no message,"—they were the first words he had spoken, and his voice was not easily manageable,—"no message that would be more than nothing compared with the fact that you have come." Rising again, he went on, "Won't you let me take your hat? Then the back of that chair won't be in the way."

It was certainly a point in his favor that she took it off and gave it to him without demur. That meant that there would be time; yet her very docility frightened him. She seemed quite relaxed now that her head could lie back against the leather cushion, and her gaze traveled about the dingy littered room with a kind of tender inquisitiveness as if she were memorizing its contents.

He gazed at her until a gush of tears blinded his eyes and he turned, blinking them away, to the untidy quires of score paper which he had tried to choose instead. It could not be that it was too late to alter that choice. The terror, for a moment, became articulate. She believed that it was too late. That was why she had come.

She spoke reflectively. "It would be called an accident, I suppose, that I came. I wrote to you but there was more to the message than would go easily in a note so I took it myself to your house. There was just a chance, I thought, that I'd find you there. I didn't find you, but I found Miss MacArthur. That was the only thing about it that could be called accidental. Your mother and sister were worried about you. They said it had been much longer than such periods usually were since they had heard from you. So I left my note and was coming away. Miss MacArthur said she would come with me and offered to drive me back to town. When we got into her car she said she thought she knew where you were and would take me to you. She did not say anything more nor ask any questions until she had stopped outside here at the curb, when she looked up and saw the lighted windows and said you were surely here. Then she pointed out the place in the dark where the stairs were and told me how to find your door. She waited, though, to make sure before she drove away. I heard her go."

He had no word to say in the little pause she made there. He felt the pulse beating in his temples and clutched with tremulous hands the wooden arms of his chair. Until she had mentioned Jennie MacArthur's name it had not occurred to him to wonder how she had been enabled to come to him. It could only have been through Jennie, of course. Jennie was the only person who knew. But why had Jennie disclosed his secret (her own at the same time, he was sure; she never would have expected Mary's clear eyes even to try to evade the unescapable inference)—why had she revealed to Mary, whom she had never seen before, a fact which she had guarded with so impregnable a loyalty all these many years?

The only possible answer was that Jennie had divined, under the girl's well-bred poise, the desperation which was now terrifying him. It was no nightmare then of his own overwrought imagination. Jennie had perceived the emergency—the actual life-or-death emergency—and with courageous inspiration had done, unhesitatingly, the one thing that could possibly meet the case. She had given him his chance. Jennie!

He arrived at that terminus just as Mary finished speaking. In the pause that followed she did not at first look at him. Her gaze had come to rest upon that abortive musical typewriter of his. Not quite in focus upon it, but as if in some corner of her mind she was wondering what it might be. But as the pause spun itself out, her glance, seeking his face, moved quickly enough to catch the look of consternation that it wore. She read it—misread it luckily—and her own lighted amazingly with a beam of pure amusement.

"I suppose it is rather overwhelming," she said; "a conjunction like that. I mean, that it should have been she who brought me here. But really, unless one accepts all the traditional motives and explanations that one finds in books, it shouldn't be surprising that she should undertake a friendly service for some one else she saw was fond of you, too. Not when one considers the wonderful person she is."

If his sheer adoration of her were enough to save her then she was safe, whatever the peril. But he doubted if it would be enough.

"Jennie and I were lovers once," he said. "But that came to an end for both of us a good while ago. Two or three years. And the last time she came to this room—one day in April it was—I told her about you and about *The Dumb Princess*." He laid his hand upon the stack of manuscript. "This. I had come home from that night at your father's house when you and I heard that song together, with my head full of it. I went nearly mad fighting it out of my head while I tried to make over that other opera for Paula."

*"The Dumb Princess...?"*

He nodded. "You see you hardly spoke that night, only at the end to say we mustn't talk. So I came away thinking of some one under a spell. A princess, the fairy sort of princess who could not speak until her true lover came to her. But instead of that I tried to go on working at that Belgian horror and stuck at it until it was unendurable. And then, when I came to the house to tell Paula so, it was you who came to me again, the first time since that night."

There had come a faintly visible color into her cheeks and once more she smiled, reflectively. "That's what you meant then," she mused. "I couldn't make it out. You said just before you went away, 'That's why it was so incredible when you came down the stairs instead.'"

She had remembered that!

"I ran away," he confessed, "the moment I had said it, for fear of betraying myself. And I went to work on *The Dumb Princess* that day."

"You've done all that, a whole opera, since the fourteenth of May?"

"I worked on it," he said, "until I had to stop for the little vacation that—that ended at Hickory Hill. And I came straight back to it from there. I've been working at it all the time since. Now, except for the scoring in the second part of the third act, it's finished. I thought it was the thing I wanted more than anything else in the world. Just to get it written down on paper, the thing which that moment with you up in that little anteroom started. I've pretty well done it. As far as the music itself is concerned, I think I have done it."

He paused there and pressed his lips together. Then he went on speaking, stiffly, one word at a time. "And I was saying to myself when you knocked that I would tear it up, every sheet of it, and set it alight in the stove yonder if it would take me back to that hour we had together at Hickory Hill."

The tenderness of her voice when she replied (it had some of the characteristic qualities of his beloved woodwinds) did not preclude a bead of humor, almost mischief, from gilding the salient points of its modeling.

"I know," she said. "I can guess what that feeling must be; the perfect emptiness and despair of having a great work done. I suspect there aren't many great masterpieces that one couldn't have bought cheap by offering the mess of pottage at the right moment. Oh, no, I didn't mean a sneer when I said cheap. I really understand. That very next morning out in the orchard, thinking over it, I managed to be glad you'd gone—alone. Your own way, rather than back with me to Ravinia. But—I'm glad I came to-night and I'm glad I know about—*The Dumb Princess.*"

Watching her as her unfocused reminiscent gaze made it easy for him to do, he saw her go suddenly pale, saw the perspiration bead out on her forehead as if some thought her mind had found itself confronting actually sickened her. He waited an instant, breathless in an agony of doubt whether to notice or to go on pretending to ignore. After a moment the wave passed.

"I know that was a figure of speech," she resumed,—her voice was deadened a little in timbre but its inflections were as light as before. "But I wish—I'd really be ever so much—happier—if you'd give me a promise; a perfectly serious, solemn,"—she hesitated for a word and smiled,—"death-bed promise, that you never will burn up *The Dumb Princess.* At least until she's all published and produced. And I wish that as soon as you've got a copy made, you'd put this manuscript in a really safe place."

He turned away from her, baffled, bewildered. She had evaded the issue he had tried to confront her with. She had taken the passionate declaration of his wish to retrieve the great error of his life as a passing emotion familiar to all creative artists at certain stages in their work. It was a natural, almost inevitable, way of looking at it! He sat for a moment gazing abstractedly at his littered table, clutching the edges of it with both hands, resisting a momentary vertigo of his own.

She left her chair and came and stood beside him. She picked up one of the quires of manuscript, opened it and gazed a while at the many-staved score. He was aware of a catch in her breathing, like an inaudible sob, but presently she spoke, quite steadily.

"I wish I could sit here to-night and read this. I wish it made even unheard melodies to me. I'm not dumb but I am deaf to this. *There's* a spell beyond your powers to lift, my dear."

She laid her hand lightly upon his shoulder and at her touch his taut-drawn muscles relaxed into a tremulous weakness. After a little silence:

"Now give me my promise," she said.

He did not immediately answer and the hand upon his shoulder took hold. Under its compulsion, "I'll promise anything you ask," he said.

She spoke slowly as if measuring her words. "Never to destroy this work of yours that you call *The Dumb Princess* whatever may conceivably happen, however discouraged you may be about it."

"Very well," he said, "I won't."

"Say it as a promise," she commanded. "Quite explicitly."

So he repeated a form of words which satisfied her. She held him tight in both hands for an instant. Then swiftly went back to her chair.

"Don't think me too foolish," she apologized. "I haven't been sleeping much of late and I couldn't have slept to-night with a misgiving like that to wonder about."

His own misgiving obscurely deepened. He did not know whether it was the reason she had offered for exacting that promise from him or the mere tone of her voice which was lighter and more brittle than he felt it should have been. She must have read the troubled look in his face for she said at once and on a warmer note:

"Oh, my dear, don't! Don't let my vagaries trouble you. Let me tell you the message I came with. It's about the other opera. They want to put it on at once up at Ravinia. With Fournier as the officer and that little Spanish soprano as 'Dolores.' Just as you wrote it without any of the terrible things you tried to put in for Paula. It will have to be sung in French of course, because neither of them sings English. They want you there just as soon as you can come, to sign the contract and help with the rehearsals."

Once more with an utterly unexpected shift she left him floundering, speechless.

He had forgotten *The Outcry* except for his nightmare efforts to revamp it for Paula; had charged it off his books altogether. What Mary had told him at Hickory Hill about her labors in its behalf had signified simply, how rapturously delicious it was that she should have been so concerned for him. The possibility of a successful outcome to her efforts hadn't occurred to him.

She said, smiling with an amused tenderness over his confusion, "I haven't been too officious, have I?"

He knew he was being mocked at and he managed to smile but he had to blink and press his hand to his eyes again before he could see her clearly.

"It's not astonishing that you can work miracles," he said. "The wonder would be if you could not."

"There was nothing in the least miraculous about this," she declared. "It wasn't done by folding my wings and weaving mystic circles with a wand. Besides making that translation,—oh, terribly bad, I'm afraid,—into French, I've cajoled and intrigued industriously for weeks like one of those patient wicked little spiders of Henri Fabre's. I found a silly flirtation between Fournier and a married woman I knew and I encouraged it, helped it along and made it useful. I've used everybody I could lay my hands on."

What an instrument of ineffable delight that voice of hers was,— its chalumeau tenderness just relieved with the sparkle of irony. But he was smitten now with the memory of his own refusal to go to Ravinia so that Paula would remember him again. He blurted out something of his contrition over this but she stopped him.

"It was only because I wanted you there. I would not for any conceivable advantage in the world have let you—oh, even touch these devices that I've been concerned with. But I've reveled in them myself. In doing them for you, even though I could not see that they were getting anywhere.

"Everything seemed quite at a standstill when I left Ravinia Thursday, but on Thursday night the Williamsons dined with Mr. Eckstein and went to the park with him; and they all went home with father and Paula afterward, Fournier and LaChaise, too; and everything happened at once. I got a note from Paula this morning written yesterday, asking where my translation was, but not telling me anything. And as she wasn't at home when I telephoned to answer her question I didn't know until to-night.

"But about six o'clock James Wallace telephoned from the park and told me all about it. He wanted you found and sent to Ravinia at once. Having wasted half the season and more, they're now quite frantic over the thought of losing a minute. And Jimmy says immensely enthusiastic. So, all you have to do now is to go up there and lord it over them. You'll hear it sung; you'll hear the orchestra play it. You will make a beginning toward coming into your own, my dear. Because even if you don't care for it as you did, it will be a step toward—the princess, won't it?"

She dropped back against the cushion as from weariness, and sudden tears brimmed into her eyes and spilled down her cheeks. He came to her at that in spite of the gesture that would have held him away.

"You must believe—it's nothing—but happiness," she gasped.

He sat down upon the arm of the chair and a little timidly took her in his hands, caressed her eyes and her wet face until at last she met his lips in a long kiss and sank back quieted.

He stayed on the chair arm however and their hands remained clasped through a recollecting silence. She said presently:

"There are two or three practical things for you to remember. You mustn't be irritated with Violet Williamson. She has let herself become a little more sentimental about Fournier than I think in the beginning she meant to be and you may find her under foot more than you like. You mustn't mind that. And you'll find a very friendly helper in James Wallace. There is something a little caustic about his wit, and he suspects musicians on principle; but he will like you and he's thoroughly committed to *The Outcry*. He is a very good French scholar and over difficulties with the translation, where passages have to be changed, he'll be a present help."

He took her face in both his hands and turned it up to him. "Mary," he demanded when their eyes met, "why are you saying good-by to me?"

# CHAPTER XXIV
# THE WHOLE STORY

The shot told. The harried, desperate look of panic with which she gazed at him and tried, tugging at his hands, to turn away, revealed to him that he had leaped upon the truth. Part of it anyhow. He closed his eyes, for an instant, for another unaddressed prayer that he might not falter nor let himself be turned aside until he had sounded the full depth of it.

When he looked at her again she had recovered her poise. "It was silly," she said, "to think that I could hide that from you. I am going away—to-morrow. For quite a long while."

"Are you going away—physically? In the ordinary literal sense, I mean; or is it that you are just—going away from me?"

Once more it was as if a trap had been sprung upon her. But this time he ignored the gasp and the sudden cold slackness of the hands he held and went on speaking with hardly a pause.

"I asked that question, put it that way, thinking perhaps I understood and that I could make it easier for you to tell me." He broke off, there, for an instant to get his voice under control. Then he asked, steadily, "Are you going to marry Graham Stannard?"

She gasped again, but when he looked up at her there was nothing in her face but an incredulous astonishment.

So there was one alternative shorn away; one that he had not conceived as more than a very faint possibility. It was not into matrimony that her long journey was to take her. He pulled himself up with a jerk to answer—and it must be done smoothly and comfortably—the question she had just asked him. How in the world had he ever come to think of a thing like that?

"Why, it was in the air at Hickory Hill those days before you came. And then Sylvia was explicit about it, as something every one was hoping for."

"Was that why you went away?" she asked with an intent look into his face. "Because he had a—prior claim, and it wouldn't be fair to—poach upon his preserves?"

He gave an ironic monosyllable laugh. "I tried, for the next few days to bamboozle myself into adopting that explanation but I couldn't. The truth was, of course, that I ran away simply because I was frightened. Sheer panic terror of the thing that had taken hold of me. The thought of meeting you that next morning was—unendurable."

She too uttered a little laugh but it sounded like one of pure happiness. She buried her face in his hands and touched each palm with her lips. "I couldn't have borne it if you'd said the other thing," she told him. "But I might have trusted you not to. Because you're not a sentimentalist. You're almost the only person I know who is not."

She added a moment later, with a sudden tightening of her grip upon his hands, "Have you, too, discovered that sentimentality is the crudest thing in the world? It is. It is perfectly ruthless. It makes more tragedies than malice. Ludicrous tragedies—which are less endurable than the other sort. Unless one were enough of an Olympian so that he could laugh." She relaxed again and made a nestling movement toward him. "I thought for a while of you that way."

He managed to speak as if the idea amused him. "As an Olympian? No, if I had a mountain it wouldn't be that one. But I like the valleys better, anyhow."

"I know," she said contentedly. Then her voice darkened. "I'm just at the beginning of you—now..." The sentence ended unnaturally, though he had done nothing to interrupt it.

Deliberately he startled her. "What time does your train go, to-morrow?" he asked. "Or haven't you selected one? You haven't even told me where it is you are going."

Through his hands which held her he felt the shock, the momentary agony of the effort to recover the threatened balance, the resolute relaxation of the muscles and the steadying breath she drew.

"Oh, there are plenty of trains," she said. "You mustn't bother.—Why, Wallace Hood has a sister living in Omaha. (Wallace Hood, not James Wallace. It would be terrible if you confused them.) She's been trying for months to find a nursery governess. And I've been trying—perhaps you didn't know; the family have been very unpleasant about it—to find a job.— Oh, for the most realistic of reasons, among others. Well, it occurred to me the other day that Wallace's sister and I might be looking for each other."

There she paused, but only for a moment. Then she added, very explicitly, "So I'm going to Omaha to-morrow."

Even her lying she had to do honestly. She preferred, he saw, that he should remember she had lied to having him recall that she had tricked him by an evasion.

One need not invoke clairvoyance to account for his incandescent certainty that she had lied. The mere unconscious synthesis of the things she had said and left unsaid along the earlier stages of their talk, would have amounted to a demonstration. Her moment of panic over his discovery that she was saying good-by, her irrespressible shudder at the question whether she was going away in the ordinary literal sense of the phrase; finally, her pitiful attempt to avoid, in answer to his last question, a categorical untruth and then her acceptance of it as, after all, preferable to the other. But it was by no such pedestrian process as this that he reached the truth.

He knew, now, why he had been terrified from the moment she came into the room. He knew why she had wrung that promise from him—a death-bed promise she had dared with a smile to call it—that he would not, whatever happened, destroy *The Dumb Princess*. It would be a likely enough thing for him to do, she had perceived, when he learned the truth. She could not—sleep, she had told him, until that surmise was laid.

There were, as she had said, plenty of trains to that unknown destination of hers, but he thought that that word sleep offered the true clue. She was a physician's daughter; there must be, somewhere in that house, a chest or cupboard that would supply what she needed. They'd find her in her own bed, in that room he had once cast a glance into on his way up-stairs to Paula.

The conviction grew upon him that she had her plans completely laid; yes, and her preparations accomplished. That quiet leisureliness of hers would not have been humanly possible if either her resolution or the means for executing it had remained in doubt. It was likely that she had whatever it was—a narcotic, probably; morphine; she wouldn't, conceivably, resort to any of the corrosives—upon her person at this moment. In that little silken bag which hung from her wrist.

He clenched the finger-nails into the palms of his hands. This thing was a nightmare. He had fallen asleep over his table; had only to wake himself.— It would not do to play with an idea like that. Nor with the possibility that he had misread her mind. He knew. He was not mistaken. Let him never glance aside from that.

For one moment he thought wildly of trying to call in help from outside, of frustrating her design by sheer force. But that could not be done. As between them, he would be reckoned the madman. Her project might be deferred by that means, perhaps. It could not be prevented.

It was that terrible self-possession of hers that gave the last turn to the screw. She could not be dealt with as one frantic, beside herself, to be wooed and quieted back into a state of sanity. She was at this moment as sane as he. She was not to be held back, either, by a mere assurance of his love for her. She had never, it appeared, lacked that assurance. But her life, warmed even as it was by their love, presented itself to her somehow as something that it was not possible to go on with.

This was very strange. All of its externals that were visible to him made up, one would have said, a pattern singularly gracious and untroubled. Buried in it somewhere there must be some toxic focus that poisoned everything. He must meet her on her own ground. He must show her another remedy than the desperate one she was now resolved upon. And before he could find the remedy he must discover the virus. The only clue he had was the thing she said about sentimentalists, and the tragedies they caused. More tragedies than malice was responsible for. He thought she was probably right about that. It was some such tragedy anyhow, ludicrous, unendurable, that had driven her to this acquiescence in defeat.

He said, in as even a tone as he could manage, "I asked about trains because I wondered whether there was anything to hurry you to-night. Packing to do or such a matter; or whether we mightn't have a really leisurely visit. I haven't much idea what time it is except that I don't think I've eaten anything since around the middle of the day. Have you? If you'd stay and have supper with me ... But I suppose you're expected somewhere else."

She smiled ironically at this, then laughed at herself. "It happens rather funnily that I haven't been so little expected or looked after, since I came home from New York, as I am to-night. I'm not—in a hurry at all. I'll stay as long as you like."

"Is that a promise?" he asked. "As long as I liked would be a long while."

"I'll stay," she said, "as long as I can see I'm making you happy. When I find myself beginning to be a—torment to you, I shall—vanish."

He was almost overmastered by the temptation to forget everything except his love for her; to let himself be persuaded that his ghastly surmise was a product of his own fatigue and sleepless nights. Even supposing there were a basis for it, could he not keep her safe by just holding her fast in his arms?

He dashed the thought out of his mind. She would surrender to his embrace, how eagerly he already knew. For a matter of moments, for a few swift hours she might forget. She had perhaps come to him meaning to forget for a while in just that way. But no embrace could be eternal. He'd have to let her go at last and nothing would be changed save that she would have a memory of him to take with her into her long sleep.

No, love must wait. That obscure unendurable nightmare tragedy of hers must be brought out into the light first and shorn of its horrors.

So he managed for the moment a lighter note. He would not let her help in the preparation of the meager little meal which was all that his immediate resources ran to. He hadn't quite realized how exiguous it was going to be when he spoke of it as supper. It was nothing but a slice of Swiss cheese, a fresh carton of biscuits and a flagon of so-called Chianti illicitly procured from the Italian grocery downstairs.

He cleared his work table and anchored her in the easy chair at the same time by putting into her lap the bulky manuscript of *The Dumb Princess*, and it was this they talked about while he laid the cloth—a clean towel—and set out his scanty array of dishes. He feared when they drew up to the table that she was not going to be able to eat at all, and he was convinced that she was even more in need of food than he. But the wine, thin and acidulous as it was, helped, and he saw to it that for a while she had no chance to talk. He told her the story of *The Dumb Princess* in detail and dwelt a little upon the half formulated symbolism of it.

When at last he paused, she said, "I think I know why the princess was dumb. Because when she tried to speak no one wanted to hear what she had to say. They insisted on keeping her an image merely, so that they could go on attributing to her just the thoughts they wished her to think and just the desires they wanted her to feel. That's the spell that has made many a woman dumb upon all the essentials."

He gripped his hands together between his knees, leaned a little forward, drew a steadying breath and said, "There's something I wish you'd do for me just while we're sitting quietly like this. It has been so momentary, this life of ours together,—the times I mean when we've been bodily together. The whole of it could be reckoned quite easily in minutes. There has been more packed into them, of course, than into many a lover's months and years, but one effect it has had on me has been to make you, when you aren't here physically with me, like this, where by merely reaching out I can touch you, a little—visionary to me. I confuse you with the Dumb Princess over there whom you made me create. I get misgivings that you're just a sort of wraith. Well, if you're going away and we aren't to be within—touching distance of each other again for a long while—perhaps months, I want more of you, that my memory can hold on by. The real every-day person that you are instead, as you say, of the image I've had to make of you. So I wish you'd tell me as nearly as you can remember everything that you've done—everything that has happened to you—to-day."

That last word was like the touch of a spur. She shuddered as she cried, "Not to-day!"

He did not press for a reason and the next moment she went on in her natural manner again. "That's a strange thing for you to wish. At least the strangeness of it strikes me after some of the things that have been happening lately. Yet I don't believe it happens often that a lover asks as specifically as that to be—disillusioned. And that is what you would be. Because the complete story of a day,—any day,—with no suppressions, nothing tucked decently away out of sight, would be a pretty searching test."

"That's why I asked for it," he said, "I'd like to be disillusioned; just as completely as possible."

"That's because you're so sure you wouldn't be." The raggedness of her voice betrayed a strong emotion. With a leap of the pulse he told himself that it was as if she were crying out against some unforeseen hope. "You think it would merely be that lovely little image of yours—the Dumb Princess, coming to life."

"I'd rather have the reality," he told her, "whatever it is. I think I can make you see that that must be true. The person I love is you who are sitting there across the table from me. I don't believe that any one in the world was ever more completely and utterly adored than you are being adored at this moment. I love the things I know you by. The things I've come to recognize as yours. I know some of your qualities that way; your sensitiveness, your uprightness, your fastidious honesty that makes you hate evasions and substitutes,—everything you mean when you say sentimentality. And I know your resolution that carries you along even when you are afraid,—when your sensitiveness makes you afraid. I admire all those qualities, but it isn't their intrinsic worth that makes me love them. I love them because they're the things I know you by. I can't be mistaken about them because I've felt them. Just as I've felt your hands and your mouth and your hair. Well, then, whatever your days have been, one day after another, they have in the end produced you sitting there as you sit now. Whatever your—ingredients are they're your ingredients. The total works out to you. Whereas my illusions work out to nothing better than my little image of the Dumb Princess."

"Would it surprise you," she asked, "to know that I could be cruel? I mean exactly what the word means. Like a little boy who tears the legs off a beetle. Can you imagine me hurting some one frightfully, whom I needn't have hurt at all? Some one who was trying in his own way to be kind to me?"

He smiled. "I can imagine your being cruel to a sentimentalist," he said. "Not deliberately, of course. Only after you had been hounded, like a little white cat, into a corner. By some one who wanted you for an image, merely, that he himself could attribute all the appropriate thoughts and desires to. I can imagine you turning, at last, and rending him;—limb from limb, if you like."

She gazed at him, wide-eyed, for a long moment; then she drooped forward over the table and cradled her head in her arms. With his hands he tried to comfort her but he felt that they were clumsy and ineffectual.

"I've hurt you horribly," he said, when he could command his voice. "Probing in like that."

This must be the unendurable tragedy she had referred to a while ago. She was speaking, voicelessly and he bent down to listen.

"... if you knew the comfort! I suppose I ought to be frightened—at your guessing like that, but it seems natural, to-night, that you should.— You know who it was, don't you?"

"Yes," he told her confidently. "It happened just to-day, didn't it?"

"It was yesterday he asked me to marry him," she said. "That wasn't hounding. He had a right to, I mean. I thought I would marry him, once. I told him I would if I could. I meant, I would if I could make him understand what I really was. He thought I meant something altogether different, something that his image of me might have meant quite nicely. Yesterday when he asked me again, I flew into a fury and told him what I am really like. I needn't have done it. I could have told him that the reason I wouldn't marry him was because I was in love with you. That would have been true— in a way. I mean, it wasn't the reason in the beginning; nor even after I was in love with you—so long as you didn't know. But I never thought of telling him that. I just wanted to—smash that image of his. And I did. I knew it was cruel when I did it, but not how terrible until this morning when Rush got a letter from him."

She had to stop there to master a sob. He went around the table and took her in his arms. "Come over to the big chair," he said, "where I can— hold you. I can't let you go on like this. You can tell me the rest of it there."

Mary Wollaston | 225

She released herself from his hands by taking them in her own and pressing them for a moment tight. Then she let them go.

"I couldn't," she said. "I couldn't be comforted like that while I was telling you about him."

He understood instantly. "That's like you," he commented. "You're always like yourself, thank God." He walked away to the chair he had invited her to and stood behind it, gripping its padded leather back. "He wrote your brother a letter then." He had spoken, he thought, quietly and evenly enough, but the indignation he felt must have betrayed itself in his voice for she answered instantly:

"You mustn't be angry about that. He had to write to Rush, you see. Rush had been in his confidence about it all the while. Rush knew his hopes and his explanations. Rush knew of his coming yesterday, was waiting up at Wallace Hood's apartment for his news. Now, do you see how horrible it was? He couldn't tell Rush what I had said to him. There was nothing he could tell him. He couldn't even face him. He did the only thing I'd left for him to do."

March asked, "What has he done?"

"We don't know, exactly. Just gone away, I suppose. The letter was written about midnight from the University Club. He said he wasn't coming back to Hickory Hill. That he couldn't possibly come back. He'd arrange things, somehow, later. He told Rush not to try to find him nor make any sort of fuss, and to be very kind to me; not to question nor worry me."

She broke off there and looked intently up at him. In her eyes he thought he saw incredulity fighting against a dawning hope. "I wonder," she went breathlessly on, "if you can understand this, too. Can you see that, for him, the unbearable thing about it—was that it was ludicrous? The contrast between what he had believed me to be and—what I am?"

He interrupted sharply, with a frown of irritation, "Don't put it like that!"

"Well, then," she amended, "the contrast between his explanation of the way I had been treating him, and the true one?"

"That is a thing I think I can understand," he said. "It was a sort of— awakening of Don Quixote. To a fine sensitive boy nothing could give a sharper wrench than that.—I'm moving in the dark," he added. Yet he knew he was drawing near the light. The secret he had set out to discover was not very far away.

"You see well enough," she said. "Better than Rush, though I tried to explain it to him. He'd caught a surmise of the truth, too, I think, in New York, when he came back from France and brought me home. But he wouldn't look. Father wouldn't, either, once when I tried to tell him about it. It was too horrible to be thought,—let alone believed.—I don't quite see how I can have gone on believing it myself."

The look he saw in her eyes made him wonder how she could. He managed to hold his own gaze steady. It gave him a sense of somehow supporting her.

"But you," she said,—"you, of all people in the world, don't seem to feel that way about it. You were there—waiting for me—before I even tried to tell you. Oh, you do understand, don't you?"

"I think," he told her—and the smile that came with the words was spontaneous enough, though it did feel rather tremulous—"I think I could almost repeat the sentence you demolished young Stannard with in your own words. But can't you see why it doesn't demolish me? It's because I love you."

"So did he. So do father and Rush."

"Not you. Not quite you. Don't you see? It's just the thing I was trying to tell you a while ago. What they insist on loving is—oh, partly you, of course, but partly a sort of—projection of themselves that they call you, dress you out in, try to compel you to fit. One can fight hard to preserve an outlying bit of one's self like that. But there would be a limit I should think. How your brother, with a letter like that in his hands, could refuse to look at what you were trying to make him see ..."

"He had a theory, that began when we were in New York together as a sort of joke, that I was a case of shell-shock. So whenever there has been anything really uncomfortable to face, he has always had that to fall back upon."

A momentary outburst of anger escaped him. "You've been tortured!" he cried furiously. He reined in at once, however. "You've never, then," he went on quietly, "been able to tell the story to any one. I'm sure you didn't tell it to Graham Stannard. You didn't even try to."

She shook her head. The pitifulness of her, sitting there so spent, so white, blurred his vision again with sudden tears. But after he had disposed of them, he managed a smile and sat down comfortably in his easy chair.

"You couldn't find a better person than me to tell it to," he said.

"You know already," she protested. "At least, you know what it comes to."

"I know the brute fact," he admitted, "but that and the whole truth are seldom quite the same thing."

He saw the way her hands locked and twisted together and remembered with a heart-arresting pang, her half-choked cry, "Don't! Don't hurt them like that!" when his own had agonized in such a grip. But no caress of his could help her now. He held himself still in his chair and waited.

"The whole truth of this story isn't any—prettier than the brute fact. There weren't any extenuating circumstances."

Then she sat erect and faced him. He was amazed to see a flush of color come creeping into her cheeks. Her eyes brightened, the brows drew down a little, her voice steadied itself and the words came swiftly.

"I think I must make sure you understand that it isn't the sort of story that you usually find enveloping that particular brute fact. I wasn't deceived nor betrayed by anybody. There isn't anybody you can take as a villain. Just a nice, rather inarticulate boy, whom I met at a dance the evening before he went overseas."

She broke off there to ask him shortly, "When was it that you went over?"

"Not until September," he said, "when it looked like a very long chance if we ever got to the front at all. Of course, you know, we didn't. But this was a lot earlier, wasn't it?"

"The seventeenth of April," she said. "We'll never forget those weeks, any of us, who were in New York doing what we called war work, but it's hard not to feel that we weren't different persons somehow. I don't mean that to sound like making excuses. We were more our real selves perhaps than we will ever be again. Anyhow, we worked harder all day long, and never felt tired, and in the evening most of the people I knew went out a lot, to dinners and dances.

"We could always make ourselves believe, of course, that we were doing that to cheer up the men who were going to France—and were very likely never coming back. Like the English women one read about. The only thing that used to trouble me in those days was a perfectly scorching self-contempt that used to come when I realized that I was enjoying it all; enjoying the emotional thrill of it. I knew I was getting off cheap.

"I suppose I needn't have told you all that. You'd have understood it anyhow. But that was how I felt when I went to that dance. As if it would be a relief to do something — costly.

"It was a uniform dance as far as the men were concerned. We made ourselves, of course, as — attractive as we knew how. Somebody introduced this boy to me with just the look that said, 'Do be kind to him,' and that's what I set out, very resolutely and virtuously, to be. He couldn't talk much beyond monosyllables and he couldn't dance, — even with me. I mean, I've danced so much ..."

"I've seen you dance, my dear," he reminded her, and saw how, with a deep-drawn breath, the memory of that night at Hickory Hill came back to her.

"Don't," she gasped. "Let me go on." But it was the better part of a minute before she could.

"We sat out two or three dances together and then, when I might decently enough have passed him on to some one else with that same sort of explanatory look — I didn't. Partly because of the feeling I have told you about and partly because I was attracted to him. He was big and young and good-looking, and his voice — oh, one can't explain those things. It wasn't pure altruism. That's what you must see. And then he got up suddenly and said, 'Good-by.' It was early, you know, and I asked him why he was going. He said he wanted to get out of there. Rather savagely.

"I got up too and said I felt the same way about it. So he asked if he might 'see me home.' The dance was in the East Sixties. There had been a shower but it was clear then and warm. There weren't any taxis about and, anyhow, he didn't seem to think of looking for one, and we went over and took a Lexington Avenue car. When we turned at Twenty-third Street I said we'd get out and walk. He'd said hardly anything, but we had sat rather close in the car and he had been holding a fold of my cloak between his fingers.

"We went on down Lexington to Gramercy Park. There was shrubbery in flower inside the iron fence and some of the trees had been leafing out that day and the air was very still and sweet. We both stopped for a minute without saying anything and I slipped my hand farther through his arm and took his.

"He gave a sort of sob and said, 'You wouldn't do that if you knew about me.' I said, 'You'd better tell me and see.'

"We walked on again, around the park and across Twentieth Street and down
Fifth Avenue. When we got to my door he hadn't told me.

"My flat was just the second story of an old made-over house. There was no one about, I mean, to stare or wonder, and I asked him to come in. When we were inside I looked at my watch and asked him what time he had to report. He said not until seven o'clock in the morning. He was going over detached. There was nothing but a hotel to go back to.

"If I'd asked him that question out on the sidewalk, and got that answer, I don't know whether I'd have asked him in or not.

"He just stood looking at me for a minute after telling me he hadn't anywhere to report that night. Then he turned away and sat down on the edge of my couch and bent his face down on his hands and began to talk. He told me what was the matter with him. Of course, the same thing must have tormented thousands of them,—the terror of being afraid. He felt pretty sure he was a coward.

"Mostly, I think, that fear was pretty sensibly dealt with in this war. It got talked out openly. But he must have been a terribly lonely person. He came from Iowa, but somehow he got sent to one of the southern cantonments, and had his officer's training, such as it was, down there. Then he was sent along to fill in somewhere else. I don't remember all the details. He'd come to New York alone. The men he had gone to the dance with he had only met that afternoon.

"I tried to help him. I told him how some of the officers in the French and English armies, who had the highest decorations for courage, had suffered most horribly, in advance, from fear. I could tell him two or three that I knew about personally; men who had told their own stories to me. Well, that helped a little, roused him out of his daze, gave him a little gleam of hope perhaps. But it wasn't much; words can't be, sometimes.

"He wanted more than that. He wanted me. He didn't want to go back alone to that hotel. So I kept him. Early in the morning, about six o'clock, I cooked his breakfast and ate it with him and kissed him good-by."

She made a sudden savage gesture of impatience. "I didn't mean to make it sound like that. That sounds noble and self-sacrificial and sickening. I suppose because that's the half of the truth that is easiest to tell. I *did* want to make an end of perpetually getting off cheap. I did have a sort of feeling of establishing my good faith with myself. I wanted to comfort him and make him happy. But it's also true that I'd been attracted to him from the very first minute, and that it thrilled me when I first touched his hand, there by the park railing, and afterward when he took me in his arms."

Since his last interruption he had sat motionless, even breathing small in the extremity of his effort not to hinder. But now he rose and without speaking, came to her and bending down, kissed her forehead, her eyes, her mouth. Then he seated himself on the table close beside her and took possession, thoughtfully, of one of her hands.

"Did you ever hear anything more of him?" he asked.

She shook her head. "I don't think he remarked my name at all when we were introduced," she said, "nor asked what it was afterward. I think it must all have seemed afterward a little unreal to him. The girls he'd known at home don't smoke cigarettes nor drink champagne—nor wear their dresses as low as we do. He couldn't once have thought of people like father and Rush and Aunt Lucile as belonging to me. I remembered his name and used to look to see if it was there when I read the casualty lists, but I never did see it again.—No, that's the whole story; just what I have told you."

# CHAPTER XXV
# DAYBREAK

There followed the conclusion of the story, an interval of ease. It gave March, to begin with, a new access of courage, almost of confidence, to note that she did not fade white again and that the sick look of horror, banished from her eyes by the mere intensity of her determination to convey the whole truth to him, did not return to them. She substituted her other hand for the one he held in order to shift her position a little and lean against his knees.

Her mind had not detached itself from the story as she made evident by the reflective way in which she went on thinking aloud about it; dwelling on some of the curious consequences of the adventure. It was surprising—she wondered if it indicated anything really abnormal in her—the way she had felt about it afterward.

She'd felt nothing in the least like shame. Certainly not at first. On the contrary, she'd taken a deep soul-satisfying pride in it, a kind of warm sense of readiness for anything.

She told him with a little clutch of embarrassment and resolution, about another incident that happened somewhat later, attributing an importance to it which he conceded while he reflected with a smile that most people, men and women virtuous or otherwise, would have regarded as ridiculously disproportionate. The incident concerned a man whom she didn't much like, she said, but found somehow, fascinating. He had been paying her attentions of a rather experimental sort for weeks, maneuvering, arranging. He knew she lived by herself and had been angling for an invitation to come to see her, alone. Finally, he telephoned her office one day and asked point-blank if he mightn't come to tea that afternoon. She said he might without telling him that she was expecting Christabel Baldwin at the same time. An hour later, a restless hour it had been, she had telephoned Christabel and put her off so that when her other guest came he found just what he had expected. In the manner of one sure of his welcome and intent on wasting no time, he had begun making love to her (she apologized for the employment of that phrase but said she knew no other that was usable). She admitted that she had never had any real doubt that this was what he had meant to do and conceded him the right to think that she had invited it. But she found it, nevertheless, unendurable. She felt unspeakably degraded by it and presently flew into a rage and turned the man out of the house, feeling, she added, as much ashamed of that part of the performance as of anything else.

This encounter, she told March, made a profound change in her feeling about the other episode—closed a door upon it. Nothing like that could happen to her again. She simply stopped thinking about it after that, buried it and it had stayed buried comfortably for the better part of a year, until Rush came home from France. At least she wasn't aware that it had troubled her. The twinges of discomfort she'd felt whenever she'd faced the prospect of coming home, she had attributed to another cause altogether.

"Paula," he observed. "That's easy enough to see."

"Oh, you are a comfort," she said; "only not Paula by herself. Paula and father and I, in a sort of awkward triangle, all doing our best and all nagging one another. That has got terribly worse in the last few days."

She seemed to find no difficulty at all in informing him fully about this home situation; needed only a question or surmise dropped here and there to develop the whole story.

It wasn't a chronological narrative. Her mind drifted like a soaring kingfisher over the whole area between her childhood and the events of this very morning, swooping down here or there to pick up some incident wherever a gleam of memory attracted her.

Her spirit was finding compensation for the agonies of the past hours in a complete detachment. Nothing she told him, no matter how close home it came, seemed to involve any painful emotion. Her body, pressed so close against his that he could have felt the faintest muscle quiver, conveyed no message to him but the relaxation of complete security.

About himself there was a curious duality. One of him was lulled irresistibly into sharing her mood of serene detachment. The other, recognizing the transitoriness of hers, knowing that when this interlude came to an end, as come it must, the storm would break upon them once more, was casting about desperately for the means of saving her.

He had come to see the situation with her own eyes, fairly felt the clutch of it upon his own heart. She or some impish power acting through her agency had certainly made a mess of things. Her father's happiness destroyed; Rush's partnership broken; and the whole Hickory Hill project ruined unless some one could be found to buy into it in Graham's place;

Graham humiliated, utterly cast adrift, irreparably hurt. And the prospect for the future….

She had told him of her tramp about the streets yesterday with her newspaper clipping and he was able to feel the full terror of it; and, beyond the terror, the gray emptiness.

There was only one way out of the tangle and this was to marry the man she loved and knew loved her. Well, he knew with merciless certainty what her answer would be when he asked her—begged her—to do that. He had provided her with the answer himself, with his sophomoric talk about traveling light and refusing to wear harness. And he'd worse than talked. His flight from her at Hickory Hill was enough to show that these weren't mere empty phrases. And yet her life depended to-night upon his ability to persuade her, in the face of those phrases and that fact, to marry him. So he sat very still, wondering how soon she would divine these undercurrents of his thought, listening while she talked to him.

The hours were slipping away, too. A glance at the watch braceleted upon the wrist he held startled him and he covered it with his hand. Had they already, he wondered, begun a search for her? Her words supplied presently the answer to that question. She was talking, with a dry sort of humor, about the commotions of that day.

He could not be sure he was getting it quite straight, for she was commenting upon events rather than narrating them. Apparently she had telephoned to her brother at Hood's apartment immediately after young Stannard left the house the evening or afternoon before, telling him not to bother about her, as she was going straight to bed. Let him go to a show and be careful not to wake her when he came in. She'd done this and gone to sleep at once, not waking until she'd heard him getting ready for bed in the adjoining room. But after that she hadn't been able to get off again.

March reflected, with a shudder, what a ghastly procession of hours those must have been. Had it been then, he wondered, that, looking for some harmless thing to help her sleep, she had come upon the deadlier stuff?

Her encounter with her brother at breakfast, which she had prepared, was their first, it seemed, since her visit to Hickory Hill and Rush had been shocked at her wan, lifeless appearance. He'd guessed, of course, that his friend's suit hadn't prospered and now took the line, which no doubt seemed to him the most tactful and comforting one available, that she was too ill to attempt any final decision on such a subject just now and that things would look different when better health had driven morbid thoughts away.

Her vehemence in trying to convince him that she had acted finally in the matter, that Graham now acquiesced fully in her decision and no longer wanted to marry her, and that Rush *must* let him alone—not even try to talk with him about it—had only made him the more confident in his diagnosis.

It must have been pat in the middle of this scene that Graham's midnight-written letter arrived. Rush's attitude toward his partner's flight—after the first moments of mere incredulity—had been one of contemptuous irritation, the natural attitude for any young man who sees a comrade taking no more of a matter than a disappointment in love with an evident lack of fortitude. This was heightened, too, by a rapidly developed sense of personal grievance. What the devil did Graham think was going to happen to him with Hickory Hill left on his hands like that? There was more than enough work for the two of them. And then the financial aspect of it! Mr. Stannard, who had just been brought to the point of loosening up and letting them have a little more money, would of course leave Rush to his fate. If he didn't call his loans and sell him out! Ruin them altogether! Graham must simply be found and dragged back before his father learned of his flight.

He couldn't have been paying his sister much attention while he ran on like that! Unwisely, perhaps, but inevitably, Mary attempted to defend the fugitive—in the only way she thought of as possible; namely, by showing her brother what the true situation was.

She didn't try to tell March what she said. The thing which, with a forlorn smile, she dwelt upon, was the terrified vehemence with which Rush had stopped her at his first inkling of what she was trying to make him see. She was simply out of her head. A bad case, he pronounced, of neurasthenia. Her having set out yesterday to find a job should have made that plain enough. What she needed was a nurse and a doctor—and he meant to provide both within the next few hours. He then compromised by saying that the nurse he had in mind was for the moment Aunt Lucile and the doctor their father.

With an alternation of truculence and cajolery, he had got her to lie down and to promise not to talk—that was the important thing—and this accomplished he devoted half an hour to the composition of a note to Miss Wollaston (whom it was difficult to tell anything to over the telephone, particularly with long distance rural connections) which he despatched, in charge of Pete, in the big car. Pete would get back with her by three at the latest.

Rush then had a long talk by telephone with his father at Ravinia. Mary didn't know, of course, what they had said, beyond that John had promised to come down immediately after lunch, but she got the idea that the professional medical attitude had been one of less alarm than the amateur one. Mary confessed to March, with a flicker of ironic amusement, that she had supported this lighter view so successfully that, a little before noon, Rush had confided to her his wish—if she were perfectly sure she didn't need him—to take the one o'clock train to Lake Geneva. He and Graham were still expected there for the week-end and on a good many accounts it would be well if he didn't fail them. He dreaded going, of course, but he felt he could meet the situation better on the ground whatever turned up. He could wait for the three o'clock train, but this was the one Mr. Stannard always took and he'd like to get in a talk with Sylvia first. She was a great pal of her brother's and might well have some real information about He'd have Pete's wife come in and look after Mary—get lunch and so on. And father would be down about two.

March thought the forlorn smile with which she told him this the most heart-breaking thing he had ever seen. Damn Rush! Damn all the sentimentalists in the world. Dressing up their desires in altruistic clothes. Loving themselves in a lot of crooked mirrors!

The rest of the story told itself in very few words. John Wollaston telephoned, about three, from Ravinia, to say that Paula wasn't well—meant to sing to-night as she was billed to do (she took great pride in never disappointing her audiences)—but very much wanted him at hand through the ordeal. If Mary was feeling as much better as her voice sounded would she mind his not coming until to-morrow morning.

She'd assured him, of course, that she wouldn't mind a bit. Aunt Lucile hadn't arrived yet but she would be coming any minute now. Rush had been making a great fuss about nothing, anyway. She did not volunteer the information that Rush had already gone to Lake Geneva.

At five o'clock a telegram, addressed to Rush, had come from Miss Wollaston. Pete had broken one of the springs of the big car and had had to go to Durham for another. She hoped Rush and his father would be able to take care of Mary until to-morrow morning when she would arrive with one of the servants and take charge.

That cleared the board. To-morrow they would descend upon her with their fussy attentions, their medical solemnities, their farcical search for something—for anything except the truth they wouldn't let her tell—to account for her nervous breakdown. But for a dozen hours she was, miraculously, to be let alone, with blessed open spaces round her. No need for any frantic haste. Plenty of time. The whole of that hot still summer night.

And then, at six o'clock, a man named James Wallace had telephoned! And Jennie MacArthur had decided to drop in that evening for a visit with Sarah! Fate had played its part; given March his chance.

"So that's why you decided to go away," he said.

He had been nerving himself during a long slow silence for that. He could almost as easily have struck her a blow, and indeed the effect of it was precisely that. But though she tried to shrink away he held her tighter and went on. "I don't believe there's anything in the whole picture now that I don't see and understand. But—but the way out … Oh, Mary darling, it isn't the one you are trying to take. There's happiness for both of us if you'll take the other way—with me."

She was struggling now to get free from his hands. "No!" she gasped wildly. "I won't do that. I'll do anything—*anything* else rather than that. Let me go now."

But he held her fast. Presently she relaxed and lay back panting in her chair. "Won't you please let me go?" she pleaded. "You haven't understood at all if you don't see that you must. Oh, but you do understand! You've comforted me … I didn't think there could be any comfort like that. Let me go now—in peace. Don't ask the other. I've spoiled things for everybody else, but I won't for you. I couldn't endure that."

All the pleas, the arguments, the convincing phrases which he had been mustering while she talked to him so contentedly, to convince her of the truth, the blinding truth that he wanted her now for his wife, that life no longer seemed a possible thing for him upon any other terms—all that feeble scaffolding of words was, to his despair, swept now clean away in the very torrent of his passion. He could do nothing for a while but go on holding her. At last, words burst from him.

"I won't let you go. Not alone. Wherever you go, I'll go with you."

She looked up, staring into his face and he saw an incredulous surmise deepen into certainty. She had seen, heard in that cry of his, the truth—that he understood what she meant to do. Then her face contorted itself like a child's, ineffectually struggling to keep back tears, and she broke down, weeping.

That broke the spell that had fallen upon him. He took her up, carried her over to the big armchair and sat down with her in his arms.

His own terror, which had never more than momentarily receded since she had first spoken to him from the doorway, was, he realized, gone;

replaced by an inexplicable thrilling confidence that he had won his victory. He didn't speak a word.

The tempest was soon spent. It was a matter only of minutes before the sobbing ceased. But for a long while after she was quiet, all muscles relaxed, she lay just as he held her, a soft dead weight like a sleeping child. He wondered, indeed, if she had not fallen asleep and finally moved his head so that he could see her eyes. They were open, though, and at that movement of his she stirred, sighed and sat erect.

"I think I would have dropped off in another minute," she said. Then she put her hands upon his shoulders. "I won't do that. I promise, solemnly, I won't do what—what we both thought I meant to do. I don't believe I could now, anyway. Now that the nightmare is gone."

She smiled then and bent down and kissed him. "But I won't do the other thing either, my dear. I'll find some other way. Really go to Omaha perhaps. But I won't marry you. You see why, don't you?"

"Oh, yes," he said. "I can tell you exactly why. You don't want to take away my freedom. You want me to be a sort of—what was that opera you spoke about at Hickory Hill?—*Chemineau*. Doing nothing but what I please. Wandering off wherever I like." He smiled. "Mary, dear, do you realize that you're proposing to deal with me exactly as Graham Stannard would have dealt with you? Trying to make an image of me?"

She started from his knees, retreated a pace or two and turned and confronted him.

"That's not true," she protested. "That can't possibly be true!"

He did not answer. He had plenty of arguments with which to establish the parallel, his mind was aflame with phrases in which to plead his cause with her. Somehow they wouldn't come to his tongue. It didn't occur to him that fatigue had anything to do with this. He was filled with a sudden fury that he could not talk to her.

She had turned away, restlessly, and moved to one of the dormer windows. Following her with his eyes he saw the dawn coming.

He rose stiffly from his chair. "I guess I had better take you home now," he said.

She nodded and got her hat. When he found her at the door after he had put out the lamp she clung to him for a moment in the dark and he thought she meant to speak, but she did not.

He helped her down the irregular shaky stair and then, along the gray cool empty street he walked with her toward the brightened sky.

She said, at last, "Graham wouldn't let me tell him what the real me was like. Tell me the truth about the real you."

"There isn't much to tell. I guess I'm pretty much like any one else when it comes down to—to ... I don't want to go on, alone. I want to be woven in with you. I want..."

He stood still in a vain effort to make the words come. "I can't talk!" he cried, and his voice broke in a sob.

"You needn't," she said; and pressing his hand against her breast she led him on again. She was trembling and her hand was cold.

Nothing more was said between them, all the way. But when they reached her door and managed to open it she stood for a moment peering through the dusk into his face.

"If it's true..." she said. "If you really want a home and a wife—like me... Oh, yes, I know it's true!"

# CHAPTER XXVI
# JOHN ARRIVES

Two or three hours after March and Mary came to the Dearborn Avenue house that Sunday morning, a little before eight o'clock to be precise, John Wollaston, deterred by humane considerations from ringing the door-bell, tried his latch-key first and found it sufficient. Rather surprisingly since his sister was particular about bolts and chains. But this mild sensation was engulfed the next moment in clear astonishment when he encountered in the drawing-room doorway, Anthony March.

The piano tuner was coatless and in his socks. Evidently it was no less recent an event than the sound of the latchkey which had roused him from sleep.

"Oh," he said. "It's you, sir." And added as he came a little wider awake, "I'm very glad you've come."

John detected a reservation of some sort in this afterthought; faintly ironic perhaps. There was, at any rate, a conspicuous absence of any implication that his presence was urgently needed just then, or eagerly waited for.

He replied with an irony a little more marked, "It's an unexpected pleasure to find you here. They're wanting you rather badly up at Ravinia these days, I understand."

March nodded, cast a glance in the direction of the stairs and led the way decisively into the drawing-room. His pantomime made it clear that he did not wish the rest of the slumbering household aroused. Considerate of him, of course, and all that, but the decisiveness of the action—as if he somehow felt himself in charge, despite the arrival of his host—roused in John a faint hostility.

He followed nevertheless. He saw at once where his unaccountable visitor had made his bed. A big cane davenport had been dragged into the bay window, its velvet cushions neatly stacked on the piano bench, and the composer's coat, rolled with his deftness of experience, had served him for a pillow. Not a bad bed for such a night as this that John himself had sweltered through so unsuccessfully. Probably the coolest place in the house, right by those open south windows. But all, the same ...

"Couldn't Rush do better for you than that?" he said. "There must be a dozen beds in the house."

"Rush isn't here," March answered. "I believe he went to Lake Geneva yesterday, for over Sunday."

John Wollaston felt the blood come up into his face as the conviction sprang into his mind that Lucile wasn't here, either. She'd never have left the front door unbolted. She'd never have permitted a guest, however explicit his preferences, to sleep upon the cane davenport in the drawing-room with his coat for a pillow.

It was as if March had followed his train of thought step by step.

"Miss Wollaston isn't here either," he said. "She was detained by a broken spring in the car. I believe she expects to arrive this morning."

A faint amusement showed in his face and presently brightened into a smile. "I'm really very relieved," he added, "that it was you who got here first."

And then the smile vanished and his voice took a new timbre, not of challenge, certainly not of defiance, but all the more for that of authority. "The only other person in the house is Mary."

A sudden weakness of the legs caused John to seat himself, with what appearance of deliberation he could manage, in the nearest chair. March, however, remained on his feet.

"I brought her home last night," he went on, "very late—early this morning rather—with the intention of leaving her here alone. But I decided to stay. Also it was her preference that I should. I suspect she's asleep. She promised, at least, to call me if she didn't."

That, apparently, finished for the present what he had to say. He turned—it really was rather gentle the way he disengaged himself from the fixity of John's look,—replaced the cushions on the cane davenport; and then, seating himself, began putting on his shoes.

Precisely that gentleness, though it checked on John's tongue the angry question, "What the devil were you doing with her until early this morning?" only added to his anger by depriving it of a target. For a minute he sat inarticulate, boiling.

It was an outrageous piece of slacking on Rush's part that he should have deserted his sister before the arrival of one or the other of his promised reenforcements relieved him of his duty. It was inexcusable of Lucile to let a trivial matter like a broken spring keep her at Hickory Hill. There were plenty of trains, weren't there? And the third rail every hour? It was shockingly disengenuous of Mary, when she talked with him over the telephone yesterday afternoon, to have suppressed the essential fact that Rush had already deserted her and that she was at that moment alone.

And then his anger turned upon himself, as a voice within him asked whether, on his conscience, he could affirm that this knowledge would have made a difference in his own actions. Could he be sure he wouldn't have clutched at the assurance that his sister was already on the way rather than have exacerbated his quarrel with Paula by doing the one thing that would annoy her most.

Laboriously he got himself together, steadied himself. "You mustn't think," he said, "that I'm not grateful. We're all grateful, of course, to you for having done what our combined negligence appears to have made necessary." Then his voice hardened and the ring of anger crept into it as he added, "You may be sure that nothing of the sort will occur again."

"No," March said dryly. "It won't occur again." He straightened up and faced John Wollaston squarely. "I've persuaded Mary to marry me," he said.

"To marry—*you*!" John echoed blankly. For a moment before his mind began to work, he merely stared. The first thought that struggled through was a reluctant recognition of the fact that there was a sort of dignity in the man which not even the stale look, inevitable about one who has just slept in his clothes, could overcome. No more than his pallor and the lines of fatigue deeply marked in his face could impeach his air of authority. There was something to him not quite accountable under any of the categories John was in the habit of applying. So much John had conceded from the first; from that morning in this very room when he had found him tuning the Circassian grand and had gone away, shutting the door over yonder, so that Paula shouldn't hear.

But that Mary should seriously contemplate marrying him! Mary! Good God!

Once more March disengaged himself from John's fixed gaze. Not at all as if he couldn't support it; gently again, by way of giving the older man time to recover from his astonishment. He went into the bay and stood looking out the window into the bright hot empty street. From where he sat John could see his face in profile. He certainly was damned cool about it.

There recurred to John's mind, a moment during that day's drive he had taken with Mary, down South, when he had leaped to the wild surmise that there might be something between those two. She'd been talking about the piano tuner with what struck him as a surprisingly confident understanding.

She had instantly, he remembered, divined his thought and as swiftly set it at rest. March wasn't, she had said, a person who saved himself up for special people. He was there for anybody, like a public drinking fountain.

But had she been ingenuous in making that reply to him? Had he really been in her confidence about the man? Obviously not. The only encounter between them that he had ever heard about was the one she had upon that day described to him. And Lucile and Rush were evidently as completely in the dark about the affair as he himself had been. Their meetings, their numerous meetings, must have been clandestine. That Mary, his own white little daughter, should be capable of an affair like that!

Another memory flashed into his mind. The evening of that same day when she had tried to tell him why she couldn't marry Graham. She wasn't, she had said, innocent enough for Graham; she wasn't even quite—good.

The horror of the conclusion he seemed to be drifting upon literally, for a moment, nauseated John Wollaston. The sweat felt cold upon his forehead. And then, white hot, bracing him like brandy, a wave of anger.

Some preliminary move toward speaking evidently caught March's ear, for he turned alertly and looked. It was one of the oddest experiences John Wollaston had ever had. The moment he met March's gaze, the whole infernal pattern, like an old-fashioned set-piece in fireworks, extinguished itself as suddenly as it had flared. There was something indescribable in this man's face that simply made grotesque the notion that he could be a blackguard. John felt himself clutching at his anger to keep him up but the momentary belief which had fed it was gone.

March's face darkened, too. "If you have any idea," he said, "that I've taken any advantage—or attempted to take any…"

"No," John said quickly. "I don't believe anything like that. I confess there was a moment just now when it looked like that; when I couldn't make it look like anything else. It is still quite unaccountable to me. That explanation is discarded—but I'd like the real one."

"I don't believe," March said, reflecting over it for a moment, "that there is any explanation I could give that would make it much more accountable. We love each other. That is a fact that, accountable or not, we both had to recognize a number of weeks ago. I didn't ask her to marry me until last night. I wouldn't have asked her then if it hadn't become clear to me that her happiness depended upon it as much as mine did. When she was able to see that the converse was also true, we—agreed upon it."

"What I asked for," John said, "was an explanation. What you have offered is altogether inadequate—if it can be called an explanation at all." He wrenched his eyes away from March's face. "I've liked you," he went on, "I've liked you despite the fact that I've had some excuse for entertaining a contradictory feeling. And I concede your extraordinary talents. But it remains true that you're not—the sort of man I'd expect my daughter to marry. Nor, unless I could see some better reason than I see now, permit her to marry."

This was further than, in cool blood, he'd have gone. But the finding of a stranger here in his own place (any man would have been a stranger when it came as close as this to Mary) professing to understand her needs, to see with the clear eye of certainty where her happiness lay, angered and outraged him. The more for an irresistible conviction that the profession was true. But that word permit went too far. He wasn't enough of an old-fashioned parent to believe, at all whole-heartedly, that Mary was his to dispose of.

Again, he looked up at the man's face, braced for the retort his challenge had laid him open to, and once more the expression he saw there—a thing as momentary as a shimmer of summer lightning,—told him more than anything within the resources of rhetoric could have effected. It was something a little less than a smile that flashed across March's face, a look half pitiful, half ironic. It told John Wollaston that his permission was not needed. Events had got beyond him. He was superseded.

He dropped back limp in his chair. March seated himself, too, and leaned forward, his elbows on his knees, his hands clasped.

"I know how it must look to you, sir," he said gravely. "Even the social aspect of the thing in the narrowest sense of the word is serious. And there are other difficulties harder to get over than that. I don't think I minimize any of them. And I don't believe that Mary does. But the main thing is a fact that can't be escaped. If we face that first ..."

He broke off there for a moment and John saw him grip his hands together. It was with a visible effort that he went on.

"One of the things Mary said last night was that sentimentality was the crudest thing in the world. It caused more tragedies, she said, than malice. She had learned the cruelty of it by experience. It's not an experience she can safely go through again."

It was in an automatic effort to defend himself against the conviction he felt closing down upon him that John lashed out here with a reply.

"The fact you're asking me to face is, I suppose, that you two have discovered you're in love with each other to a degree that makes all other considerations negligible."

"That's not quite it," March replied patiently. "A part of it is, that it would have been just as impossible for Mary to marry Graham Stannard if she had never seen me. And if she could forget me completely it would still be impossible for her to marry any one else like him."

John didn't follow that very closely. His mind was still upon the last sentence of March's former speech. "It's not an experience she can safely go through again." What did he mean by that? How much did he mean by that? Would John, if he could, plumb the full depth of that meaning? There was no use fighting any longer.

"The simplest way of stating the fact, I suppose," he said, "is that you two mean to marry and that you're satisfied that your reasons for making the decision are valid. Well, if Mary corroborates you, as I have no doubt she will, I'll face that fact as realistically as possible. I'll agree not to, as you put it, sentimentalize."

Then he got up and held out his hand. "I mean that for a better welcome that it sounds," he concluded. And if there was no real feeling of kindliness for his prospective son-in-law behind the words, there was what came to the same thing, a realization that this feeling was bound to come in time. No candid-minded person could keep alive, for very long, a grievance against Anthony March.

The physician in him spoke automatically while their hands were gripped. "Good lord, man! You're about at the end of your rope. Exhausted — that's what I mean. How long is it since you've fed?"

March was vague about this; wouldn't be drawn into the line John had been diverted into. He answered another question or two of the same tenor with half his mind and finally said—with the first touch of impatience he had betrayed, "I'm all right! That can wait. There's one more thing I want to say before you talk to Mary."

He seemed grateful for John's permission to sit down again, dropped into his chair in a way that suggested he might have fallen into it in another minute, and took the time he visibly needed for getting his wits into working order again.

"I think I can see how the prospect must look to you," he began. "The difficulties and objections that you see are, I guess, the same ones that appeared to me. The fact that I'm not in her world, at all. That I've never even tried to succeed nor get on, nor even to earn a decent living. And that, however hard I work to change all that, it will only be by perfectly extraordinary luck if I can contrive to make a life for her that will be—externally anywhere near as good a life as the one she's always taken for granted.

"It won't be as much worse, though, as you are likely to think. With the help she'll give me I shall be able to earn a decent living. Unless that opera of mine fails—laughably, and I don't believe it will, up at Ravinia, it will help quite a lot. Make it possible for me to get some pupils in composition. And I know I can write some songs that will be publishable and singable—for persons who aren't musicians like Paula. I did write two or three for the boys in Bordeaux that went pretty well. That sort of thing didn't seem worth while to me then and I never went on with it.

"Oh, you know how I've felt about it. How I've talked about traveling light and not letting my life get cluttered up. But that isn't really the thing that's changed. I've never been willing to pay, in liberty and leisure, for things I didn't want. The only difference is that there's something now that I do want. And I shan't shirk paying for it. I want you to understand that."

He stressed the word you in a way that puzzled John a little, but what he went on to say after a moment's hesitation made his meaning clear.

"That's preliminary. You'll find that Mary's misgivings—she's not without them and they won't be easy to overcome—aren't the same as ours. Those aren't the things that she's afraid of. She's afraid of taking my liberty away from me. She won't be able to believe, easily, that my old vagabond ways have lost their importance for me; that they're a phase I can afford to outgrow. She's likely to think I've sacrificed something essential in going regularly to work, giving lessons, writing popular songs. Of course, it will rest mostly with me to satisfy her that that isn't true, but any help you can give her along that line, I'll be grateful for. Last night she seemed convinced—far enough to give me her promise but..."

Words faded away there into an uneasy silence. John, looking intently into the man's face, saw him wrestling, he thought, with same idea, some fear, some sort of nightmare horror which with all the power of his will he was struggling not to give access to. He pressed his clenched hands against his eyes.

"What is it?" John asked sharply. "What's the matter?"

"It's nothing," March said between his teeth. "She promised, as I said. She told me I needn't be afraid." Then he came to his feet with a gesture of surrender. "Will you let me see her?" he asked John. "Now. Just for a minute before I go."

John, by that time, was on his feet, too, staring. "What do you mean, man? Afraid of what? What is it you're afraid of?"

March didn't answer the question in words, but for a moment he met her father's gaze eye to eye and what John saw was enough.

"Good God!" he whispered. "Why—why didn't you ..." Then turning swiftly toward the door. "Come along."

"I'm really not afraid," March panted as he followed him up the stairs, "because of her promise. It was just a twinge."

Her door at the foot of the stairs which led to the music room stood wide open, but both men came to an involuntary breathless pause outside it. Then John went in, looked for a brief moment at the figure that slept so gently in the narrow little bed, gave a reassuring nod to March who had hung back in the doorway, a nod that invited him in; then turned away and covered his face with his hands just for one steadying instant until the shock of that abominable fear should pass away.

When he looked again March stood at the bedside gazing down into the girl's face. It was as if his presence there were palpable to her. She opened her eyes sleepily, smiled a fleeting contented smile and held up her arms to her lover. He smiled, too, and bent down and kissed her. Then as the arms that had clasped his neck slipped down he straightened, nodded to John and went back to the door. John followed and for a moment, outside the room, they talked in whispers.

"I'm going home now," March said. "To my father's house—not the other place. There's a telephone there if she wants me. But I'll call anyhow before I go to Ravina this afternoon."

It was he, this time, who held out his hand.

"You can trust her with me in the meantime, I think," John said as he took it, but the irony of that was softened by a smile. March smiled, too, and with no more words went away.

Her eyes turned upon John when he came back into the room, wide open but still full of sleep. When he stood once more beside her bed a pat of her hand invited him to sit down upon the edge of it.

"He really was here, wasn't he?" she asked. "I wasn't dreaming?"

"No, he was here," John said.

Her eyelids drooped again. "I'm having the loveliest dreams," she told him. "I suppose I ought to be waking up. What time is it?"

"It's still very early. Only about half past eight. Go back to sleep."

"Have you had breakfast? Pete's wife, out in the garage, will come in and get it for you."

"When I feel like breakfast, I'll see to it that I get some," he said, rising.

Once more she roused herself a little. "Stay here, then, for a while," she said. "Pull that chair up close."

When he had planted the easy chair in the place she indicated and seated himself in it she gave him one of her hands to hold. But in another minute she was fast asleep.

And that, you know, was the hottest, most intolerable sting of all. He was sore, of course, all over. He had been badly battered during the last four days. Some of those moments with March down-stairs had been like blows from a bludgeon. But his daughter's sleepy attempt to concern herself about his breakfast and the perfunctory caress of that slack unconscious hand had the effect of the climax of it all.

She'd just been through the crisis of her life. She'd been down chin-deep in the black waters of tragedy (he didn't yet know, he told himself, what the elements of the crisis were nor the poisonous springs of the tragedy) and all her father meant to her was a domestic responsibility, some one that breakfast must be provided for!

He managed to control his release of her hand and his rising from his chair so that these actions should not be so brusk as to waken her again and, leaving the room, went down to his own.

That was the way with children. They remained a part of you but you were never a part of them. Mary having awakened for her lover, smiled at him, been reassured by his kiss, had been content to drop off to sleep again. Her father didn't matter. Not even his derelictions mattered.

He had been derelict. He didn't pretend to evade that. He could have forgiven her reproaches; welcomed them. But thanks to March, she had nothing to reproach him for The presence of a man she had known a matter of weeks obliterated past years like the writing on a child's slate. He tried to erect an active resentment against the composer. Didn't all his troubles go back to the day the man had come, to tune the drawing-room piano? First Paula and then Mary.

None of this was very real and he knew it. There was an underlying stratum of his consciousness that this didn't get down to at all, which, when it managed to get a word in, labeled it mere petulance, a childish attempt to find solace for his hurts in building up a grievance, a whole fortress of grievances to take shelter in against the bombardment of facts.

Was this the quality of his bitter four days' quarrel with Paula? Was the last accusation she had hurled at him last night before she shut herself in her room, a fact? "Of course, I'm jealous of Mary," she had acknowledged furiously when he charged her with it. "You don't care anything about me except for your pleasure. Down there in Tryon, when you didn't want that, you got rid of me and sent for Mary instead. If that weren't true, you wouldn't have been so anxious all these years that I shouldn't have a child."

No, that wasn't a fact, though it could be twisted into looking like one. If he had refrained from urging motherhood upon her, if he'd given her the benefit of his special knowledge, didn't her interest in her career as a singer establish the presumption that it was her wish rather than his that they were following. Had she ever said she'd like to have a baby? Or even hinted?

He pulled himself up. There was no good going over that again.

He bathed and shaved and dressed himself in fresh clothes, operations which had been perforce omitted at the cottage this morning in favor of his departure without arousing Paula. (He'd slept, or rather lain awake, upon the hammock in the veranda.) When he came down-stairs he found Pete's wife already in the kitchen, gave her directions about his breakfast and then from force of habit, thought of his morning paper. The delivery of it had been discontinued, of course, for the months the house was closed, so he walked down to Division Street to get one.

He had got his mind into a fairly quiescent state by then which made the trick it played when he first caught sight of the great stacks of *Tribunes* and *Heralds* on the corner news-stand all the more terrifying. It had the force of an hallucination; as if in the head-lines he actually saw the word suicide in thick black letters. And his daughter's name underneath.

He had managed, somehow, to evade that word; to refrain from putting into any words at all the peril Mary had so narrowly escaped, although the fact had hung, undisguised, between him and March during the moment they stared at each other before they went up-stairs together. It avenged that evasion by leaping upon him now. He bought his paper and hurried home with it under his arm, feeling as if it might still contain the news of that tragedy.

Reacting from this irrational panic he tried to discount the whole thing. March hadn't lied, of course, but, being a lover, he had exaggerated. As John sat over his breakfast he got to feeling quite comfortable about this. His mind went back to the breakfast he had had with Mary at Ravinia — breakfast after much such an abominable night as this last had been—the breakfast they had left for that talk under the trees beside the lake. And then his own words came back and stabbed him.

He had been arguing with her his right to extinguish himself if he chose. He had said he had no religion real enough to make a valid denial of that right. It was a question no one else could presume to decide. How much more had he said to that sensitive nerve-drawn child of his? He remembered how white she had gone for a moment, a little later. And he had pretended not to see! Just as he had been pretending, a few minutes back, to doubt the reality of the peril March had saved her from. What a liar he was!

Sentimentality, March had quoted Mary as saying, was the cruelest thing in the world. John stood convicted now of that cruelty toward his daughter. Was he guilty of it, also, toward his wife? Did their quarrel boil down to that?

# CHAPTER XXVII
## SETTLING PAULA

Anthony March might deny as much as he pleased that he was "enough of an Olympian to laugh" at life's ironies, but it remained true that his God had a sense of humor and that March himself appreciated it. When, well within that same twenty-four hours, a third member of the Wollaston family insisted upon telling him her troubles and asking him what she'd best do about them, he conceded with the flicker of an inward grin (not at all at the troubles which were serious enough nor at their sufferer who was in despair), that the great Disposer, having set out to demolish that philosophy, enjoyed making a thorough job of it.

It was about four o'clock on Sunday afternoon that he came to Paula's cottage at Ravinia to get the score to *The Outcry*. The maid who opened the door informed him that her mistress wasn't at home, but when he told her what he wanted, and she had gone rather dubiously up-stairs to see about it, it was Paula herself who, after a wait of ten minutes or so, came down with the manuscript in her hand.

He was, perhaps, just the one person in the world she'd have come down to see. All the explanation she volunteered to herself was that he didn't matter. It didn't matter, this was to say, if he did perceive that she had been crying for days and days and looked an utter wreck.

And then his errand brought her a touch of comfort. The acceptance of *The Outcry* for production restored the proprietary feeling she once had had about it. She was the discoverer of *The Outcry* and if you'd asked her who was responsible for the revival of interest in it and for the fact that it was now to be produced, I think she'd have told you quite honestly that she was. Hadn't she asked them all to come to her house to hear it? And sung the part of "Dolores" herself at that very informal audition?

And I'll hazard one further guess. It is that her quarrel with John made March's opera a rather pleasanter thing to dwell on a little. She had taken it up in defiance of his wish in the first place; her abandonment of it had acquired from its context the color of a self-sacrificial impulse. She would carry out her contract, she had told John down in Tryon, but she wouldn't sing "Dolores" for anybody. Well, now that her love-life with John was irremediably wrecked, there was a sort of melancholy satisfaction in handling, once more, the thing that stood as the innocent symbol of the disaster.

That's neither here nor there, of course. Paula was totally unaware of any such constellation about her simple act of deciding to carry down the score herself instead of handing it over to the maid.

The sight of him standing over the piano in her sitting-room cheered her and the look of melancholy she brought down-stairs with her was replaced by a spontaneous unexpected smile. Just as Mary, out at Hickory Hill, had predicted, she remembered how well she liked him. She laid the manuscript on the piano in order to give him both hands.

"I can't tell you how pleased I am about it," she said. "I wish you all the luck in the world."

He brightened responsively at that but looked, she thought, a little surprised, too.

"I am glad you're pleased about it," he told her. "I wasn't quite sure you'd know. Of course, they telephoned."

She stepped back, puzzled. "But of course I know!" she said. "Haven't I been working on it for weeks! Why, it was right here in this room that they decided on it. Days ago. I've been trying frantically to find you ever since."

"Oh," he said, "you mean *The Outcry*. I thought you were congratulating me on my engagement to marry Mary."

She stared at him in simple blank incredulity. "To marry Mary! Mary Wollaston? You don't mean that seriously?"

"It's the only serious fact in the world," he assured her.

"But John—Does John know about it?" she demanded.

"Yes," he said.

She drew a long breath, then pounced upon him with another question. "Did you tell him about it, or was it Mary who did?"

"It was I," March said. "I was the first one to see him after it happened."

"He hadn't suspected anything, had he?" she persisted.

She was vaguely aware that he was a little puzzled and perhaps in the same degree amused by her intensity, but she had no interest in half tones of that sort.

When he answered in the sense she expected, "No, I can testify to that. He was taken completely by surprise when I broke it to him;" she heaved another long breath, turned away, and sat down heavily in the nearest chair.

"Poor old John!" she said. But she didn't let that exclamation go uninterpreted. "I didn't mean anything—personal by that," she went on. "Only—only I didn't think John could make up his mind to let her marry—anybody." Then in a rush—an aside, to be sure, but one he was welcome to hear if he chose.—"He wanted her so much all to himself."

Whether he heard it or not, he failed, she thought, to attach any special significance to that last comment of hers. He said that John had been very nice about it, though he was, as any father would be under the circumstances, taken aback. He had consented to regard the arrangement as an accomplished fact and would, March hoped, in time be fully reconciled to it. Then he went back rather quickly to the matter of his opera.

"Of course, it means more than ever to me now," he said, putting his hand on the manuscript, "to get this produced. If it goes moderately well it will help in a good many ways."

She found some difficulty in again turning her mind to this theme and answered absently and rather at random, until she perceived that he was getting ready to take his leave. He was saying something about an appointment with LaChaise.

"Is it at once?" she asked. "Do you have to go right away?"

"I'm to have dinner with him and his secretary, who can talk English, at six," March said, "but I thought I'd carry this off somewhere and read it before I talked with them. It's been a long way out of my mind this last three months."

"Don't go," Paula said. "It seems so—so nice to have you here. Sit down and read your score. Then you'll have a piano handy in case you want to hear anything." She added as she saw him hesitate, "I won't bother you—but I'm feeling awfully lonely to-day."

At that, of course, he relinquished, though a little dubiously she thought, his intention to go. She set about energetically making matters convenient for him, cleared a small table of its litter and set it in the window where he would have the best light; chose a chair for him to sit in; urged him to take off his coat; and began looking about for something for him to smoke—but not quite successfully. She was sure there were cigarettes of Mary's somewhere about.

He didn't care to smoke just now, he said. If he felt later like resorting to a pipe he would.

Was there anything else? Didn't he want a pencil and paper to make notes on? No, he was supplied with everything, he said.

But for all the ardor of these preparations of hers, she was a little disconcerted and aggrieved at the way he took her at her word and plunged into the study of his score.

She found herself a novel and managed, for five minutes or so, to pretend to read. Then she flung it aside and drifted over to the piano bench and after gazing moodily a while at the keyboard, began in a fragmentary way to play bits of nothing that came into her head. But she stopped herself short in manifest contrition when, happening to look around at him, she saw a knot of baffled concentration in his forehead.

"Of course, you can't read if I do that," she said. "I'm sorry." Then under cover of the same interruption, "How did John look when you saw him this morning? Like a wreck? What time was it, anyway? It must have been frightfully early that he left here because I waked as soon as it was really light and he was gone by then."

"I don't know that he looked particularly a wreck," March said. "Not any worse, I mean, than he looked out at Hickory Hill the day you opened the season here."

"He didn't say anything about me, did he?" she asked.

"No," March said, "I don't think he did."

"I suppose you'd remember it if he'd happened to tell you that he loathed and hated me and never wanted to see me again." Then she rose and went over to the opposite side of his little table and leaning down spread her hands out over his score.

"Oh, I know I said I wouldn't bother, but do stop thinking about this and talk to me for a minute. We're having—we're having a perfectly hideous time. He and I. We've been fighting like cat and dog for four days. I don't exactly know what it's all about, except that it seems we hate each other and can't go on. You've got to tell me what to do. It all started with you anyway. With the time you brought around those Whitman songs.—That was the day Mary came home from New York, too," she added.

"All right," he said, shutting down the cover upon his manuscript, "then Mary and I will try to patch you up. That is, if we haven't already done it."

Her face darkened. "Don't try to talk the way they do," she commanded. "I'm not intelligent enough to take hints. Do you mean that the whole trouble is that I'm jealous of Mary? And that now she's going to marry you I'll have nothing to be jealous of? Well, you're wrong both ways. There's more to it than that. And that isn't going to stop just because she's marrying you. She'll always be there for him. And he'll be there for her. You'll find that out before you've gone far."

He didn't seem disposed to dispute this, nor to be much perturbed about it, either. He annoyed her by saying, "Well, if it's a permanent fact, like snow in February, what's the good of taking it so hard?"

"You can go south in February," she retorted. Then she went on, "I want to know if you don't think I've a right to be jealous of her. I'd saved his life. He admitted that. But when we went south, afterward, he simply didn't want me around. Sent me home pretending I'd be wanted for rehearsals. And then he sent for her. They spent a week together—talking! As far as that goes, they could have done it just as well if I'd been there. They can talk right over my head and I never know what it's all about. Wait till they begin doing that with you! I don't suppose they will though. You're a talker, too. He told her things he'd never told me-about his money troubles. What he said to me was that he didn't want to stand in the way of my career. He left her to tell me the truth about it, later,—after I'd told him I didn't want any career—though I'd just been offered the best chance I ever had. And then, when he came and found that I'd done—for him—what he'd been trying to make me do for myself, he was furious. We fought all night about it. And when I came down the next morning, ready to do anything he wanted me to, he'd wandered off with Mary. To talk me over with her again.—Tell her some more things, I suppose, that I didn't know about."

March had nothing to interpose here, it seemed, in Mary's defense, for her pause gave him ample opportunity to do so. He merely nodded reflectively and loaded and lighted his pipe.

"Well," she demanded presently, "can you see now that there's something more to it than jealousy? Whatever I try to do, he fights. When I wanted to begin singing again last spring, he fought that. And when I wanted to give it all up, after he'd so nearly died, he wouldn't let me. And when I'd refused the best chance I'd ever had, for him, and then changed around and accepted it because of him, he seemed to hate me for doing that. And he simply boiled when I told him I'd gone and got the money, myself, from Wallace Hood."

"Yes," March said, so decisively that he startled her, "I know all about it up to there. That was Thursday afternoon, wasn't it? Go on from then."

The interruption disconcerted her. "There isn't much more—to tell," she went on, but a good deal less impetuously. "Except that we fought and fought and fought. About eight o'clock that night I said I was going to the park to see the performance;—just to get a rest from talking. Mr. Eckstein was there and the Williamsons and James Wallace, so I asked them all to come home with us. And Fournier and LaChaise, too. And we got on your opera and LaChaise played part of it and then I read a lot of it with Fournier. So they didn't go home till after three. John thought I was keeping them there in order not to be left alone with him.—Well, what was the good of talking, anyhow? We did get started again on Friday, though; all day long. And Friday night we—made up, in a way. At least, I thought we did.

"Well, and then yesterday morning Rush telephoned out from town and said he thought John ought to come in to see Mary. She wasn't very well. I told him to go if he liked. I was feeling perfectly awful, yesterday, myself—and I was billed for *Thaïs* last night. There isn't another soprano up here who wouldn't have cancelled it, feeling the way I did. But I told John that if he thought Mary needed him more than I did, he'd better go.—I wish he had gone. After he'd telephoned to say he wasn't coming—he'd talked to Mary herself, that time—he kept getting colder and gloomier and more—unendurable from hour to hour. And after the performance, we had the most horrible fight of all. He told me I had kept him away from Mary on purpose,—because I was jealous of her. He said he could never forgive himself for the way he'd treated her—in order to curry favor with me. And he said that the first thing in the morning he was going to her. That's all.— Oh, well, I said a few things to him, too. Do you wonder?"

By way of a flourish, she flashed to her feet again at this conclusion (she'd been up and down half a dozen times in the course of her appeal to him as jury), and walked away to a window. But after the silence had spun itself out to the better part of a minute, she whipped round upon him.

"Have you been listening to a word I've said?" she demanded.

"Yes," he said, but with the contradictory air of fetching himself back from a long way off. "Truly! I've listened to every word. And I don't wonder a bit."

"Don't wonder at what?"

"That you said a few things to him, too. You've got a valid grievance, it seems to me. You couldn't be blamed for quarreling with him over it as bitterly as possible."

She barely heeded the words. They never did mean much to Paula. But his look and his tone reached her, and stung.

"Look here!" she said with sudden intensity. "Before we go any farther, I want to know this. Did Mary really need John, yesterday?"

She saw him turn pale and she had to wait two or three long breaths for her answer. But it came evenly enough at last.

"I happened to turn up instead. And she's perfectly all right, to-day."

Her eyes filled with tears. She turned forlornly away from him and dropped down upon a settee. "You hate me, too, now, I suppose. As well as he."

He sat down beside her and laid a hand upon her shoulder. "My dear," he said—and his own voice had a break of tenderness in it,—"I couldn't hate any one to-day if I wanted to. And I never could want to hate you. If there's anything I can do to help with John Wollaston.... But you see, if you want to keep your grievance you don't need any help. Nobody can take it away from you. It's only if you want to get rid of it—because it's making you beastly unhappy, no matter how valid it is—that you need any help from me or any one else. If that's what you want, I'll take a shot at writing you a prescription."

"Go crawling back to him on my knees, I suppose," she said in a tone not quite so genuinely resentful as she felt it ought to be. "And ask him to forgive me. What's the good of that when he doesn't love me?—Oh, of course I know he does—in a way."

His hand dropped absently from her shoulder. After a thoughtful moment he sprang up and took a turn of the room. "Do you know," he said, halting before her, "'in a way' is the only way there is. The only way any two people ever do love each other. That's what makes half the trouble, I believe. Trying to define it as if it were a standard thing. Like sterling silver; so many and so many hundredths per cent. pure. Love's whatever the personal emotion is that draws two people together. It may be anything. It may make them kind to each other, or it may make them nag each other into the mad-house, or it may make them shoot each other dead. It's probably never exactly the same thing between any two pairs of people..."

"Don't talk nonsense," she said petulantly.

"I'm not a bit sure it's nonsense," he persisted. "I only just thought of it, but I believe I've got on to something. Well, if I'm right, then the problem is to adjust that emotion to your life, or your life to that emotion, in such a way that the thing will work. There aren't any rules. There can't be any. It's a matter of—well, that's the word—adjustment."

She could not see that this was helping her much. It was not at all the line she'd projected for him. Yet she was finding it hard not to feel less tragic. She had even caught herself, just now, upon the brink of being amused. "Wait till you've tried to adjust something, as you say, with John, and have had him tell you what you think until you believe you do. When he's really being perfectly unreasonable all the while."

"Of course," March observed with the air of one making a material concession, "he is a good bit of a prima donna himself."

"What do you mean by that?" she demanded. And then, petulantly, she accused him of laughing at her, of refusing to take her seriously, of trying to be clever like the Wollastons.

"Look here, Paula," he said, and he put so much edge into his tone that she did, "have you ever spent five minutes out of the last five years trying to think what John was, besides your husband? I don't believe it. When I spoke of him to you, months ago, as a famous person you didn't know what I was talking about. He is. He's got a better chance—say to get into the next edition of the *Encyclopaedia Britannica*, than you have. He's got a career. He had it long before he knew you existed.—How old was he when he came to Vienna? About fifty, wasn't he?"

"Forty-nine," she said with the air of one making a serious contradiction; but her, "Oh, well,—" and a little laugh that followed it conceded that it was not.

"He'd had a career then for a long time," March went on. "He was established. He had things about as he wanted them. And then, out of nowhere, an irresistible thing like you came along and torpedoed him. He must have realized that he had gone clean out of his head about you. A man of that age doesn't fall in love unconsciously, nor easily either. He must have had frightful misgivings about persuading you to marry him. On your account as well as his own. Because he is that, you know. Conscientious, I mean. Almost to a morbid degree."

"Oh, yes," she conceded, "they're both like that. They spend half their time working things out trying to be fair."

He gave her a quick look, then came and sat down beside her again. "Well, then," he said, "we're on the right track. Just follow it along. You're the one big refractory thing in his life. The thing that constantly wants reconciling with something else,—at the same time that you're the delight of it, and the center and core of it. And while he's trying to deal with those problems justly, you know, he's taking on all of yours, too. He's trying to see things with your eyes, feeling them with your nerves, and since he's got a kind of uncanny penetration, I'd be willing to bet that he can tell you, half the time, what you're thinking about better than you could yourself. No wonder, between his conscience and his desire—your mutual desire—he's unreasonable. And since he's too old to be reformed out of his conscience that leaves the adjustment up to you."

"I don't know what more I can do," she said. "I've offered to give up everything."

"Yes," he said with a grunt, "that's it. I don't wonder he flew at you. *That's* the thing you'll have to give up!"

He rose and stood over her and thumped home, his point with one fist in the palm of the other hand. "Why, you've got to give up the nobility," he said. "The self-sacrificial attitude. You've got to chuck the heroine's rôle altogether, Paula. That's what you've been playing, naturally enough. It makes good drama for you, but look where it leaves him! First you give up your career for him, and then you give him up for the career you've undertaken for his sake. You've contrived to put him in the wrong both ways. Oh, not meaning to, I know; just by instinct. Well, give that up. Give up the renunciatory gesture. Go to him and tell him the truth. That you want, in a perfectly human selfish way, all you can get, both of him and of a career. They aren't mutually exclusive really. It ought to be possible to have quite a lot of each."

"You think you know such a lot," she protested rebelliously, "but there's only one thing I want, just the same, and that's John, himself."

"No doubt that's true this afternoon," he admitted. "You sang *Thais* last night and several thousand people, according to this morning's paper, cheered you at the end of the second act. But I believe I can tell you your day-dream. It's to be the greatest dramatic soprano in the world—home for a vacation. With John and perhaps one or two small children of the affectionate age around you."

Her face flamed at that. "John *has* been talking about me this morning!" she cried.

He shook his head. "It was only a chance shot," he told her. "I'm sorry if it came close enough home to hurt. But there couldn't be a better day-dream than that and there's no reason I can see why it shouldn't come reasonably true, if you'll honestly try for as much of it as you can get. That's the prescription, anyhow. Give up nobility and all the heroic poses that go with it and practise a little enlightened selfishness instead. Perhaps by force of example you may persuade John Wollaston to abandon about half of his conscience. Then you *would* be settled."

With that he went back to his score and by no protest or expostulation could she provoke another word out of him. She fidgeted about the room for a quarter of an hour or so. Then with the announcement that she was going to dress, left it and went up-stairs.

When she came down a while later in street things and a hat she presented him with a new perplexity.

"I've been trying everywhere I can think of to get a car," she said, "and there simply isn't one to be had. I even tried to borrow one."

He asked her what she wanted of a car. Where she wanted to go.

"Oh, can't you see!" she cried, "I don't want to send for John again to come to me. I want to go to him. It's too maddening!"

"Well," he said, with a grin, "if you really want—desperately—to go to him, of course there's the trolley."

She stared at him for a moment and then perceiving, or thinking she perceived, something allegorical about the suggestion, she gave a laugh, swooped down and kissed him and went.

# CHAPTER XXVIII
# THE KALEIDOSCOPE

It was the next Sunday morning that Miss Wollaston, who had decided to stay in town even though the emergency she had been summoned to meet was found mysteriously to have evanesced when she arrived, asked Wallace Hood, walking home with her from church, to come in to lunch.

"I haven't the least idea," she said, "whether we shall be quite by ourselves or whether the entire family, including the latest addition to it, will come straggling in before we've finished."

She would not have considered it quite delicate to have owned to him how very clearly she hoped to have him, for an hour or two, all to herself. He would be found, she was confident, not to have gone through the looking-glass into the world of topsy-turvey that all the rest of them seemed to be inhabiting, these days. It would be comforting to talk with somebody who was still capable of regarding things right side to.

She was much too penetrating a person not to have been perfectly aware from the first that, astonishing as were the facts John had communicated to her, upon her arrival from Hickory Hill a week ago, other facts of major importance were being suppressed.

She had found her brother apparently occupied in the normal Sunday morning manner with his newspaper, and he had answered her rather breathless inquiries about Mary by saying that she was all right. She was finishing off her night's sleep but would, he supposed, be down by and by. There was nothing the matter. Rush had been unnecessarily alarmed, lacking the fact which explained the case. And then he sprang his mine, informing her that Mary was engaged to marry Anthony March.

When, after a speechless interval, she had asked him, feebly, whether he didn't mean Graham Stannard, he had been very short with her indeed. The engagement to March was an accomplished fact, and the sooner we took it for granted the better. He showed a great reluctance to go further into detail about the matter and he flinched impatiently from the innocent question;—

when had he himself been informed of this astounding state of things. Well, naturally, since in the train of his answer the fact had been elicited that he hadn't come to town until this morning and that Mary had spent another night alone. And it was not Mary but March who had, already this morning, told him about it.

Beyond that John couldn't be driven to go. He concluded by putting a categorical injunction upon her. She wasn't to expostulate with Mary nor to attempt to examine either into her reasons for this step nor into her state of mind in making it. He was satisfied that the girl knew what she was doing and that it represented her real wishes. His sister's satisfaction on these points would have to be vicarious.

The surmise had formed itself irresistibly in Lucile's mind that John himself was involved in this decision of Mary's. Had she done this thing—involved herself in the beginnings of it, anyhow,—as a desperate measure to bring her father and his wife together again? By removing a temptation that Paula was still in danger of yielding to? She didn't put it to herself quite as crudely as that to be sure.

Certainly she had no intention of asking Wallace Hood what he thought about it. But perhaps he might have some other explanation of her niece's sacrifice. It must have been a sacrifice to something. An answer to some fancied call of duty. Unless it were a freak of sheer perversity. But this was dangerous ground for Lucile.

The queerest thing about it all was the way it seemed—magically—to be producing such beneficent results. John and Paula were reconciled by it,—or at least as soon as it happened. Paula had come down from Ravinia that very day, had had some sort of scene with her husband, and the two had been almost annoyingly at one upon every conceivable subject since. Something had happened also during the week to Rush, which lightened the gloom that had been hanging on him so long,—some utterly surprising interview with Graham Stannard's father. Pure coincidence one must suppose this to be, of course. Mary's engagement couldn't have anything to do with it. And then Mary herself! The girl was a new person. Absolutely radiant. Orthodox conduct of course for a just engaged girl—but in the circumstances one would think...

Lucile saw that Wallace hesitated a little about accepting her invitation to lunch and recalled the fact that he hadn't dropped in on them once during the week though he had known that they were more or less back in town.

"Why, yes, I'll come with pleasure," he said. "I don't know precisely what sort of terms I'm on with John. He felt for a few days, I know, that I'd been rather officious, but I may as well have it out with him now as later. And I shall be glad of an opportunity to give Mary my best wishes. I wrote her a note, of course, the day I read the announcement of the engagement in the newspapers." He added, "I certainly was in the dark as to that affair."

"Aren't you—still more or less, in the dark about it?" Miss Wollaston inquired. "I don't mind owning that I am. Mary's sense of social values always seemed to me to be at least adequately developed. On the surface one would have to call her rather worldly, I think."

"On the surface perhaps," Wallace interposed, "but not really; not at heart. Still, I'll grant it isn't easy to understand. There's a certain attraction about the man of course. And then there's his music."

"And Mary," Miss Wollaston observed, "happens to be the one utterly unmusical person in the family. She's completely absorbed in the preparation for his opera however." Then after a little pause, "She may prove rather more explanatory with you than she has been with me. She seems to take a certain pleasure in mystifying me. In saying things in a matter-of-fact way that are quite astounding. That's the new generation, of course. They talk a different language from mine. It will be a comfort," she concluded, rather pathetically, as they mounted the high steps to her brother's door, "to talk the matter over quietly with some one to whom my ideas and standards are still intelligible."

But this comfort was, for the present, to be denied her. Mary had spent the morning in her room writing notes and was coming down the stairs when the church-goers came in.

She negotiated what were left of the steps in a single swoop, gave her visitor both hands along with the "Wallace! How nice!" that welcomed him, and then, drawing back with a gesture which invited his scrutiny, said, "Well? What do you think?—Oh, but thanks for your note, first. I've just answered it."

Radiant was the word. There couldn't be any doubt of that. And younger. There was a twinkle of mischief that he had to go back-five years, anyhow, to remember the like of.

He had none of Lucile's feeling that decency required one's joy over an event of this sort to be of the chastened variety and he brightened in instantaneous response to the girl's mood, but the mere impact of her left him for a moment wordless.

"You needn't try to make me a speech," she said. "I know you're pleased. Not as pleased as you would be if you knew all about it, but ..."

"As pleased as possible, anyhow," he said. On that, amicably arm in arm, they followed Miss Wollaston into the drawing-room.

"I don't believe we've seen each other," she said, "since the night we had dinner together at the Saddle and Cycle, weeks and weeks ago."

"No," he said. "I remember very well that we haven't."

Miss Wollaston had drifted away from them (occupied, as she so often was when there were no persons present in the formal status of guests, in making minute readjustments of pillows and things as a sort of standing protest against the demon of disorder), and having noted this fact he went on:

"I didn't come for the picnic tea you invited me to the other day. If I'd known how the land lay, I shouldn't have sent a substitute. I'm afraid, perhaps, that was rather—tactless of me."

He saw the queerest look come into her face,—enough in itself to startle him rather though it wasn't without a gleam of humor.

"I was just wondering," she explained, "whether if you had come that particular day, I mightn't be engaged to you now instead of to Tony."

Unluckily Lucile heard that and froze rigid for a moment with horror. Then recovering her motor faculties, she moved in a stately manner toward the door.

"I think if you will excuse me," she said, "I'll go up and prepare for luncheon."

Mary gazed conscience-stricken from her to Wallace who was blushing like a boy caught stealing apples. "I'm sorry," she gasped, but not quickly enough for the apology to overtake her aunt. "It's terrible of me to say things like that and I do, every now and then. Can you bear with me until I've had time to quiet down? It's all so new, to be happy like this, I'm a little—wild with it."

In his nice neutral unexaggerated way he told her that her happiness could never be anything but a joy to him; and after that, when they were seated side by side upon the cane davenport he asked about her plans; when they were going to be married, where they meant to live, and so on.

"Why, we'll be married, I suppose," she said, "at the end of the customary six weeks' engagement. There isn't a thing to wait for, really."

"I'm glad of that," he remarked.

Anybody but Mary would have taken that at its face value; he was glad that they would have to wait no longer. But he flinched as she glanced round toward him and at that she laughed and patted his hand reassuringly.

"We're doing everything correctly," she told him; "beginning with father's announcement of the engagement in the papers, Tuesday. We remain on exhibition during the conventional six weeks and then we're married at noon over in the Fourth Church. Impeccable! That's going to be our middle name."

Mary used so very little slang that she was able to produce quite extraordinary effects with it when she did.

"I'm glad," Wallace said, a little ruffled by the start she had given him, "that you have not been persuaded to do anything—differently."

"Who do you suppose it was," she asked, "who insisted, in an adamantine manner, that it be done like that? It wasn't me and it wasn't Aunt Lucile. It was Anthony March." She added, after a reflective silence, "He was right about it, of course, because when that's over it's done with. And then—what he hasn't thought of, and I wouldn't have, most likely until it was too late—he'll have a friendlier audience next Tuesday night than if he'd given me my way and made a trip to the City Hall with me last Monday. I wanted to burn my bridges, you see;—and he laughed at me. I haven't told that to any one but you.—All the same, if he thinks, from that, that he can go on accumulating—millstones ..."

"Tell me where you are planning to live," Wallace said, getting back as he was always glad to do, to firm ground again. "Not too far away, I hope, for us to go on seeing a lot of you."

"Oh, it's very sad about that," she told him. "I was hoping to live with him in his secret lair over the Italian grocery. No, but it was really delightful. One big room, bigger than this, with dormers and dusty beams and an outside stair. He's had it for years. It's not half a mile from here—and Paula could never find out where it was! But, unexpectedly, he's being turned out. I could have wept when he told me."

"Unexpectedly!" quoted Wallace, the professional real estate man in him touched by this evidence of lay negligence. "March hadn't any lease, I suppose."

"He didn't need any," said Mary. "He owned it."

"If he owns it how can they turn him out—unexpectedly?"

"What he owned was the second story. Well, he still does, of course. But when they tear the first floor and the basement out from under him, as they're going to do next week, his second story won't do him much good."

"But, good gracious, they can't do that!" Wallace cried. "They must leave him his floor and his ceiling just where they are now. And his light. They can build above and below—I suppose that's what they're tearing the old building down for—but that layer of space, if he really bought it and has got anything to show that he really bought it, belongs to him."

"Do you mean seriously," she demanded, "that it's possible to buy the second story of a building? It's like Pudd'n-'head Wilson's joke about buying half a dog and killing his half."

"Of course I mean it," he insisted. "An easement like that cost our estate thousands of dollars only a year or two ago. Serious! I should think it was! Ask Rodney Aldrich. See what he says.—Of course, it's nothing unless he can show some instrument that proves his title. But if he can it might be worth … Well, it's just a question how badly they happen to need that particular bit of land. Those people we fell foul of managed to hold us up for a tidy sum."

She was looking at him thoughtfully, a faint, rather wry smile just touching her lips. "A minute ago," she said, "I was about to fling myself upon your neck and thank you for so wonderful a wedding present to us as that would be. And now I'm wondering … Wallace, I don't suppose it would strike you that there would be anything—shady about doing a thing like that."

"Shady!" He was, for a moment, deeply affronted by the mere suggestion. Then, remembering her total ignorance of all such matters, he smiled at her. "My dear Mary, do you think—leaving my rectitude aside—that I'd have referred you to Rodney Aldrich if I'd felt that there was anything questionable about it?"

"I know," she conceded. "And Martin Whitney would feel the same way. And father, I suppose, and Rush. Everybody we know. Yet I was wondering whether I'd say anything to Tony about it. I've decided I will, but I'm going to ask you not to, nor to anybody else, until I've talked to him. I'd like it left—altogether to him, you see."

He agreed, rather blankly to this. Presently she went on:

"I'm glad he's a real genius, not just a fragment of one as so many of them are. There's something—robust about him. And since that's so, I don't believe we'll do him any real harm; we—advantage-snatchers, you know. That's so very largely how we live, we nice people (it's why we're able to be nice, of course)—that we get perfectly blind to it. But he's so strong, and he can see in so deep, that I guess he's safe. That's the belief I have to go on, anyhow."

She sprang up and gave him another pat upon the shoulder. "He'll be getting here in a few minutes, I suspect. Father telephoned that he and Paula were going to bring him down as soon as his rehearsal was over. I'm going up now to try to make my peace with Aunt Lucile."

After lunch she told the family that she had matters to talk over with Tony and meant to take him for a walk. His father and mother expected them to drop in at their house about five and the intervening two hours would give them just about time to "cover the ground." She was openly laughing at her own pretense at being matter-of-fact.

It was pretty hot for walking, her father thought. Why not let Pete drive them around a while in the car? Or take the small car and drive herself? But she was feeling pedestrian, she said, and, anyhow, the topic she had in mind couldn't be discussed in a motor-car. They'd go to Lincoln Park and stroll around in the shade.

"And if we get tired," she added with a flicker, in response to her aunt's movement of protest, "we can squeeze in among the other couples on some grassy bank.—Oh, Aunt Lucile, don't mind! We *won't* do anything—disgraceful."

"You see what a cat I am," she told March as they set out. "I make her squirm without meaning to, and then, when she squirms, I scratch. Now talk to me until I can get in good humor with myself again."

"I've two or three things to tell you," he said. "I saw Sylvia Stannard this morning. She came to rehearsal with the little Williamson girl, and carried me off bodily for a talk. She's had a long letter from Graham.

"He's quite well," he went on swiftly, ignoring the gasp she gave, "and doesn't want to be, as he says, fussed over."

"Where is he?" she asked. "I'll write him a letter, of course. Only you'll have to tell me what to say."

"He's visiting a friend—a college classmate—on Long Island. And he's already had a job offered him by his friend's father, in an engineering office. He's a pretty good engineer, I believe. He thinks he'll accept it. Anyhow, he is definitely not coming back to Hickory Hill. Sylvia attaches some significance to the fact that his friend also has a pretty sister, but that's just the cynicism of youth, I suspect."

This last suggestion silenced her—with another gasp, as perhaps he had meant it to do. He added, presently:

"As for writing, I've already done that myself."

"You!" she exclaimed. "Where's the letter?"

"It's already despatched. I wrote it as soon as the rehearsal was over. But I'll tell you what I said in it. I told him I supposed he had heard of our engagement, but that I knew you wished him to be told of it personally. You were very fond of him, I said, and the only thing that clouded your happiness was a fear that he might not be able to share it. I assured him that I was completely in your confidence and knew that you had been through a period of very severe nervous stress, verging upon a nervous breakdown, but that I believed you were on the way to a speedy recovery. And I ended by saying that I believed a line from him to you, setting some of your misgivings at rest, would hasten it. And I was his most cordially."

She didn't try to pretend she wasn't aghast at this. "But what an— extraordinary letter. Won't he be—furious? At you for writing?—Speaking for me in a case like that. Telling him you knew all about it!"

"Well, that was more or less the idea," he confessed, with a rueful grin. "He'll think I stole you away from him; he'll think I gave you the nervous prostration I hinted at. Heaven knows what he won't think! But, of course, the more of a villain I am the less you're to be held responsible. And there's nothing insupportable or—ludicrous about a grievance against another man. At all events it enables him to get round the statement you demolished him with. No, you'll see. He'll write you a letter, correctly affectionate but rather chilly, and after that you'll be off his mind. And if the pretty sister Sylvia alleges doesn't exist, there'll be another one along pretty soon, who will."

She was obviously a little dazed by all this. It was the first time they had talked of Graham since that night in his room and he knew the bruise from that experience must still be painful to touch. So he hastened to produce his other item of news—also provided by Sylvia.

"This is a perfectly dead secret of hers," he began. "Told me in sacred confidence. She finished, however, by saying that she knew, of course, I'd go straight and tell you. So to justify her penetration, I will. Sylvia has accounted for her father's amazing change of attitude toward Hickory Hill. It seems she's persuaded her father to give Graham's share of it to her. She told him—what's obviously true—that she's a better farmer now than Graham would ever be. She hates town and society and all that, she says, and never will be happy anywhere but on a farm—anywhere, indeed, but on that farm. He was very rough and boisterous about the suggestion, she says, for a day or two, but finally he quieted down like a lamb and gave in. He never has refused her anything, of course."

"But a partnership between her and Rush!" Mary cried. "It's perfectly impossibly mad. Unless, of course ... You don't mean...?"

"Yes, that's the idea, exactly," March said. "Only Rush, as yet, knows nothing about it. Hence the need for secrecy. Sylvia acknowledged to her father that she couldn't possibly own a farm in partnership with a young man of twenty-three unless she married him, but she said she'd intended to marry Rush ever since she was twelve years old. She's confident that he's only waiting for her eighteenth birthday to ask her to marry him, but she says that if he doesn't, she means to ask him. And if he refuses, she pointed out to her father, he can't do less than consent to sell the other half of the farm to her. She treats that alternative, though, as derisory.—And I haven't a doubt she's right. Evidently her father has none, either.

"Well, it accounts for the change in Mr. Stannard's attitude toward the farm, of course," he concluded. "A son's supposed to thrive on adversity. It wouldn't be good morals not to make things difficult for him by way of developing his character. But where a mere daughter is involved he can chuckle and write checks. Under his tradition, he's entitled to regard her as a luxury. Anyhow, your father has nothing more to worry about as far as Rush and Hickory Hill are concerned."

"Life's a kaleidoscope," Mary said. "I'm tired. Let's sit down."—They were half-way up the park by that time.—"Oh, here on the grass. What does it matter?" When they were thus disposed she went back to her figure. "There's just a little turn, by some big wrist that we don't know anything about, and a little click, and the whole pattern changes."

"There are some patterns that don't change," he said soberly, but he didn't try to argue the point with her. He knew too exactly how she felt. "Tell me," he said, "what it was that you wanted to talk to me about."

She acknowledged that she'd been hoping he'd forgotten that, of the momentousness of his two items of news had left her, as her talk about kaleidoscopes indicated, rather disoriented. So he threw in, to give her time to get round to it, the information that both Sylvia and the little Williamson girl had decided they wanted to study music with him. "I agreed," he added, "to take them on, when I got around to it."

"Tony," she said, "I won't let you do that. Not music lessons to little girls. I won't."

"Afternoons?" he asked gently. "When I'm through the real day's work? It would be pretty good fun, trying to show a few people—young unspoiled people—what music really is. Dynamite some of their sentimental ideas about it; shake them loose from some of the schoolmasters' niggling rules about it; make them write it themselves; show 'em the big shapes of it; make a piano keyboard something they knew their way about in. That wouldn't be a contemptible job for anybody.—Oh, well, we can talk that out later. But you needn't be afraid for me, my dear."

"That's what I said to Wallace Hood," she told him; "just before lunch. When I was trying to decide to tell you what he'd been saying.—About your room that they're turning you out of."

With that, she repeated the whole of the talk with Wallace and the serio-fantastic idea that it had led up to.

He grinned over it a while in silence, then asked, "Are you willing to leave it entirely to me?"

"Of course," she said.

"Well, then," he decided, "if I've still got that paper—and I think I have … I copied it, I remember, out of an old law-book, and to satisfy Luigi's passion for the picturesque and the liturgical we took it to a notary and got it sealed with a big red wafer—Well, if I've got it and it's any good, I'll let Aldrich,—is that his name?—make what he can of it. I'll square it with Luigi afterward of course."

"It's a compromise for you," she said gravely. "You wouldn't have done that two weeks ago."

He laughed. "Folks use the word uncompromising as if it were always a praiseworthy thing to be. But it hardly ever is, if you stop to think. Certainly if life's an art, like composing music or painting pictures, then compromise is in the very fabric of it. Getting different themes or colors that would like to be contradictory, to work together; developing a give and take. What's the important thing? To have a life that's full and good and serviceable, or to mince along through it with two or three sacred attitudes?—Wait a minute."

She waited contentedly enough, watching him with a misty smile as he lay upon the grass beside her wrestling with his idea.

"All right," he said presently. "Here's the test that I'll agree to. I'll agree to do things or to leave them undone, to the end that when I'm—sixty, say, I'll have packed more of real value into my life—my life as your husband and the father of your children—than that vagabond you're so concerned about would have had in his if—if ..."

"If I hadn't gone to him a week ago last night?" She said it steadily enough, where he could not say it at all.

"Yes," he said. "That's what I mean."

He reached out for her hand and she gave it to him. Presently his face brightened once more into a grin. "I'll even promise to write more music. Lord, if I've really got anything, you couldn't stop me. Come along. Father and mother will be looking for us before very long now."

The critics agreed that the *première* of March's opera was a "distinct success," and then proceeded to disagree about everything else. The dean of the corps found it somewhat too heavily scored in the orchestra and the vocal parts rather ungrateful, technically. The reactionary put up his regular plaintive plea for melody but supposed this was too much to ask, these days. The chauvinist detected German influence in the music (he had missed the parodic satire in March's quotations), and asked Heaven to answer why an American composer should have availed himself of a decadent French libretto.

The audience showed a friendly bias toward it at the beginning and were plainly moved by the dramatic power of it as it progressed, but they seemed shocked and bewildered by the bludgeon blows of the conclusion and the curtain fell upon a rather panicky silence. Then they rallied and gave both the performers and the composer what would pass in current journalese for an ovation.

The Wollastons' friends, who were out in pretty good force, crowded forward to be introduced to Mary's fiancé and to offer him their double congratulations. They found him rather unresponsive and decided that he was temperamental (a judgment which did him no serious disservice with most of them), though the kindlier ones thought he might be shy. Mary herself found something not quite accountable in his manner, but she forbore to press for an explanation and let him off, good-humoredly enough, from the little celebration of his triumph which she had had in mind.

The fact was that he had come through the experience, which no one who has not shared it with him can possibly understand, of discovering the enormous difference between the effect of a thing on paper, or even in its last rehearsal, and the effect of it when it is performed before an audience which has paid to see it. It was no wonder he was dazed, for the opera he found himself listening to seemed like a changeling.

He worked all night over it and told LaChaise the next morning that he had made serious alterations in it and would need more rehearsals. The opera had been billed in advance for a repetition on the following Saturday night, the understanding among the powers being that if it failed to get a sufficient measure of favor the bill should be changed. It was touch and go, but the final decision was that it should have another chance.

So LaChaise agreed to March's request, ran over the composer's revised manuscript with a subtle French smile, sent for the timpani player, who was an expert copyist, and put him to work getting the altered parts ready, instanter. March told Mary he was making a few changes and asked her to stay away from rehearsals so that on Saturday night, from out in front, she might get the full effect.

Really, as it turned out, he did not need any individual testimony, for one could have learned the effect of the new ending from half a mile away. When he came back into the wings from his fourth recall he saw her face shining with joy through her tears. But his heart sank when he saw, standing beside her, Paula. He thanked his gods that Mary had a sense of humor.

Paula was smiling in high satisfaction, and she spoke first. "Well, stupid," she demanded, "what have you got to say for yourself, now?"

"Not a word," he answered, smiling too, "except that we have to live to learn."

Then he explained to Mary. "That ending—having the girl come back to life again, to sing some more after she'd been shot—was one of the things

Paula was trying to make me do, all the while. And some of the other changes were, too."

"But not that trumpet," said Paula, and he could only blush.

In a moment of dead silence, just before the crash that accompanied the descent of the curtain, he had scored for the C trumpet, muted and pianissimo, a phrase in the rhythm of the first three bars of the *Marsellaise*, but going up on the open tones and sustaining the high G, so that it carried also, a suggestion of *The Star Spangled Banner*. A flagrant trick, but it had served to remind the audience, bruised by the horror of abomination it had just witnessed, of the vengeance which, afar off, was gathering.

"I'd like to know what you'd have said to me," Paula went on, "if I'd asked you to do that!"

Mary laughed, and pushed her lover toward the stage. "Oh, go back," she said. "They want you again, my dear."

They gave *The Outcry* two more performances during the next week, one of them being the closing performance of the season, and by that time, so far as a single success could be said to establish any one, March was established. He and Mary discussed this rather soberly as they drove home in the small car after the convivial wind-up supper at the Moraine, where this fact had been effusively dwelt upon. Their wedding was now less than a month off.

"I know," she admitted, "it looks as if I were all wrong. To go on being afraid of—harness and millstones and all that. But just the same ... Oh, you can live my sort of life. That's been made plain enough. But I wish I could think of some way of making you sure that I could live yours, as well. Your old one; the *Chemineau* one. The way it was when you came to Hickory Hill."

A few minutes later she gave a sudden laugh. "Tony," she said, "will you swear you will do something for me—without knowing what it is? Oh, it's nothing very serious. It's about our honeymoon. A girl has a right to decide about that, hasn't she?"

"You've got something up your sleeve, all right," he said dubiously; but she remained severely silent until he gave in and promised.

"Well, then," she said, "this is what our honeymoon is going to be. We'll take one of the farm Fords-Rush can spare one, I'm sure, in October-and we'll get some camping things and start out—oh, along any one of your old routes—without one single cent of money. And we'll tune pianos as we go. We'll live off the country. Really and honestly take to the road. For a month. If we can't find any pianos we'll go hungry—or beg! The one thing we won't do, whatever happens, is to telegraph. After we've done that we'll come back and be—regular people. And I won't mind, then. Because, don't you see, you'll know. And if it's ever necessary to do it again, we'll do it again."

"There's no one in the world," he remarked in a voice that wanted to break, "—no one in the world who'd have thought of that but you. But, my dear, I don't need any reassurance like that."

"Tony, dearest, don't be solemn," she admonished him. "Won't it be *fun!*"